A Small Thing –
Like an Earthquake

A Small Thing –
Like an Earthquake

Memoirs by Ned Sherrin

Weidenfeld and Nicolson
London

For my mother and father

First published in Great Britain by
George Weidenfeld & Nicolson Ltd
91 Clapham High Street, London SW4 7TA
1983

ISBN 0 297 78211 8

Printed and bound in Great Britain by
Butler & Tanner Ltd, Frome and London

Contents

Illustrations vii

Author's Note ix

Introduction xi

Entering the Sixties 1

A Birmingham Person 12

Tonight and Every Night 33

Light Entertainment 48

That Was The Week That Was 55

Not So Much A Sequel 96

Virgin Producer 126

Virgin Films 138

Brahms and Sherrin 163

Side by Side 185

Beecham to Mitford 202

Performing 214

Father of the Man 232

Index 258

Illustrations

My parents on their wedding day (author)
My brother, Alfred, and me (author)
Lower Farm, Kingweston (author)
Going out to bat for the cricket club (author)
Two undergraduate poses for *Isis* (Edmark)
Maggie Smith's first solo lines on the London stage (John Vickers)
Pamela Harrington and Maggie Smith (Keystone)
Early days at ATV (author)
Members of the *TW3* team (Planet News)
David Frost watching a *TW3* playback (John Timbers)
Eating oysters with Caryl Brahms (Michael York)
Discussing the Wolfit obituary programme (Richard Levin)
Virgin Soldiers on location (author)
Party for *The National Health* crew and cast (author)
With Zsa Zsa Gabor (author)
A scene from *The Mitford Girls* (Reg Wilson)
Cindy-Ella or I Gotta Shoe (BBC Television)
Side by Side by Sondheim (Donald Cooper)
Rehearsing an American news quiz (PBS Television)

Author's Note

Mrs Willowherb was the consort of the caretaker of a block of flats where I lived in the 1950s. Occasionally she 'did' on a modest scale. One day Mrs Willowherb appeared in our apartment distraught. Her only daughter, Aurelia, had disappeared, Mrs Willowherb knew not where. Long into the night she borrowed the telephone to call far-flung relatives all over the British Isles with whom the unfortunate Aurelia might be. No luck. The next day Aurelia returned, having gone to Brighton on a whim with the daughter of the caretaker next door. Her return hardly diminished Mrs Willowherb's hysteria. 'How could she go off like that without a word? Go off to Brighton and me not knowing! Anything could have happened!' She hit her most piteous note, 'Even a small thing – like an earthquake . . .!'

Mrs Willowherb's phrase has stayed with me through some thirty years, long after my memory of Aurelia and her mother has faded. Beleaguered by the nigh impossible quest for a title – happy collections of words like *That Was The Week That Was* do not tumble felicitously on to a luncheon table every day of the week – it occurred to me that *A Small Thing* was about right; but since my career has been attended by two or three disturbances which, if not earthquakes on the seismograph of history, did provide enjoyable local tremors at the time, it could take the extra qualification. Hence
A Small Thing – Like an Earthquake

Introduction

For many of my generation the 1960s were a period of prodigious excitement which we were ripe to enjoy. For that reason I have chosen to start this book with a detailed account of some of the world events and some of the trivia which concerned us in the early weeks of 1960. I hope that this brief, personal picture of how it was may help to put into perspective the changes which followed. Small events tangential to the main issues of the day often evoke the temper of an earlier time more vividly than great occasions – hence the trivia.

From this sketch of the beginning of a decade I have gone back to my first job, which was with ATV in the early days of commercial television. Just before the 1960s I moved to the BBC, and two chapters cover my work on the *Tonight* programme and with the Light Entertainment department. Then I moved on to devise, produce and direct *That Was The Week That Was* or, *TW3* as it became generally known. Another chapter deals with my work on other television programmes, those which followed in the tradition of *TW3* and those which had a different character. When I left the BBC I spent some years producing films and a chapter tells how I helped to embalm the twitching corpse of the British movie.

Another legendary invalid, the British musical, features prominently in my memories of the theatre. Rather late in life I embarked, almost by accident but not unwillingly, on a career of occasional performances. Some of the lessons learned on these occasions fill the penultimate chapter. The early stages of most lives are either of compulsive fascination, brilliantly described by an Emlyn Williams, a Charles Chaplin or a John Mortimer, or they are eminently skippable in the hands of lesser writers. For this reason I have relegated my early years to the back of the book and only the really curious and conscientious reader need bother to dwell on my bucolic beginnings.

I am grateful to many people, but particularly on this occasion to writers who have allowed me to quote from their work: Peter Lewis and Peter Dobereiner for 'The Song of Lyndon'; Robert Gillespie and Charles Lewsen for a paragraph from their 'Consumer Guide to Religion'; Keith Waterhouse and Willis Hall for lines from 'Closedown' (the 'bum and po' sketch); Herbert Kretzmer for stanzas culled from 'Teenager', 'Lullaby for an Illegitimate Child', and 'A Song of Nostalgia for an American State'; Peter Shaffer for generous slices of 'But, My Dear'; Christopher Booker for some of Disraeli's advice to Sir Alec Douglas-Home; to A.D. Peters Ltd, literary agents of the late Cecil Day Lewis for permission to quote from his thoughts on the birth of Prince Andrew; and to Graham Payn and the Noël Coward estate for permission to quote four lines from 'I Wonder What Happened to Him'.

John Curtis was extraordinarily patient for over seven years on Lord Weidenfeld's behalf, and Alex MacCormick extraordinarily speedy and helpful once the manuscript got to her desk. Mary l'Anson has been diligent and encouraging in tieing up loose ends and Dorothy Siggars tireless in deciphering my handwriting, typing the result and pointing out similar ground covered better in other books on which she has worked. Any inaccuracies, errors of fact or spelling should be blamed on Martin Tickner, who has very kindly ploughed through the text.

By embarking on her own memoirs at roughly the same time, Caryl Brahms has provided me with an incentive to finish mine first which has been as stimulating as have her friendship and collaboration over twenty-eight years. Any stories that we have both chosen to tell will read better in her book.

N.S.

Entering the Sixties

Some decades acquire a personality, a glamour, a legend of their own. In confirmation of this special status they achieve an adjective. The Nineties were 'naughty'; the Twenties were 'roaring'. The Fifties and the Seventies still lack their labels; but the Sixties were emphatically 'swinging'. In the minds and memories of those who grew up then the character of the Sixties was explosive and innovative. It seemed as if Newton, Pythagoras, Columbus, Archimedes, St Francis of Assisi, Galileo and Dr Marie Stopes were all working away happily on the same campus. 'Breakthrough' was the popular word, and the belief that a bloodless but comprehensive revolution was being fought and won was widely held. Since then many principal performers have regretted the rapture. I share some of the disappointment that those ten years did not transform the world into a perfect place; but I suspect that a longer perspective will still pronounce a favourable verdict on them.

The excitement lay not so much in originality as in the growing awareness of many people that opportunities were there for the taking. The decade saw an increase and redistribution of available wealth, and major switches of power and influence, emphasized by more sophisticated communication which made the phenomenon more easily observed and more readily recognized.

Some people had always been able to spend more, eat better, drop out more carelessly, dress more extravagantly, travel further and fornicate more graciously in wider, warmer beds. In the Sixties more people enjoyed the opportunity of indulging in these luxuries. They had to get used to the new temperature which a place in the sun gave them. In a society where potato soup was despised, vichyssoise suddenly became a mass-produced delicacy, and many 'breakthroughs' had the status of discovery conferred on them because so few people knew that they had been there all the time.

The achievements of the decade seemed less substantial to its inhabitants at the end of ten years because they had begun to live with their new knowledge and to realize that many of the most important changes had not meant change at all but rearrangement. The human condition 'was not better, it was much the same'; but more people were aware of it.

In 1960, working in the dusty warren of untidy offices in the knocked-together terraced houses which harboured the BBC's Current Affairs Department, I felt no sense of impending excitement. In retrospect all earlier ages have an innocent appearance; but the last weeks of the Fifties and the beginning of the Sixties seem particularly naive in the light of the explosion which we were about to witness.

Looking at *That Was The Week That Was* tapes some twenty years on, the minutiae on which we had commented came back to me most vividly – not the big set-pieces. Similarly, my memory of early 1960 is a jumble of world events and theatre gossip. Hindsight converts those days into a pocket prophecy of what was to follow. A chorus of names which were to be regularly reprised rang out clearly for the first time.

On the first day of the New Year, no sooner had *The Times* announced that in America there was 'a Roman Catholic aspirant for the Presidency', and also that 'Mr Nixon's hat is officially in the ring', than the *Guardian* spotted 'Mr Kennedy's hat in the ring'. Meanwhile the *Tatler*'s social columnist, Miss Muriel Bowen, reporting from New York in a rare excursion into politics, backed Mrs Patricia Nixon as the next First Lady (though she found Mrs Jacqueline Kennedy lively and refreshing, and quoted with glee her reply to President Eisenhower, who had been rash enough to comment on the Kennedys' good fortune in living near a golf course: 'Oh,' she said tartly, 'but Mr President, my husband doesn't have time for that sort of thing.').

Jennifer, Miss Bowen's opposite number in *Queen*, had also seen in the new decade in New York: 'I thought *Gypsy* one of the worst shows I've seen for years. I had been warned, but I am an Ethel Merman fan.' She returned hopefully to England via Jamaica ('The barometer looks set fair for a bumper social year'). Ian Fleming, author of several books with Jamaica as a setting, was there with his wife. Bond's creator could still be mentioned without his brand label in January 1960 in *Queen*, a magazine which perhaps more than any other was to hunt, package and peddle the extremes of fashion which dressed the image of the age. Bond's interpreter, Sean Connery, was at this time acting very well, no doubt for a modest sum, in a BBC-TV revival of Anouilh's *Colombe*, equally unaware of the celebrity that was to hit, make and harass him.

'Suddenly it's 1960,' announced the editor of *Queen*, and, welcoming a new associate, 'Suddenly it's Norman Parkinson – England's tallest, gayest, most impeccably dressed photographer ... enemy of dead-pan and pretension ... he will bring a lively and untrammelled mind ... not only into fashion but to every aspect of 1960 living.'

The glossy guns were primed. The post-war upheaval and the Butler Education Act had produced a generation which found its voice in the mid-Fifties and its spokesmen were beginning to shout from the rooftops of the Royal Court Theatre, the universities, and the television studios. Another decade of youth was under way. Colin MacInnes anticipated it in his book *Absolute Beginners*: 'As for the boys and girls, the dear young absolute beginners, I sometimes feel that if they only knew this fact, the very simple fact, namely how powerful they really are, then they could rise up overnight and enslave the old taxpayers, the whole damn lot of them – *toupets* and falsies and rejuvenators and all.' By 1970 they understood.

In 1960 the homage to youth was still only lip-service. The *Daily Mirror* threw a 'Teenage Ball' at the Waldorf. Tommy Steele embarked on a 'Youth Venture' with Frank Pakenham, not yet Lord Longford, who had still to link hands with his later colleague, Cliff Richard. Richard himself set off to America as an 'Ambassador of Youth', a role he was still undertaking twenty years later but which the Beatles were confidently to usurp in the meantime. There was a Chelsea set and there was preludin, a drug for it to take. The drug inspired questions in the House of Commons and articles in university newspapers on its advantages and disadvantages compared with marijuana – a word with which the media was coming to terms after a long conspiracy of nervous silence. The Noel Baker Committee sought to restrict the sale of all drugs, 'stimulant, sedative and euphoriant', though not of alcohol, which so often combines all three.

Alongside the explosion of youth came the flamboyant manufacture of huge fortunes. Six more traditional millionaires profiled in the *Sunday Times* were Alfred Krupp, Charles Clore, Aristotle Onassis, Simon Marks, Marcel Boussac and John Paul Getty; the financial columns noted that the exciting new phenomenon of Unit Trusts had seen a doubling of investment in the previous year from one hundred to two hundred million pounds; John Bloom etched an early wrinkle on the unacceptable face of capitalism by giving a dinner at the Talk of the Town for a large party of guests at £7 a head. The dimly remembered names of Jasper, Murray, Grunwald and Lintang Investments jostled for attention on the news pages.

Harold Macmillan, the Prime Minister, who seemed, paradoxically, to be most out of touch with the age and best able to manipulate it, let off a few barrels of shot at Lord Astor of Hever's flying pheasants and took wing himself to say goodbye to the Queen, who was at Balmoral. His departure on an African excursion was typical of his flair for stage management. He left behind him a press and a public expecting nothing but anachronistic postures and empty words. They smiled tolerantly at his farewell message, 'These are exciting days for Africa.' Cassandra, the hasty sage who was required to fulminate regularly in the *Daily Mirror*, was soon thundering, 'Mr Macmillan has tiptoed through the Apartheid tulips ... the red badge of courage does not seem to be upon him'; and *The Times* dismissed his first speech in Lagos as 'a masterpiece of non-commitment'.

In Bulawayo seven hotels said there was no room at the inn for Indian businessmen and Sir Roy Welensky's New Year message promised the abolition of any right which the British Government had to veto Federal Legislation. South Africa declined to let Mr Tom Mboya change planes at Johannesburg, making it impossible for him to travel from Kenya to Basutoland to open the National Congress there. In the Belgian Congo a call went out to men to refuse to shave and for women to let their hair down until independence was achieved; naturally, King Baudouin promised it. Lumumba stayed in prison and Kasavubu came out. The Cameroon Republics, which had already achieved independence, celebrated it with such vigour that forty people were killed in the merry-making. In Egypt, Nasser was pressing the button to start the turbines on the Aswan high dam. In Algeria, the French fought the Algerians and fought each other; and, when the International Red Cross reported that torture continued to be practised in French prisons, the French Government replied frankly that this was regrettable but that it used to be much worse.

On getting out of his aeroplane Macmillan, 'the old crofter', added to the flurry of activity. Garbed in a leopard-skin, he was adopted as a son-in-law of the Bantu – an honour that meant that his feet were not allowed to touch the ground and so speeded him on to the dénouement he had carefully planned. He progressed non-committally through

Nigeria, dutifully shaking hands with Nnandi Azikiwe, Obafemi Awolowi and Abubakar Tafawa Balewa, bowing with patrician courtesy and managing the unfamiliar names as though they were obscure authors on his publishing list. Further south the *Malawi News* advised a boycott: 'He should not be given any welcome. No one should line the streets to cheer him up. No one should go up to Chipoka to cheer him up. No one should go to Zomba to cheer him up. Before we can be happy with him he must release our Dr Hastings Banda.'

By the time he reached South Africa, liberal opinion had been further inflamed by police treatment of native demonstrators at Blantyre. The incident was fresh in African minds when Macmillan rose to make his speech to the South African Parliament. 'There is a wind of change blowing through Africa....' The words had been drafted two months before in London (by Sir David Hunt, who was to be acclaimed Master of Masterminds twenty-two years later). They had been designed to be the climax of the tour and were guarded as carefully as if one of Agatha Christie's ingenious twists depended on them. They made no new statement; their strength was that they were clear and unambiguous, and that they were made in South Africa.

The Old Crofter flew off before South Africa could realize the extent of the outrage; flew back to England where actors, sportsmen, politicians and clerics were mounting a boycott on South African goods, and Randolph Churchill (his father was sunning himself in Monte Carlo) declared his intention of 'consuming all the South African produce I conveniently can'. At home, upon a smaller stage, promoted by Professor Trevor-Roper, the Crofter was contesting the chancellorship of the University of Oxford against Sir Oliver Franks, who had the Master of Pembroke in his corner.

Cherwell, the undergraduate magazine, had the last word on both campaigns: 'Banda is not English, but nor is Macmillan. Macmillan is not a Negro, but Banda was not at Balliol. Banda is in gaol, but Macmillan put him there.... If Oxford is the home of lost causes, surely the chancellorship must go to Banda.' It went to Macmillan.

His long absence was made easier by unrest among the Labour opposition. Easy targets like Blue Streak (one of a line of sophisticated weapons costly to a degree and, by the time they were produced, already naive to a fault and as obsolete as mere conventional weapons) could not provide a rallying point.

Clause Four of the Labour Party constitution – a provision that committed the Party to increasing public ownership of the means of production – excited Labour as readily as it left the country listless. An early example of trial by television – John Freeman confronting Frank Foulkes of the ETU – was a spectacle that the voter found easier to watch. Mr Foulkes had threatened to suspend all elections to his union if members did not stop complaining about the conduct of recent elections.

The passionate abuse by the young socialist Dennis Potter (who was to become one of the most prolific and polemical of playwrights) in his book *The Glittering Coffin* aroused no answering concern in the Labour Party. Potter dismissed the Labour leaders as 'hypocritical, stinking, pin-striped, slovenly, stupid, tatty', and Hugh Gaitskell as 'a fun-fair barker with a false nose'. But these were words the Party did not want to hear. Bevan was dying; Gaitskell was to die three years later. Potter, in a quieter mood, pinpointed a left-wing problem of 1960: 'the dilemma of working-class students who are unsure of the class to which they belong, culturally divorced from the one in which they grew up, resentful of and still outside the one into which their ability has thrown them. Some are quickly assimilated, others alienated and it seems re-tribalized.' That condition was hardly to survive a decade in which many found a new chic in working-class backgrounds, real or assumed. There would be other influences – age, acquisitiveness, affluence – to make the switch from Left to Right tempting for many in ten years' time.

The BBC announced the significant appointment of Hugh Carleton Greene as Director General in the same week as an unfortunate headline appeared declaring 'Now Reith takes over State'. It meant no more than that the onlie begetter of the BBC (who was soon to view his successor with some suspicion) had accepted the chairmanship of the State Building Society. Hugh Greene's appointment represented a radical change of policy at the BBC. He was a professional broadcaster and a skilful enough politician to attempt to change the Corporation. Time proved that he could achieve little more than a facelift, but he allowed programme building – the public aspect of the BBC – to grow and mature. He was not to strike at the BBC's monolithic structure and when he was replaced, old features, warts and disfigurations broke out again through his cosmetic operation; but in the early Sixties his confidence and the lead he gave created an atmosphere of change.

John Betjeman (CBE in the New Year Honours List) protested in vain that he 'wouldn't mind if all television programmes were just breaking waves and sea noises'. The assault on his ears was compounded by the imaginative appointment of William Glock as Head of Music. In the same week two future television queens staked their bids for recognition.

Ngaire Dawn Porter (later cruelly dismissed by Noël Coward as 'the three worst actresses in the English-speaking world', but loved by millions in *The Forsyte Saga*) was heralded in a little revue as 'the girl from down under who looks like being tops'; and Millicent Martin, who in the dignified phrasing of the day 'made such a success of her role in *The Crooked Mile*'.

Commercial television had already shaken up the BBC in 1956 and this phenomenon, together with the shock waves sent out from the Royal Court Theatre in the same year, had begun to produce more interesting and varied programmes; but there was still room for *This Is Your Life*, *Dancing Club*, Hans and Lotte Haas, *Do It Yourself*, *Picture Parade*, *Juke Box Jury* and a *Panorama* to which Robin Day and Ludovic Kennedy had just been added, kidnapped from the opposition ranks. Johnny Speight was contributing whimsical comedy for Arthur Haynes and for Eric Sykes, Hattie Jacques and Richard Wattis, 'a new comedy team on Fridays'; and Hancock's return to the screen with Sid James was welcomed.

In the theatre, Chichester took a step towards a festival and Peter Hall announced his first Stratford season. John Mortimer's stage play *The Wrong Side of the Park* provoked his dismissal by Alan Brien in the *Spectator* as, 'the Christopher Fry of Prose Drama'. 'There are some *tours de force*', Brien continued, 'which can only be described as ghost art. I mean those productions of men with quicksilver talents – Kodak eyes, stereo ears and a copywriter's fluency – which never quite add up to genius. I mean the paintings of Annigoni, the verse plays of Christopher Fry, the poetry of Dylan Thomas, the novels of L.P. Hartley – all these okay names are creators of middle-brow masterpieces.'

The instinct to assemble lists of okay names was powerful. Osborne, Wesker, Arden, Behan, Mortimer, Willis Hall, Shaffer, were defined as leading playwrights by the *Radio Times*, which added cautiously, 'and perhaps also J.P. Donleavy and Harold Pinter – whose future is still a controversial question.' *The Times* shared the caution in announcing two of Pinter's plays, *The Dumb Waiter* and *The Room*, at the Hampstead Theatre Club: 'Mr Pinter is of course well known to a wide public through his brilliant contributions to revues and also as the writer of *The Birthday Party*.' Its drama critic was bolder in his assessment of the two plays: 'Like Webern he has a taste for short, compressed forms and like Webern he inclines towards etiolated, *pointilliste* textures, forever trembling on the edge of silence and to structures elusive, yet so precisely organized that they possess an inner tension nonetheless potent because its sources are not completely understood.' But the heady wine of the Fifties breakthrough pioneered by the Royal Court Theatre was going sour in some parts of London. Alan Brien again: 'The old audience for playwrights is gradually disintegrating like an army without a general. It is bewildered by N.F. Simpson, bored by John Arden, depressed by Arnold Wesker, infuriated by John Osborne, perturbed by Brendan Behan, disgusted by Shelagh Delaney – none of them is an acceptable indigestion tablet after an early dinner. . . . The West End Managements still know nothing about art; but now they don't even know what they like.'

Various sages attempted prophecy. Richard Hoggart in *Encounter* felt sure that 'art will emerge more closely from non-commercial sources'. Harold Hobson predicted that 'a specific kind of English musical will develop'. Lindsay Anderson opted for 'a theatre of poetry and prophecy and obstinate aggression which disturbs and exhilarates'. His production of *The Lily White Boys* at the Royal Court Theatre was clubbed down by Brien: 'The English musical comes to immaturity'. A commercial manager, Donald Albery, saw 'more and more plays with colour and music' and, slipping in a little special pleading, conditioned no doubt by wounds to pride and pocket-book suffered at the hands of leading performers, 'fewer and fewer of the "show me a star and I will show you a good play" sort'.

At the universities a clutch of Sixties names were already sparring with celebrity. Alan Bennett, Peter Cook, Jonathan Miller and Dudley Moore, all down from Oxford and Cambridge, were preparing their assault on Edinburgh and London with *Beyond The Fringe*. At Cambridge, Corin Redgrave was guiding Eleanor Bron in and out of Beckett's dustbins watched by Waris Hussein – then Waris Habibullah ('I wish I were more depraved,' he told *Varsity*); and David Frost was practising jokes which still stand him in good stead. At Oxford, Ken Loach as Angelo 'did not make his part interesting, though as co-director he did achieve audibility and a general ease of movement'. His later partner in revolutionary television films, Tony Garnett, was at London University. According to the critic of the *Sunday Times*, 'the verse came off poorly' in his Hamlet, 'which more closely resembled a low-spirited sailor on leave after the pubs have shut than a Prince of Denmark'. Plainly a house-style was being established.

Brigitte Bardot had a baby and Diana Dors gave double birth – to a son and to her memoirs in the *News of the World*: 'I hate nothing in my story – I write it because I am currently a wife and about to become a mother.' She was often to write and sell it again, without the onset of any change of marital or parental status.

In the midst of all this life Constance Spry died and so did Albert Camus – *The Times* obituary recorded that 'the clue to his character was that he once played in goal for Algiers'. Football fans at home could still watch 'Mr Alf Ramsey's Ipswich Town', and a critic could still write that 'Revie of Leeds showed signs of his form in the mid-Fifties with Manchester City'.

The French achieved a Bomb at last and in America fall-out shelters were being fitted with 'rumpus rooms'; 'What blows up must come down' was the salesman's catchphrase. 'I can see nothing objectionable in the total destruction of the earth', observed Evelyn Waugh, 'provided it is done, as seems likely, inadvertently.'

A clutch of prophecies were to prove remarkably accurate. The *Sunday Times* risked forecasting a golden age of youth, heart transplants, travel to New York in two hours, even home video-recorders. A less convincing foretaste of what lay ahead was provided by the declaration of the results of a competition to find a new alphabet, inspired by Bernard Shaw. None of the finalists, not Dr Pugmire, Mr Magrath, Mr Kingsley Read, nor Mrs Barrett of Nova Scotia, has seen the winning entry pass into the language.

The language was stretching to accommodate *Clea*, the final volume of Durrell's 'Alexandrian Quartet'. The writer could not entirely escape the charge, levelled by Pursewarden, one of his characters, at D.H. Lawrence: 'I am simply trying not to copy your habit of building a Taj Mahal around anything as simple as a good f..k.' David Storey's *This Sporting Life* and Clancy Sigal's *Weekend at Dimlock* were more in the mood of the time, sharper, sparer observations of life in the North, natural successors to the novels of Kingsley Amis, Keith Waterhouse, John Braine and Alan Sillitoe which had appeared in the late Fifties. Sillitoe's *Saturday Night and Sunday Morning* was already on the way to the cinema screen and Waterhouse's *Billy Liar* to the stage.

The British cinema was seeing one of its false dawns. As the year opened a number of movie houses were converted into skittle alleys and the old guard, represented by Sir Michael Balcon, clashed in print with the Young Turks led by Tony Richardson, whose Woodfall company had already produced *Look Back in Anger* and was in the process of making *Saturday Night and Sunday Morning*. However, Richardson, with Karel Reisz and Lindsay Anderson, headed a group of film-makers who seemed to come some way towards promising a British film revolution to match the exciting flair of French films, which were beginning to arrive in England under the blanket label *nouvelle vague*.

The use of this journalistic label was as lazy as had been the easy resort to the earlier phrase, 'angry young man', to cover writers as disparate as John Osborne, Kingsley Amis and Colin Wilson; but it served to classify a group of film-makers who were at least French and had done less than twenty years' service in the cinema. Louis Malle, Claude Chabrol, François Truffaut and Alain Resnais were the most familiar names. Truffaut's *Les Quatre Cents Coups* and Resnais's *Hiroshima, Mon Amour* both opened in London in January 1960. 'Personally I prefer *Gigi*,' said the French Ambassador disloyally, but expectation ran high for *Les Amants*, *Les Cousins*, *Les Mistons* and *Le Beau Serge*.

By the end of the Sixties one man, Nat Cohen, was to be for a moment the most powerful influence in the almost defunct British cinema. In 1960 *Kinematograph Weekly*, a trade paper, devoted a special issue to this 'fruity fifty-three-year-old with a Guy Middleton moustache' and his then partner, Stuart Levy. 'Two of the greatest guys in the industry,' one colleague bought space to testify; another chorused, 'The best pals I ever had.' It was still a *Boy's Own* industry.

As if to semaphore its survival into the new decade there was a flurry of royal activity. The Queen produced a third child and, although the Empress of Japan managed the same feat, it was loyally noted that ours was bigger (seven pounds three ounces). Ours was called Andrew; they called theirs Naruhito Hironomiya. C. Day Lewis, poet but not yet laureate, staked a claim for consideration for the job:

> Today we sing
> Like sunbeams carolling
> The hearts of commoner and Queen
> Break out in happiest green
> You princely babe, you pretty dear,
> For you we bring
> The birthday honours of the quickening year.

Sir Arthur Bliss, Master of the Queen's Musick, set it to music, Novello published it, but somehow it was not much sung.

Lady Carisbrooke and Lady (Edwina) Mountbatten both died, but Lady (Pamela) Mountbatten married interior decorator Mr David Nightingale Hicks, thus conferring the first royal blessing on one of the 'new professions' at the altar of Romsey Abbey. The next profession to be honoured had not long to wait. Cecil Beaton had been clicking with chic for years, but the first undeniably royal photographer took the stage with the announcement of the engagement of Princess Margaret to Antony Armstrong-Jones. No one had guessed, not a gossip column had had wind of it. Newspapers had a field day all over the world:

'Meg to wed court Fotog' (*New York Daily News*)

'She'll be the most famous Jones of all' (*Toronto Star*)

'He really clicked' (*Journal American*)

'I do not know the gentleman,' commented the Duke of Windsor, 'but wish my niece and her betrothed every happiness.'

There was a spate of 'my friend Tony' articles. 'She will have three mothers-in-law. The newest (until she married a few days ago) was an air hostess,' was another fruitful line. Already the marriage was compounding the belief of the decade that anyone could get anywhere. Exciting jobs were in anyone's reach. With a handsome face and social manner the commonest in the land could gain access to the most select circles. The way was being prepared for the barbers, models, graphic designers, footballers and pop singers, the new rich about to become the new fashionable.

There were rumours that the Royal Family had not embraced the new son-in-law quite as readily as the euphoric newspaper reports suggested. One told the story of Macmillan, back from his African tour, retiring early to bed, tucked up with his Trollope, startled by a phone call. Pulling his tweeds over his pyjamas he obeyed an urgent summons to Sandringham. Driving through the night he speculated on the nature of the constitutional crisis that could be causing this uncomfortable break in routine. The confusion in the drawing-room on his entry was painted dramatically: the Queen frozen and fretful in one corner, the Duke of Edinburgh pacing and swearing, Princess Margaret sobbing, the Queen Mother sipping gin to steady herself. Suddenly a door opened and the Old Crofter was confronted by a small man whom he recognized vaguely as a photographer and who, throwing him a look, hastened out of another door without a word. Whatever the nature of the constitutional crisis, plainly Her Majesty's Chief Minister had not arrived a moment too soon. 'By God,' he was said to murmur, 'the press are here already!'

A Birmingham Person

To watch the world from a media perch in Lime Grove in 1960 was to have a privileged vantage point, one to which I had clambered by a series of fortunate accidents. The luckiest was to be born in 1931 and to finish Army service, Oxford and Bar exams conveniently in time for the opening of commercial television.

In my last year at Oxford I assembled and produced a revue for BBC television called, I think, *Oxford Accents*. The BBC Outside Broadcasts Department had decided to do an Oxford week. They would go to the Union, they would eavesdrop on conversations in a don's room over dinner, and they would cover various sporting events. One of these was to be an undergraduate boxing match. However, almost too late, it was discovered that on the night fixed for the boxing there was to be a professional bout in Limehouse. The BBC's agreement with the boxing authorities was that they would not compete for audiences. If undergraduates were trying to maim one another on television, it was considered unlikely that the people of Limehouse and thereabouts would turn out to see bloodshed on their own doorstep. In deference to the promoters' pockets the BBC had to cancel and look around for an alternative attraction. They considered fencing and rejected it; it sounded suitably undergraduate, but insufficiently crowd-pulling. Eventually Anthony Craxton, the producer, and Brian Johnston, the commentator, decided on a revue, and Desmond O'Donovan and I – having done two or three – were asked to devise one drawn from our best previous shows. Among the cast was Maggie Smith, an ASM at the Oxford Playhouse, already showing sure signs of her potential as a comedienne. Most of the revue was written by Jeremy Bullmore, who had gone down the year before and was devoting all his time to writing.

The show went out live, as shows did at this time, and next day the television critics used us as a stick with which to beat professional entertainers. The adjectives reserved for these occasions – fresh, high-spirited, witty, bright, intelligent – were taken down and dusted off, and I was invited to go to Television Centre to talk to Ronald Waldman, the Head of Light Entertainment, who received me solemnly, regretted that he had not seen the show himself (no recordings), and advised me very sensibly to go into a good repertory company and learn the job from the bottom.

Suitably chastened, I returned to Oxford to find an invitation to meet George Dixon, a director at J. Walter Thompson, the advertising agency. I suggested that he should interview Jeremy Bullmore as well, as Bullmore had been understandably miffed at being left off the closing credits of the television programme. Separately we visited 40 Berkeley Square and submitted to various tests of creative writing and fashionable psychological battles with ink-blobs. Bullmore proved infinitely more inventive and, presumably, more stable, and was hired on the spot. I was told that it might be worth applying again, but much later on. Bullmore is now head of JWT in England, so it is unwise to mock ink-blob tests.

I finished my time at Oxford, just managing to scrape a Second by furious cramming in the last term to make up for two and two-thirds years of enjoyable idleness. It was a hot, happy summer and I started a routine of rising very early, working very hard and lunching lightly in my rooms with half a bottle of claret. I napped and worked until dinner, and then sat in Wadham Garden for half an hour after supper. It was quiet, with only the mildest murmur of traffic from outside. The huge, dark, heavily laden trees were cool and reassuring, and since I knew almost no one in the college, the business of committing the Law to memory proceeded without interruption. I continued in this fashion throughout the examinations and the only moment of genuine anxiety was when I was called for a *viva*. I had a secret weapon if stumped: there is a Victorian case, 'Regina *v*. Dodds', which concerns a sexual assault on a duck, and I felt that if I dragged the 'Fuck-a-Duck' case into my *viva* it would provoke an embarrassed change of gear and a switch to another question which I had a better hope of answering.

I knew that my *viva* could not be to confirm a First; it could only be to spoil my chance of a Second – or worse. Eventually, without recourse to Regina *v*. Dodds, I got my Second and faced the prospect of finding real work. I had no idea what I wanted to do, but I did know that if I enrolled at Gibson and Weldon's cramming school for barristers in Chancery Lane I could get six months' grace before having to make a decision. I had already been eating dinners at Gray's Inn for some two years. They made a pleasant break in undergraduate life. Three times a term we left Oxford in the late afternoon, British Rail tea took us to Paddington, and Henekey's sherry filled the waiting time until the Inn offered its very average dinner (Gray's kitchens were, however, supposed to provide better food than those of its rivals); then we caught the late train back to Oxford – nicknamed the Flying Fornicator by those who had not come to London for the serious purpose of eating dinners.

I fainted for the only time in my life after one of them. A 'moot' had been mounted, an elaborate debate presided over by a real live judge (Norman Skelhorn), in which four junior members of the Inn argued an abstruse legal point. I was two nights underslept and totally ill-prepared, and those arguments which I had rehearsed were pre-empted by 'leading counsel', leaving me nothing to say before an increasingly irritated judge. Suddenly a heavenly choir started to sing, bright colours danced in my eyes and the room revolved gently and gracefully. I fell to the floor and, when I came round a minute or two later, I received nothing but help and encouragement from the learned judge. I realized I could not rely on frequent fainting fits in a long career at the Bar, and if I had any lingering hopes of a legal career this dispelled them. However, with my Oxford Law degree the whole feeding fiction meant that I could be called as a barrister almost as soon as I had completed Gibson and Weldon's course, which would give me breathing space of some six months to think about a job.

Meanwhile, with other unemployed graduates I brought a couple of revues to the Watergate – a club theatre now covered by the widened Strand – and provided Maggie Smith with her first solo lines on the London stage. She played a cinema usherette overcome with nerves on her first appearance in the spotlight at the local Odeon. I can only recall the first two lines:

> It's my première tonight
> And I'm scared as scared can be ...

Miss Smith, challenged twenty-five years later, went on a lot longer.

The Watergate concentrated on small revues and boasted a minute theatre restaurant which started the Fifties fashion for apparently amateur restaurants staffed by tight-trousered waiters. The specialities were Scampi Bill (after the owner) and Banana Beryl Reid (after Miss Reid).

It was the beginning of the restaurant revolution, masterminded by a volatile personality called Bill Staughton, who went on to open La Popote and the Hungry Horse among others. His finest hour at the Watergate was a confrontation with a temperamental chef. Diners could hear but not see the row building up in the kitchen or the dénouement when the chef flung a large, freshly-prepared chocolate sponge at his employer and covered his face in deep brown cream. Unflurried, Staughton looked through the hatch into the dining room. We waited in uneasy silence as he delicately picked the goo from his eyes. 'Chocolate gâteau is off!' he said.

I settled in Chelsea in a large flat on the Embankment owned by a writer, Michel Raper, and an actor, Kenneth Fortescue. In the early days they were ambitious to serve breakfast, which was included in the rent, but the enthusiasm soon wore off and fish cakes passed out of my life with no regrets. They had room for three lodgers and, during the eight years I was there, Peter Nichols (then an actor, not yet a playwright), Roderick Cook, Jeremy Sandford and Julian Pettifer were among my fellow tenants. We called it the Chelsea Palace.

Nichols's tenancy was illuminated by occasional visits from Kenneth Williams, with whom Peter had served in an ENSA troupe along with John Schlesinger and Stanley Baxter. Nichols, a good mimic and an excellent raconteur, fumed in impotent rage whenever Kenneth took over his stories half-told and embroidered and developed them to some extravagantly bawdy punch line. He was playing the Dauphin to Siobhan McKenna's Saint Joan at the Arts Theatre at the time and relished a fruity impersonation of an elderly actor-laddie, Frank Royde, playing the Archbishop, who had been directed to spend most of the play downstage, with his back to the audience, looking upstage at Saint Joan. Asked some question about his make-up he boomed back at the director, 'Don't know! Never had to make up me arse before!'

Kenneth was the worst hospital visitor I ever had. He came to see me in St Mary's, Paddington, after my hernia operation. Laughing is bad for post-hernia patients and my surgeon, Arthur Dickson-Wright, also an after-dinner speaker, was already a risk. Kenneth, though, was definitely dangerous and had to be made to listen for once. I wish he had been there after my only other confrontation with the surgeon's knife (apart from loosing my tonsils to a Mr Arthur Miller (no relation) at the Italian Hospital in Queen Square, where I felt cheated by having to send out for my own Italian ice cream). The daunting second operation was for piles at the London Clinic. Afterwards, on the day when I was judged ready to risk an evacuation, I was warned by the nurses that they had the whole business down to a fine art. They gave me pills the night before. After a good sleep I would be woken early, given breakfast and at nine o'clock precisely lowered onto a portable throne for the painful climax. Waking as advised, I realized that I was more than ready for the dreaded seat. However, loyalty to my nurses made me conform to their programme and I had my breakfast and held my peace with increasing discomfort. Just before nine the throne arrived and all hell broke loose. Every available nurse materialized with the plain intention of seeing how I stood up to suffering; the searing pain started; and at the same time I could hear my secretary outside the door insisting that she had to deliver my mail at nine exactly. At that precise moment *Housewives' Choice* struck up 'All Things Bright and Beautiful'. Thank God no second operation has been necessary.

The most eccentric tenant at 6 Chelsea Embankment was Jeremy Sandford, who was just starting his career as a writer. He spent a great deal of time in bed, fully clothed, peering at empty sheets of paper. One day, when water poured through the ceiling of his landlord's sitting-room below, it took precious minutes to get Jeremy to open the bedroom door, acknowledge that his hand basin was running over, and turn off the tap.

His encounter with a burglar was hardly less eccentric. Strange people were always coming and going in that house, and it was considered gauche to question a guest. Jeremy returned to it one day to find one of these strangers leaving with a pile of clothes and a typewriter. Jeremy was with Nell Dunn, who was to become his wife, and they greeted the 'new tenant' politely. When the theft was discovered later, the police were keen to interview Jeremy, the only man who had seen the thief. Could he identify him? He certainly could. Notebooks poised, they waited while Jeremy thought long and deep. At last he found the words. 'He looked like a rather bad journalist.' No more could they elicit.

It was some six or seven years before King's Road began to epitomize the urge to 'swing'. Bakers, greengrocers and family butchers still confirmed the village atmosphere. Boutiques were a phenomenon of the future, although espresso coffee bars were appearing – notably Roy's, heavy with *trompe l'oeil* on the outside, near the Pheasantry. On my first excursion along the pleasant, shabby street, the Chelsea Palace was still active and Monty Norman, 'the Singing Barber', topped the bill. Chelsea love affairs filled the newspapers, whether they were explosive and elderly like Sir Mortimer Wheeler's or romantic and raffish like those in which James Goldsmith snapped up Isabel Patino, and Dominic Elwes eloped with Tessa Kennedy and settled in a basement in Tite Street, or dashing, like the series of amorous advances made to the young, rich, beautiful and impressionable by Edward Langley.

By the time I finished Gibson and Weldon's cramming course and was due to take the Bar exams, I had adopted Caletta's Restaurant in King's Road as a perfect place from which to plan my assault on the examiners. Unlike many King's Road eating places it has had only one change of face. It is now a Chinese restaurant called Marco Polo, which it became on Caletta's demise. Caletta's walls were brown and discoloured, partly through age and partly due to a vague sepia mural which was supposed to have been painted many years before by a non-paying diner. The *table d'hôte* at luncheon was a legendary three shillings all included. The table-cloths were white and soup stained. Even the soup was soup-stained. It was also thick and gravelly. Unappetizing things were done to lamb and chicken, and yet the spindly chairs and creaking tables had their *aficionados*.

I used it a great deal and, when examinations loomed, the routine of steak and salad, claret and cheese, with books propped up and perfect peace in the sparsely attended room, was all conducive to committing the longer and more complicated passages of the law to memory. Above all, the room was presided over by a benign, shaky old gentleman – a transplanted Italian version of the waiter in *You Never Can Tell*. Madame Caletta commanded from a cash desk, and a young Mr Caletta divided his time between the restaurant and the tobacconist-cum-sweet-shop next door; but it was the old gentleman to whom all the regulars reported and who fussed over and coddled and was considerate of them. When Caletta's changed hands the new owners engaged him and he greeted his old customers with frail warmth at the opening party, but the variety of new and mysterious Chinese dishes brought fear and confusion into his eyes, and I never found the courage to go back and see how he was doing.

The last night of Bar exams ended with a bang. I had a couple of drinks with fellow victims in Chancery Lane and went to the Haymarket Theatre to see *The Matchmaker*. Ruth Gordon, Sam Levene and Eileen Herlie were starring in a magical production by Tyrone Guthrie of the play that was to be the basis for *Hello Dolly*; Arthur Hill and Alec McCowen played the two apprentices. The evening started badly – I cannot remember whom I had invited to go with me, only that I was stood up – but the play quickly dispelled irritation. Afterwards I took a bus home and it crashed into the front of the Ritz Hotel, producing jovial jokes about caviar and chips.

I went to my parents' home in Somerset to await the exam results and when I heard that I had passed, I returned to London to look for a job, with no more excuses up my sleeve. I had no wish to starve, as I certainly would do, at least for a few years, if I stayed at the Bar; nor did I relish the idea of living off my parents any longer. In spite of my failure at J. Walter Thompson, advertising seemed the best bet. I made a few forays from Chelsea Embankment and talked without much enthusiasm to a couple of firms. Returning from one of these interviews I was walking down the Strand when I bumped into Stephen Wade, who had been the BBC's Outside Broadcast floor manager on the Oxford revue. 'What are you doing?' he asked. I explained proudly that I had become a barrister, and he asked me to lunch. He had left the BBC to take part in the great adventure of commercial television. After lunch he took me back to Television House at the end of Kingsway to meet Keith Rogers, another ex-BBC man, who was now Head of Outside Broadcasts for ATV. (He was later the recipient of one of Lew Grade's early Goldwynisms. Keith made a deal with the Amateur Athletic Association for coverage of athletics meetings. Proudly he reported to Grade, 'We've got the three As.' 'What's the three As?' 'The Amateur Athletic Association.' 'I don't want any amateurs. Get me professionals.')

Stephen Wade introduced me fulsomely and Keith Rogers asked what I was doing. I confessed to being a barrister and he looked impressed and apologetic. He could only offer me a producer's job. I had arrived with visions of starting as the traditional tea-boy and working my way up with talent, hard work and determination; but seeing a possibility that none of these qualities might be needed, I kept quiet and asked what the salary would be. Rogers looked still more embarrassed. 'Only £900,' he said. Even with my slight grasp of mathematics I could work out that this was twice the £450 that most of my contemporaries were being offered for the jobs advertised by the Oxford University Appointments Board. I said I thought I could manage on £900 for one year. I reported to ATV on the following Monday and transmission began on the Thursday. It was as easy as that.

It did not take long to discover that my legal training had fitted me for precious little in a television studio, but I was in, paid and established as a producer, and assigned to a programme. With the advent of breakfast television in this country most people have forgotten that ATV pioneered breakfast television in the 1950s. They did not pioneer it for very long or with any great success, but from October to Christmas we reported dutifully to Viking Studios in Kensington on Friday evenings and prepared for a feast of entertainment from nine to ten on Saturday mornings. The presenters were two charming actors, Daphne Anderson and David Stoll. They did chatty interviews in the cramped studio. Jerry Desmonde broadcast a live commercial for the Palladium. There was a weekly domestic sketch played by two more actors, Hannah Watt and Tom Chatto, written by Leslie Julian Jones; there must have been a cooking spot, and I have a dim memory of gardening and household hints. Noele Gordon and I were production assistants working incredibly hard at achieving amazingly little. My particular responsibility was to find out by various subterfuges what our celebrity guests would like as a gift, publicly presented on screen in lieu of a fee.

Our first guest was Gracie Fields, who was to top the bill at Val Parnell's first *Sunday Night at the London Palladium*. No detective work was required on this one: the word came down that she was to have a Parker pen. But someone had blundered; when it was presented, Boris Alperovici, her husband, took but one look at it. 'We have one already,' he said firmly.

Donald Wolfit got a combined alarm clock and tea-pot, and Dorothy Tutin a small white lambswool rug from Harrods.

On Sunday afternoons I used to hang around the London Palladium watching Parnell complain about Tommy Steele's guitar or the late George Carden, the choreographer, bawling out his dancers. 'But Mr Carden,' said one, after a severe dressing-down, 'I'm not queer!' Carden advanced on him from the stalls. 'Never mind,' he shouted, 'no one will know from the front.'

Best to listen to was Tommy Trinder, the first host of the show and of *Beat the Clock*, its game show centrepiece. Trinder remains the epitome of Cockney repartee, but he has never found the same ease and fluency on television that he achieved on the halls and in cabaret with his now almost forgotten catch-phrase, 'you lucky people', and his table-hopping, when he would hand out cards inscribed 'Trinder's the name'. The phrase got him into trouble and then triumph with Orson Welles on an occasion when Welles looked up in a surly mood and asked, 'Why don't you change it?' 'Is that an insult or a proposal of marriage?' was Trinder's reply.

I cherish one comeback less well known – since it never got on the air. Trinder was once confronted by a particularly obnoxious contestant on *Beat the Clock*. The woman was infuriating but, with a comedian's instinctive reluctance to alienate the audience, Trinder persevered with her. The more answers she got wrong, the more prizes and points he showered on her. Finally he found that he had let her through to the last round. She was in for the jackpot. Again she failed. Indecision creased his face. Again he favoured her and wheeled on the prize. It was a hairdryer. Ungracious to the last, she surveyed it balefully and said with resentful deliberation, 'I've got one already.' Trinder's patience snapped: 'Never mind, madam, one day you may have a two-headed baby!'

There was an air of happy improvisation at ATV in the early days. We camped above Associated Rediffusion at the end of Kingsway and, stiffened by a backbone of BBC professionals, most staff members seemed to have drifted into their jobs from some outpost of Moss Empires and the variety circuit. We were aware of Val Parnell, of Prince Littler and dimly already of little Mr Grade, though no one was tipping him to emerge as the ultimate survivor in the ATV power struggle. Most conspicuous, pacing intently along the corridors, was the short, pudgy, pale-grey figure of Harry Alan Towers, who was also the first to go. Norman Collins, who had done so much to lobby for commercial television, had faded into the woodwork of the boardroom. Prince Littler's group, the Incorporated Television Programme Company, combining the Grade Agency, Moss Empires, Towers's commercial radio contacts and Warburgs as merchant bankers, had been turned down by the ITA as too powerful, so they had merged with Norman Collins and devoured him in the process. (Although swallowed by the vaudevillians, Collins stayed on inside the firm until 1982 when he left the Board of ATC with Lord Grade.)

For the company it was a period of turmoil and substantial losses. In the studio it was a time of cheerful cooperation. After starting the day with the morning show I had another job as floor manager on a children's afternoon programme, masterminded by Anna Lett, another BBC refugee, who was later to marry Christopher Chataway. As well as doing my usual floor manager's chores, I was also the voice of the invisible 'Charlie'. Charlie was intended to be our secret weapon in the ratings battle with BBC children's television, and our regular uncle - Uncle Fred - indulged in whimsical conversations with him. I provided Charlie's voice by squeezing a rubber toy. Charlie got up to no end of mischief, squeaked when excited and would, we hoped, become an invisible national figure. Unfortunately on one occasion when I was nipping in deftly to arrange bare-handed Charlie's latest bit of trickery, I mixed up the cameras and enraptured tots had their illusions shattered as they saw two bare arms arranging the skullduggery for which Uncle Fred was berating Charlie. Nowadays heads would roll, but that was not the way things were in 1956.

Occasionally we used to broadcast from the New Cross Empire, making brief use of the stage before it was given over to *People Are Funny,* one of the first ITV programmes to provoke a standards scandal. Had we produced Charlie from New Cross, his secret might never have been revealed for in those autumn and winter months heavy fog used to rise from the river and there were afternoons when the white mist made it impossible to see across the makeshift studio. On its site now stand a garage and forecourt.

ATV's first Christmas Day was celebrated for children with a special live broadcast from the hospital on Paddington Green. A whole ward was taken over but on the day we moved in our equipment we found it sadly bereft of children. Most of them had been allowed to go home for Christmas! We were left with a happy and cooperative band – perhaps six children and twenty-four beds. Two problems soon defined them-selves: one of the professional entertainers displayed an unprofessional interest in the little boys; and six children did not go far to 'dress' the ward. Constant vigilance kept the risk of child molestation under con-trol, and to some extent the second problem helped solve the first. The children had to move rapidly from bed to bed to provide backgrounds which suggested a ward full of festive tots; and a moving moppet is a much harder target for a molester to hit.

Conjuring tricks were mingled with prayers, and as the *Robin Hood* series was popular in those early days, Dick James – later the Beatles' publisher – who had recorded the title song turned up to sing it. Suddenly the live programme which we thought it would be hard to spin out to thirty minutes looked like over-running. There was a rigid rule then that programmes which contained any religious content must be separated by several minutes from commercials. The danger point drew nearer – an extra prayer did not help matters – and my last memory of the afternoon is listening over my headphones as an agonized Anna Lett screamed down the line to central control pleading for more seconds. For a moment it looked as though she might have won but then her last despairing cry rang out: 'You *can't* fade a blessing!' There was not much liaison between ATV spiritual and ATV temporal in those days.

By this time I had started to collaborate on plays with Caryl Brahms and on that same Christmas weekend we were living through the excite-ment of our first television play. We had adapted an old farce which

Caryl wrote with S.J. Simon some years before. Not too sure of the durability of its immensely complicated plot, we submitted it to the BBC under the pseudonym Moss Mindelbaum. To our surprise they accepted it as a vehicle for Harry Green, whose broad farce technique was a great audience puller. We had to cut the two-and-a-half-hour stage script to seventy-five minutes. Then Harry reminded us that he was performing it live in front of an audience and that he always allowed fifteen minutes for laughter. Obediently we cut another fifteen minutes.

We went to a dress rehearsal as soon as I could get away from Paddington Green and were not greatly encouraged by what we saw. The next day we turned up to watch hours being spent on achieving a 'comic' effect. The director had come straight from radio and was devoted to exploiting sound effects on television. This particular rib-tickler was a squelching noise inserted as a criminal's head was squeezed between door and post. The director also had a theory about television comedy. It was simple and, he claimed, infallible. 'Long-shot, mid-shot, close-up, LAUGH!' he would burble happily.

We watched the seventy-five-minute transmission from Chelsea Embankment. In spite of long-shots, mid-shots and close-ups, the audience did not laugh once and apart from a couple of coughs there was no sign that anyone had turned up. Even with a delay of thirty seconds while the camera held a close-up of a door handle and we waited for the leading actress to complete her change and enter, the farce under-ran by exactly fifteen minutes.

ATV started broadcasting to the Midlands from Birmingham in February 1956. An old theatre in the suburb of Aston was adapted as a studio, with an Outside Broadcast control van drawn up by the stage door and a line of prefabricated huts attached to the side of the building for offices. On a clear day, when she was arguing a point with sufficient conviction, you could hear Noele Gordon's theatrically trained voice distinctly through three or four sets of office walls.

The breakfast programme had been cancelled – there was scant evidence that anyone had watched it – and our little group became the nucleus of Birmingham programming. With three months' experience on the floor, I was considered to be a fully trained producer/director, although I still awaited my first experience of controlling cameras. We arrived in Birmingham just before the opening night and I was relieved to be given the simple job of stage managing the inaugural ceremony at the town hall. All commercial television opening ceremonies were characterized by a pompous, respectability-seeking opening ceremony, decked out with as many lord mayors, bishops and platitudes as could reasonably be assembled under one roof. All I had to do was drop a finger, rather like starting a race, so that the lord mayor would know when to start spouting.

Early on the day I got a call at my hotel. I was to report instead to the Television Theatre at Aston, to stage manage the opening variety show. Bob Monkhouse was hosting it with Dennis Goodwin. They were also writing it. The star guests were Tyrone Power, who was touring *The Devil's Disciple*, Richard Hearne, Barbara Lyon and the Buddy Bradley dancers. I had never worked on such a show before. The director was Bill Ward, another capture from the BBC, notorious for his impatience with staff. Monkhouse realized early on how lost I was and chaperoned me through the day with fatherly patience and tact. My abiding memory is a constant barrage of noise from Bill Ward coming through my headphones. Mostly it consisted of the word 'seque'. I had no idea what or where a 'seque' was and did not like to ask. I hunted everywhere for something that looked like 'seque' sounded – all to no avail – and only some time after ATV's opening variety spectacle had ground to its undistinguished close did I find out that seque is a musical term implying smooth transition from one piece of music to another.

The evening ended with a lot of drink in Prince Littler's suite at the Queen's Hotel, at which I arrived limpet-like rather than by invitation. As the others watched the Bishop of Birmingham deliver the epilogue, I watched Prince Littler's hand creeping deeper into the cleavage of one of the ladies on his staff, the better to caress her breasts. 'May the Lord bless you and keep you ...' said the Bishop. 'This is show biz,' I was thinking.

I stayed in Birmingham for about eighteen months, and it was an invaluable baptism of fire. The production staff, under Philip Dorté, was slender. Originally it consisted of Noele Gordon, Reg Watson, an Australian director-producer, and me. At first we did very few programmes but later, as we did more, the production staff got even smaller. Noele had not spent some twenty years on stage learning her craft as a performer in order to dwindle into an executive. She came back into view and on to stardom via *Fancy That*, an advertising magazine programme. This pure kitsch art form sadly disappeared from our screens a long time ago – *aficionados* will remember *Jim's Inn* with particular reverence. After that Noele found a more permanent niche in a midday variety show called *Lunch Box*, a sort of *Family Favourites* dressed up as a Valentine card. Finally she achieved Meg Mortimer, née Richardson, in *Crossroads*. Reg Watson was Noele's personal producer, devising these programmes with her and for her, and occasionally being allowed a longer leash with a variety show in London before being returned to Birmingham for regular duties. This left me as a general dogsbody, filling in the other small nooks and crannies of programming intended to give the Midlands viewer the illusion that he was watching a station bursting with regional character.

The first programme which I could decently call my own owed its notoriety to a tabloid journalist called Douglas Warth. Douglas was a beguiling mixture of idealist and hustler, a sensitive vulgarian, a campaigner whose commitment came and went, brash and bashful, cunning and gullible. He was short, stocky and swarthy, sporting a stubbly, shaving-brush beard. I do not remember how we met, but Douglas convinced me and subsequently Philip Dorté, Controller of Programmes in Birmingham, that there was a place on television for some equivalent of controversial tabloid journalism. Douglas's range of interests was wide and his enthusiasm for debate, and in particular for devil's counselling, was infectious. Moreover, he could combine theatrical tub-thumping with Jesuitical debate, in varying proportions depending on how much – if anything – he knew about the subject he was discussing.

We called the programme *Paper Talk* and it produced ATV's first regional storm in a teacup. Douglas decided that if he was going in for hard-hitting journalism he should be seen to be going in for it. Our opening shot revealed a tousled head of hair, a shirt unbuttoned at the neck, a tie awry. As the camera pulled back the viewer took in a whisky bottle half-empty, a cigarette half-smoked, an ashtray overflowing, and a typewriter on which Douglas pounded between swigs and sentences. A monstrous talking, drinking, swearing, arguing caricature journalist was born, and phones began to ring. The impression of 'the reporter as drunkard' was compounded by the fact that Douglas's voice had almost disappeared. He had not been drinking heavily before the show, but he had been attacked by that psychosomatic assault on the vocal chords which silences many performers before a particularly nerve-racking first night. He croaked and slurred his opening diatribe in a manner which left no doubt in the minds of those who did not want to doubt.

It was the beginning, for me, of a wonderful roller-coaster ride of programmes and my introduction to the lesson – fully assimilated much later on *TW3* – that it is much better for your programme to be mentioned on the front pages of newspapers than in columns of television criticism. Douglas provided most of the ideas for the programme and a lot of the leg work, tirelessly luring local and national figures into the studio so that he could turn on them when he got them there.

We failed to work the miracle with Sir Oswald Mosley, which disappointed Douglas mightily. Mosley was due to address a public meeting at Birmingham Town Hall. The wave of prejudice against black immigrants was swelling across the country and was breaking with particular power in the Midlands. There was a strong move to ban the meeting, which looked provocative, and Douglas was particularly keen to confront Sir Oswald. On the editorial decision as to whether we should issue an invitation to Mosley, Philip Dorté preferred to refer me to Val Parnell in London. I called Mr Parnell and explained the premise of the programme. The noises which came down the line were not encouraging. I pleaded the importance of the meeting, the growing success of the programme, the sense of anticipation which would be aroused in Midlands breasts at the prospect of a Mosley–Warth confrontation.

'No, Ned,' said Mr Parnell, 'I don't think that's a good idea.'

'But everybody is talking about the meeting, Mr Parnell.'

'No, Ned, he's not a very nice man.'

'But Douglas would certainly give him a very rough time in argument, Mr Parnell.'

'No, Ned, we can't do that.'

'But, Mr Parnell, the figures for the programme are going up and ...'

'No, Ned, we can't touch it. You see, it's politics.'

'But, Mr Parnell, you broadcast another political programme on Sundays, in the afternoon. It's called *Free Speech*.'

'No, Ned, that isn't politics. That's just four impartial politicians talking.'

We did not invite Sir Oswald, but I've always enjoyed the thought of Michael Foot, A.J.P. Taylor, W.J. Brown and Woodrow Wyatt or Randolph Churchill as 'impartial politicians just talking'.

My favourite farcical show with Douglas was his 'serious' attempt to put the point of view of nudists before the Midlands public. We made a reconnaissance of a soggy nudist camp near Coventry and talked to a leading lady nudist who was only too anxious to cooperate. She chased me down a dripping wet glade on the grounds that no one was allowed in the camp with clothes on, and I could only defend myself (successfully) with my umbrella. We arranged to conduct the programme in the studio in the nude – with the nudists and Douglas discreetly photographed or carefully posed behind deck-chairs or box-hedges so that the viewer would not be outraged.

The rehearsals began tensely when the mother-hen nudist heard that photographers from the national press were in the building hoping to catch indiscreet shots of her chicks. She strode on to the set in her kimono and dropped it unattractively to her feet under my nose, threatening that that was what would happen on camera if she caught another peeping tom from the press in the building. My very young floor manager, Terry Yarwood, had entered into the spirit of the thing by deciding that anyone over thirty was a dirty old man and should not be allowed on the studio floor. Most of the older electricians and stage hands clustered at the back of the control room where the cameras were swinging about finding interesting but eventually untransmittable ana- tomical close-ups. The scent of prurience was heavy in the air and the leading lady's defiant strip had laced it with tension.

There were incidental joys in the programme – a momentary flick down of Douglas's eyes as he introduced one young woman warmly, 'I wish you could be sitting where I am tonight . . .'; a forthright statement of his job by a young, male, Midlands nude: 'I'm a tool-maker, i'n't I?'; but the grand climax was an interview with a married couple who were keen to establish the respectability and family nature of committed nudism. They sat together on a park bench, but no camera angle which we could devise solved the problem of showing him nude to the waist (acceptable) without showing her nude to the waist (unacceptable). We finally settled for a pose in which they were discovered 'casually' poring over a shared *Daily Telegraph* – the most respectable cover we could invent. After we had established this picture of domestic bliss we intended that they should, on a given cue, put down the paper and we would move into close-ups which would conform to the IBA's standards of decency. Not being professionals, they were nervous on the air and I saw the paper start to go down a fraction before we were due to cut to the next camera. The result was probably the best camera cut I ever made. Next morning half the Midlands swore they had seen and the other half swore that they had not. Fortunately in those days no recordings were made and there was no tangible evidence that anything untoward had been viewed – or, to continue in the prurient vein, nothing that would stand up in court.

Douglas's forays into sensationalism in the 1950s have left no mark on television in the 1980s, but he was a precursor of some of the best and worst trials by television which were to follow. Certainly I learned a lot from him which was useful when it came to arranging the Levin confrontations on *TW*3, developed and sometimes debased later by David Frost in his television trials of Savundra and Petro. Douglas engaged in wild attempts to provoke the unprovokable; he showed childlike joy at hearing Norman St John Stevas say 'masturbation' on *Paper Talk* in 1957 ('Is this a television first?'). He had a famous encounter with Bishop Watson of Birmingham. Asked afterwards how he felt, the Bishop said, 'I felt as though I was being mentally raped, then I realized I was being paid for it, so I simply said to myself, "Makes you a prostitute, Bishop, better get on with the job."'

Douglas delighted in being recognized, cheered or goaded in the street and more often in bars. Teddy boys were new then and he interviewed a bunch, inevitably treating them more sympathetically than he would more 'respectable' opponents. Before the programme we entertained them to dinner, as we always did our guests. The next day we were walking past a pinball alley in Birmingham and heard a row inside reaching punch-up proportions. In a flash it subsided and the two opponents were out on the pavement. The first was one of our interviewees from the night before. Grabbing Douglas and the other lad, he brought them forcibly together and yelled at Douglas to authenticate his story. 'Go on,' he said, almost in tears, 'you tell 'im. We did 'ave table wine to drink, din't we?'

And then there was the time when Douglas was accused of anti-semitism – how the charge arose on a programme about boxing and brain damage I am not sure, but Douglas was duly hauled up before Lew Grade.

'It's ridiculous,' Douglas said, 'I'm partly Jewish myself.'

'How much?' said Lew.

'A quarter.'

'It's not enough!'

I shall remember too his pride and affection in his wife and daughter. He was a mixture of pussy cat and toothless tiger; he was never dull and sometimes roared. After I left Birmingham he failed to find anyone else who enjoyed the extraordinary experience of cavorting through programmes with him and I could not find a place for him in the less buccaneering atmosphere of the BBC. For a time he became a television critic and joined that honourable band who, having more pressing things to do, publish their criticism of a programme which has not been transmitted. In the end, a disappointed man, Douglas took his own life.

By the time ATV's Birmingham station was in full swing an earnest television trainee could not have hoped for a busier apprenticeship.

Philip Dorté's ambition to increase the amount of local programming resulted in convenient little spaces of half an hour or a quarter of an hour or five minutes springing up all over the schedules. As an old television newsreel man he wanted to establish the first regional television news service.

Considering the interminable rolls of credits which follow current affairs programmes these days, I am amazed at the output which my poor overworked secretary and I used to foist on the Midlands audience; at the busiest period I used to be responsible for producing and directing three programmes each Monday: a half-hour outside broadcast hosted by Billy Wright in the afternoon, *Seeing Sport*; five minutes of news at six; and then, at ten, another live show called *The Midlands Storyteller*, in which old gentlemen reminisced about past glories, mysteries and mishaps. On Tuesday the regular local news gave way to twenty minutes of controversy with *Paper Talk*. On Wednesday afternoons Noele Gordon presided for thirty minutes over *Tea with Noele Gordon*, a couple of celebrity interviews and a few home hints to which my favourite contributors were R. St John Roper, the late spangle-king of London Palladium costumes, demonstrating to Noele, and through her to housewives, how to make a shirt – a skill he had to learn especially for the show; and the legendary principal boy – Dorothy Ward – who sang 'I never felt more like singing the blues, Hotcha!' clinging to a blue chiffon handkerchief. After *Tea with Noele* came another news programme.

On Thursday the other programme after the news was *Midlands Affairs*, a half-hour forum for local and national debate. George Brown and Gerald Nabarro were the regular stars and they were decked out with an assortment of local politicians, mayors and councillors. Friday was an easy day – only the five minutes of news unless Reg Watson was exhausted, as he occasionally was, by the time he had produced four *Lunch Boxes* in a week. *Lunch Box* was Noele's request variety show featuring various supporting singers and the Jerry Allen Trio. Failing Reg, I used to step into the breach and wetted my feet in the world of variety.

Seeing Sport had great compensations: a chance to rub shoulders with or point cameras at some of my boyhood idols, like Arthur Wellard, the great Somerset fast bowler, coaching at Alf Gover's cricket school; Billy Wright himself; and, in retrospect, the distinction of being the first person to televise Mick Jagger. Of course, I did not realize that the spotty boy, who was a member of his father's basketball class, was a future star at the time – but then how much do most people contribute to the debuts of the stars they introduce to the public?

The Midlands Storyteller, later on the same night, was an entirely congenial chore. There lived near Birmingham a distinguished elderly pathologist, Professor Webster, who had been, after Bernard Spilsbury, the most famous pathologist in the country until Camps, whom he rather despised. His career had started with the Buck Ruxton and 'Nodder' cases – both famous trials in which he had appeared for the prosecution – and his last front-page involvement was in the James Camb/Gaye Gibson 'Girl Through the Porthole' case. The professor had been educated at the University of St Andrews at the same time as the actor Lionel Mollison and had also considered going on the stage, but instead stayed at medical school and did his acting in court.

Now, through an appearance on *Paper Talk*, he was revealed as a television natural – the most compulsive talker to camera I have ever come across. He had one glass eye which was a little wayward, but he could still talk at the lens as though it was a best friend. In the introductory interview with Douglas Warth he leant forward conspiratorially and cunningly in front of a few hundred thousand viewers and said in a convincing whisper, 'Confidentially, just between you and me . . .' and proceeded to reveal some hoary, gory secret. Left to himself he was even better. He revelled in the fifteen-minute length – if a story took longer he would spread it over two weeks and make it last exactly thirty. He liked the stage manager to give him a five-minute sign, a two-minute sign, one-minute, thirty-seconds and finish. He always signed off on the dot and always with a flourish; sometimes with a twist that would have sent O. Henry to bed happy.

His kindness and concern for me were constant and we used to lunch occasionally to get a rough idea of what cases he might cover, though he preferred not to elaborate on them before telling them on the air, perfectly shaped, for the first time. One lunch-time we were disturbed by the proprietor of our regular restaurant, the Olympia in Dale End. He ushered in a policeman. The constable bent low and whispered something to Webster, who smiled briefly and excused himself. He returned with a broad grin on his face. A crowd had gathered around his car and another policeman was standing guard over it. Inside the car a blood-covered skull lay on the back seat. The cloth which covered it had slipped and the lunch-time crowd were convinced that they had stumbled on a murder. Webster covered the skull and came back to his lunch.

On another occasion he arrived at the studio chuckling. He had come from a post-mortem examination and the widow, told who was doing it, seemed much comforted and said with some pride, ''E's going to 'ave to hurry to get to ITV in time, i'n't 'ee?' So many early television programmes are not recorded, but Webster's would have been a unique record of story-telling and of provincial crime from the Twenties to the Fifties.

No other *Midlands Storyteller* achieved the same popularity, though Phil Drabble had an enjoyable run with Black Country stories. One programme scars my memory as the most embarrassing and heartbreaking in which I ever took part. I invited a distinguished old Birmingham journalist, Harry Bush, who was known for his careful, considered, amusing prose. He had a rich store of reporter's tales and seemed an ideal successor to Webster. He was a teetotaller who had, I was led to believe, been a heavy drinker some years before. In his first trial story ('pilots' took place live in those days) he was to describe a visit to a menagerie and an encounter, alone and unprotected, in a lion's cage. My professional responses should have been much quicker, but Webster's expertise had made me careless. Harry arrived at the studio carrying a closely typed, tightly constructed account of his ordeal. It was nicely timed for fifteen minutes and he had tried to commit it to memory. This would be no mean feat for a practised actor – for a seventy-year-old with no experience it was hopeless. As we rehearsed it became more and more obvious that we were in for a débâcle. I tried to persuade Harry to abandon the script and simply tell the story as he remembered it – as he first told it to me over lunch at the Press Club. We seemed to make progress. He appeared to be prepared to abandon the text.

As the time for live transmission got nearer I convinced myself that he was going to be all right. Never was there a more hopeless miscalculation and I shall not easily forget the next fifteen minutes. I counted down to transmission and gave the studio manager the cue to start. Harry looked at the camera. 'I want to tell you . . .' he said, stopped and looked wildly around. Luckily the studio manager was holding the pages the storyteller had brought with him.

'I want to tell you about the time I went into the lion's den . . .' he prompted.

'I want to tell you about the time I went into the lion's den . . .' Harry said obediently and with no conviction.

'It was unforgettable . . .'

'It was unforgettable . . .' Harry forgot again and sat looking bemused at the camera. Central control faded to an equivocal caption for some seconds and I crept into the studio. It was virtually a one-shot show so the responsibility for directing the cameras was not onerous. When they picked us up again I was sitting at Harry's feet and prompting him from out of camera range as he limped and stalled through the remaining ten minutes or so – I have never felt so helpless. The sensible solution would have been to have switched to an interview at the last moment, but the idea did not occur to me. The programme was faded out at the end of its time slot, the story half told. Harry, deeply disturbed, left for home. The experience provoked another battle against drinking for him which he eventually won by himself, no thanks to me. He was a lovely man.

One probable reason why I did not consider converting Harry's solo disaster into a limping, last-minute interview was my reluctance to appear in front of the camera, which I always felt while working as a producer and director. I did it only a couple of times in Birmingham, usually giving short arts reports on the *Midlands News* in order to get free tickets to the Shakespeare Memorial Theatre at Stratford-on-Avon. The nearest I got to television celebrity occurred on a visit to a Birmingham cinema to see the Boulting brothers' film, *Brothers in Law*. As I edged my way to my seat in the crowded theatre I had to clamber over two teddy boys. One of them looked up and a flicker of recognition crossed his face – I had been on the news earlier that night. He nudged his companion: 'Look who that is.'

'Who is it?'

'It's Ned Sherrin. He's on television. He's famous – like Lassie!'

The Mickey Mouse nature of the nation's first regional television news service which I started is another humbling experience on which to look back. The news was provided by the Birmingham *Evening Dispatch* – they simply sent across a sheaf of stories written in exactly the sort of provincial newspaper prose in which they were printed in the paper. Some were accompanied by still photographs, never more than two or three per bulletin. We also made an arrangement with a Birmingham firm of film makers whose principal business was filming weddings or occasionally recording a company outing or making unambitious advertising films. A day or so ahead we would arrange to cover the opening of a supermarket, the unveiling of a statue, the laying of a foundation stone, a village fête, a pancake race, the oldest, the fattest, the highest, the prettiest, the biggest, the smallest, the flower show, the beauty show, the fatstock show. We never got to know about real news in time to film it.

The film 'reports' averaged twenty to thirty seconds of silent footage cramming as many Midlands faces as possible on to Midlands screens in the hope of creating the illusion of Midlands coverage. As the film was silent, a long debate raged over whether we should sweeten it with sound effects as well as commentary – see a lorry, stick on an effects record of a lorry; see a field, turn up the birdsong. The essence of the debate was whether there was actually birdsong at the time? Did the lorry make more or less noise? Were we reporting faithfully or could these sound effects be said to amount to misrepresentations of the news? In the end the silent film clips became so boring that the sound effects crept in.

Very occasionally there would be a two-minute interview. On one memorable occasion the great Reginald Bosanquet, at that time a slim, tanned, dapper ITN hopeful, was specially imported to handle street interviews with strikers in the street outside our makeshift studio. The first set of live interviews went out on the national network and we swelled with pride at our contribution. The second set filled most of our very own show.

This rag-bag of items was held together by Patricia Cox, the news-reader; she was a drama student who looked a little like the Queen and was enormously dignified and reassuring. The idea of using a woman at all was considered daring; but Patricia held the job for some years. On her first holiday we thought we would try something even more daring – a black woman news-reader – especially 'brave' as Birmingham was one of the first cities to identify its 'colour' problem. After an exhaustive search we found a charming girl who looked ravishing, spoke sweetly and seemed perfect. We were only a matter of hours from unveiling her to the press and the public when we found she could not read.

After eighteen months in Birmingham – coming home to London for weekends and leaving from Euston every Monday morning – I wanted to work in London. I asked for an interview with Bill Ward, who was in day-to-day charge of ATV programmes, and I put my case. I had, I felt, given loyal service to ATV in Birmingham; it had been a valuable apprenticeship. The scope of programmes there was limited; the challenge of London was exciting. I warmed to the persuasion – all to no effect. There was a long pause from the other side of the large desk, and then, 'No, Ned, we think of you as a Birmingham person. . . .'

It was time to look towards the BBC.

Tonight and Every Night

I joined the BBC on a Monday morning in 1957, having left ATV on the previous Friday. I had an introduction from Caryl Brahms to Cecil McGivern, who was then in charge of television programmes. He handed me on to Grace Wyndham Goldie. Mrs Wyndham Goldie is one of the critical influences on the development of television. She had been the *Listener*'s first television critic and in the 1950s and 1960s she brought a ruthless and relentless intelligence to current affairs programming.

Raised on the unquestioning, optimistic pioneering spirit of early commercial television, I found an audience with her daunting. Later I learned two tricks which helped me when I could not keep up with her impatient quizzing. Sometimes, like a dubious Sunday newspaper reporter, I made an excuse and left the room, to return later having had time to think of a counter for her latest ploy, or, if I only needed a moment or so, I could usually depend on a compliment – hat, dress or hair-style – to disconcert her momentarily. As she rarely changed her basic style these ploys seemed almost too transparent to me, but they usually gave me the respite I needed.

Mrs Goldie had a better mind and higher standards than any television executive I have met before or since. She was not without humour, but only in the sense that the equator is not without ice if you ship in a refrigerator.

I was lucky in my training. The *Tonight* programme had started a few weeks earlier. It had an unlikely birth. In the early 1950s the BBC conspired with parents in the absurd fiction that television closed down early in the evening so that young children could be packed off to bed; when they were assumed to be safely asleep transmission started again.

In the infancy of Independent Television it became clear to the commercial companies that this period covered by 'the toddlers' truce' would be one of their most lucrative selling times, and where ITV led the BBC had to follow. The first plan to counter the commercial challenge was to award various time segments to different departments – Outside Broadcasts, Drama, Talks, Light Entertainment.

Donald Baverstock and Alasdair Milne had produced a novel, popular news magazine called *Highlight*, and ambitiously they advanced a scheme to fill the full hour, five nights a week. Championed by Mrs Wyndham Goldie they won the day and *Tonight* went on the air hosted by Cliff Michelmore, Derek Hart and Geoffrey Johnson Smith and employing highly idiosyncratic film reporters like Alan Whicker, Fyfe Robertson and Macdonald Hastings. Baverstock and Milne also recruited a production staff of exceptional quality. Tony Essex ran the film editing department – editors and directors who were to graduate in the major cinema and television leagues included Jack Gold, Kevin Billington, Michael Tuchner and Ken Ashton. Antony Jay, Gordon Watkins and Cynthia Judah were early associate producers. It was a dedicated and ambitious team and the amount of unyielding in-fighting between them was remarkable.

Baverstock's great virtue was a mind prodigal of ideas. In a world in which few television people can lay claim to a single original notion, he could produce a hundred in as many minutes. Of the hundred, on a good day, one might be valuable, two mundane and the rest rubbish, but Donald did not surround himself with 'Yes' men. He relied on his colleagues to sort the nuggets from the trash while chipping away remorselessly at their own suggestions himself. Each early morning conference was a free-for-all alive with acrimonious interest. After lunch screening sessions of near fine-cuts of film stories ready for transmission that night or rough-cuts being prepared for a day or so ahead were more emotional excuses for blood-lettings.

Alasdair Milne's contribution was no less important. If Baverstock sparked a flurry of ideas, Milne had a better mind for analysing the results. Of course their roles were not limited to originator and analyst, but these were the more obvious aspects of their contributions. The respect in which the members of the team held one another was extraordinary testament to their talents and the skill of their selection.

At first the programme was broadcast from the tiny 'Viking' studio off St Mary Abbot's Place, Kensington, where I had begun my television career with ATV's *Breakfast Show*. It had also been used to film commercials and Wendy Toye made her charming short film *The Twelfth Day of Christmas* there some years earlier. Already the studio had seen a classic mix-up involving Jonathan Miller. This was before *Beyond The Fringe*, but the great doctor was already established as a university comedian and caused a scandal on *Tonight* by performing an irreverent sketch about Admiral Nelson on a patriotic anniversary. Those were the days when Sir Ian Jacob was running the BBC. More farcical was Miller's misunderstanding with a cameraman who was signalling to the tracker (who pushed and pulled his camera base) to pull back so that he could take a slightly larger shot to encompass the doctor's generously flailing arms. Each time the cameraman crooked his finger and the conscientious dolly-pusher retreated, the alert comic would spot the finger and read its beckoning wave as an invitation to come nearer to the lens. Frustrated, the cameraman pulled back again and once again the doctor misinterpreted the gesture. In and out of areas of light they journeyed, further and further back across the studio floor. Very soon the cameraman found himself backed against the wall, with the gesticulating Miller shrouded in shadows, peering into the lens darkly until he finished his monologue.

I have never had occasion to work with Dr Jonathan since then but he has come in and out of my life for some thirty years, since I first saw him as the brilliant star of a Cambridge revue. Leaving his production of Chekhov's *Three Sisters* in 1976, I heard a puzzled American lady mourn to her companion: 'More a play than a show, wasn't it?', a line which I was able to put to good use later in defining *Side by Side by Sondheim* for the audience – 'More a show than a play.'

On another occasion Jonathan was directing Denis Quilley as Sir Benjamin Backbite in *The School for Scandal*. Quilley is not only a fine actor but also an honest, straightforward fellow. He found the role of an archetypal, acid gossip hard to fathom and took his troubles to Miller. 'Do you know Ned Sherrin?' the Doctor asked, and all was apparently explained. Denis was very good in the part.

Grace Wyndham Goldie, hearing that I had been directing cameras in Birmingham, thought that it was perhaps time for *Tonight* to have a full-time camera director and brought me down to look at the programme and meet my future colleagues. They were and always remained a close, elitist clique ever eager to give or take internal criticism, but equally sure about closing ranks when it came to defending their own programme against outside criticism or savaging other people's shows. We went to the pub across the road after the transmission and I talked mainly to Mrs Goldie and to Alasdair Milne, with whom I had been at Oxford. I learned in retrospect that the others felt that they had behaved very badly and given me a complete cold shoulder. I had said brashly that 'wrestling is good for ratings' and argued for a more tabloid approach – remembering *Paper Talk* no doubt. I was not aware of frostiness in the air at the time; but I saw it often enough later when others joined the team to realize that it had probably been the case.

For me, *Tonight* was an extension of my ATV apprenticeship in Birmingham, albeit a more demanding, sophisticated and metropolitan course. Again I was in a studio five days a week, planning and directing some forty-five minutes of live television a day. The difference lay in my colleagues – I now had some – their standards, and a national audience.

The editorial team met in Lime Grove each morning and ransacked the newspapers for likely stories. Topical items of national interest presented themselves automatically – the only question was who to ask to discuss them. A government minister might swish down to Lime Grove in his limousine, arriving at the last moment, and be wafted away immediately his interview was over; or an Opposition spokesman might arrive early in a BBC taxi, share BBC hospitality enthusiastically until he could be quizzed, and then linger garrulously, long after the broadcast, as though he had no home to which to go. Change the government, and the politicians would switch routines with ease. The former laggard became the man with the mission; last week's action man stayed on to prop up the bar. If we lacked a ministerial spokesman there were traditional pairings of backbenchers – a Boothby and a Foot, perhaps. Next down the line came the rival journalist-apologists: Paul Johnson and Peregrine Worsthorne were, I suppose, the Michael Denison and Dulcie Gray of *Tonight*, appearing when only less than mighty opposites were available.

One of *Tonight*'s most significant changes was to admit the ordinary person to the screen. Hitherto cameras were turned on statesmen or experts. *Tonight* pioneered the participation of people.

As the programme developed the film input became more and more ambitious. Early on Baverstock, and his film department under Tony Essex, established an approach which changed film reporting throughout the BBC. Like the rest of *Tonight* it was flowing, fluent, apparently casual – though in fact carefully thought out – and proceeded from a firmly held attitude that *Tonight* was on the side of the audience. *Tonight* interviewers asked the questions that they imagined the intelligent viewer would want to ask and not the question that the subject of the interview most wanted posed, like the classic old-BBC feed line, 'Minister, is there one jot of truth in this suggestion ...?'

In the studio this frequently led to elaborate stratagems talked through exhaustively by Baverstock and Milne and the other production assistants with Michelmore, Derek Hart, Derek Bond, Geoffrey Johnson Smith or Kenneth Allsop, on the assumption that to a certain question the subject could answer A or B. If the answer was A then ploys C or D could be followed; if he answered B then the counter stroke was E or F. Of course, after these heavily argued preparations the inconsiderate subject could always go off the rails and the interviewer needed to use his own flexibility and wit; but thrashing out the alternatives in advance primed the mind for a confrontation designed to extract the maximum amount of information during an interview which often lasted no more than four minutes and needed to be weighty or witty indeed to survive for ten.

As I remember, interviewees were paid some five or six pounds for their trouble and there was a classic encounter on one occasion when Peter Sellers arrived to plug a play in which he was opening at the Aldwych (pre-RSC, although it was directed by Peter Hall). The play, by George Tabori, concerned an oil sheikdom, and Sellers arrived in flowing robes to be interviewed, as for real, as an oil sheik. Straight faces were kept and I think some plug was given to the play once the interview was over. Sellers had improvised prodigally and the allotted five or six minutes spread to nearly ten. Everyone was delighted, Sellers left happy, and the next morning we heard from his manager – not angrily, but hooting with laughter. The relevant BBC booking lady whose job it was to negotiate the contract had been on the telephone early. 'We were so pleased with Mr Sellers last night,' she cooed. 'He was so funny – we let him go on rather longer than we agreed.' The agent could detect a note of caution through the charm. 'What we would like to suggest', said the fearless bargainer, 'is increasing his fee' – the agent waited for it – 'from six pounds to seven.'

Sellers tangled rarely with television, but the late Harvey Orkin, who was his agent for some years, told me that when Jonathan Miller was planning his television film of *Alice in Wonderland* Orkin urged him to make it in colour because of the possibility of a sale to an American network. Miller said no – he saw it in black and white like the Tenniel illustrations. After his deserved success he called Orkin again. Did Harvey think Peter would consider re-shooting in colour? The possibility of an American sale had indeed raised its head. Of course the moment had passed, Sellers had played his role and, like a child tiring of a new toy, had thrown it away. He had no wish to pick it up again.

Another favourite device which *Tonight* may not have invented but grew fond of was the 'vox pop' – grabbing passers-by on a busy street to canvass their views on an issue of the day or on some more self-conscious question dreamed up by a desperate production team short of material at the early morning conference. A favourite site was the King's Road, Chelsea – just beginning to be colourful, even in black and white – at the top of Royal Avenue and on a particularly wide stretch of pavement in front of the shop of Thomas T. Crapper, the famous indoor plumbing and sanitary engineers.

Crapper's has gone and the forecourt no longer seems fashionable for itinerant 'news 'n' views' gatherers, but during the Sixties the whole of the King's Road was their paradise. Teams of anything from two people upwards could be seen photographing the exotic natives or, more often, photographing one another with a view to reporting back to Tokyo, Berlin or even boring old New York. I remember trying to get into Alexander's, the friendly basement restaurant on the corner of Markham Square which Mary Quant – whose first shop was above it – opened with her husband Alexander Plunket Greene. The narrow steps down to the restaurant were cluttered with uniformed Nazis, some carrying camera equipment, some not. I pushed past towards the food and inquired what was going on. The waiter looked surprised that anyone should even ask. 'Is swinging King's Road movie,' he shrugged. Natch.

In recent years the down-market vox pop has migrated to the North End Road market – famous thoroughfare transformed into a shrine by Esther Rantzen's arrest for microphone-importuning. (The up-market favourite is still the north-east corner of Harrods.) In the mid-1970s I had occasion to ask questions on Esther's patch. Starting a vox pop attack is rather like going into the sea for a spring dip. It is hard work building oneself up for the first invasion of some passer-by's privacy, but once you are in and well and truly wet there is an awful fascination about it. This day was particularly lucky. Esther's special star, Annie Mizen, the little old lady who sucked, nibbled, or spat out everything Esther gave her to taste, came bustling across within seconds.

'Are you from Esther?' she asked.

'No.'

'I thought not,' she said darkly, plainly having spotted an impostor. 'She told me she wasn't coming back till January!'

I could hardly let her go. 'Is it true?' I asked, '... you must know her as well as anyone. Is it true that she's going to have her teeth shortened?'

A look of horror crossed Annie's face. She pondered the enormity and shook her head vigorously. 'No,' she said, 'no, Esther won't have her teeth done. She's known for her teeth!'

My main editorial contribution to the content of *Tonight* was on the showbiz side, easily the most thankless part of the programme. If a toothless grandmother from the Hebrides or a seraphic infant from Bude said something amusing it was always a bonus. The moment we cut to an entertainer everyone, audience and production team, became a critic. There were various ways of injecting performed items into the show. At the beginning Cynthia Judah made two inspired bookings, Robin Hall and Jimmy MacGregor, the Scottish folk singing act, and Cy Grant, whose calypsos and folk songs were equally popular. They also provided a convenient device for a programme which had to end on time and yet contained items of odd and often unpredictable length. Later I introduced Noel Harrison when we needed a replacement. He had been singing in clubs around Italy, came back for the programme and went on to make such records as *Windmills of my Mind* and to launch an apparently open-ended career around America appearing in his father's role in *My Fair Lady*.

Then there were the 'girl singers'. *Tonight*'s original concept as an all-round magazine programme always included an 'entertainment spot' – one of the few hangovers from a previous era. At first the girls were booked on a night-by-night basis after rather sketchy auditions. They were accompanied by the Ted Taylor trio, piano, bass and drums. Ted was an endearing figure, who had had a vaudeville musical act. He buttonholed me one day to recall a triumph of which he had been particularly proud: 'I had this wonderful piece of business,' he started. 'I used to cut my toenails with a pair of garden shears – of course it was a false foot!' He rocked with laughter. Some two or three hours later I found myself giving Bob Hope a lift back from Lime Grove to the West End – something had gone wrong with the limousine that should have collected him. He was charming, but the similarity at all levels in the great family of comedians was striking. He was full of his latest television sketch, performed with Robert Wagner and Natalie Wood, and the obsession with the detailed mechanics of the gags was just as single-minded as Ted's – so was the opening line: 'I had this wonderful piece of business . . .!'

After I joined *Tonight* we rationalized the girl singers a little – booking them for a week at a time. Donald liked clean, scrubbed sopranos like Diane Todd and Marion Grimaldi; Carole Carr, Maxine Daniels and Tonia Bern were others who did their weeks. We usually selected half a dozen numbers at the beginning of the week and then rehearsed one a day during the afternoon. On one chaotic day we were hardly expecting to get in a musical contribution at all – we were virtually pre-empted by a live outside broadcast from Copenhagen of a royal visit to Denmark, compèred by Richard Dimbleby. No studio interviews were planned, no interviewers, apart from Cliff, were called, and there was one short piece of standby film for an emergency. Timing in Copenhagen went wildly wrong, and after a scene-setting piece from Dimbleby we had to permute the resident folksingers (thank God folksingers always have an unlimited repertoire!) with Maxine Daniels. It was a Friday and she had used up her entire week's list of songs, so she had to busk unrehearsed, inter- rupted only by occasional admissions from Denmark that nothing was happening yet. We had just managed to last the course without repeating ourselves when the doors opened and the royal party entered in time for our sign-off.

Tonight introductions often had a shamelessness which was all their own. The presenter would look brazenly into the lens and say, 'On this day 115½ years ago ...' and no further justification for an interesting, well-researched, well-illustrated subject which had fascinated one of the production team was required. My own personal excuse was usually the death of any songwriter, however obscure. I scanned the obituary columns keenly and the moment I saw that someone had gone to the great Tin Pan Alley in the Sky I would chase up the well-known songs he had written, scratch around for a few which were less well-known, and see how quickly Peter Greenwell could cobble snatches together in a miniature version of the medleys with which he and Caryl Brahms had such a success in the *Song By Song* series twenty years later. Invariably Millicent Martin and David Kernan would arrive to coo the songs at one another – Miss Martin with iron-clad aplomb, Mr Kernan with many misgivings but always winning through in the end. Parodies, however contrived, were another favourite form. There was a four- minute saga called 'Rembrandts are a Girl's Best Friend' based on the slender thread of a news story which hinted that smart girls were investing in Old Masters.

It was possible to get away with songs and parodies on *Tonight* – much harder to get away with topical sketches. Not only were they played to silence but they had to compete with that formidable opponent, unconscious humour, which often bubbled up in interviews. We persevered with attempts to dramatize Michael Frayn's very funny columns in the *Guardian*, but the effect of fleshing them out with actors was invariably to transform them into nudging and winking moments which disturbed the rhythm of the programme. Worst of all we attempted a genuine television strip cartoon, ignoring the basic problem that readers of a newspaper have the option to turn to a strip if they like it or ignore it if they do not. Our viewers had no escape from 'Evelyn'. She came with the best credentials: Bernard Levin wrote her and Tony Hoare devised paper scenery and paper clothes for the main stars, who were Prunella Scales as Evelyn and Ronnie Barker as the irascible Uncle to whom she posed unanswerable questions. 'Evelyn' lasted some weeks and brought down much wrath on her head and ours. At the end Bernard gave me a copy of John Evelyn's diaries, from which I have had far more pleasure than out of foisting 'Evelyn' on an unwilling public.

Although it made no impression at the time, an interesting dramatization in the context of *Tonight* was Anthony Burgess's *Clockwork Orange*. We taped a ten-minute excerpt to illustrate our interview with the author, with James Bolam in what became Malcolm McDowell's role. Burgess later confessed that he had never expected it to reach the screen.

As a programme which did more than most to change the face of current affairs broadcasting and to make cracks in the traditional image of the BBC, *Tonight* has been discussed and analysed, explained and apologized for by a host of commentators – the most perceptive is Mrs Wyndham Goldie in her book on television and politics, *Facing the Nation*. My favourite memories are more peripheral. My role, apart from being a licensed importer of candy-floss, was to slicken and regularize the studio procedures; to make sure that the elaborate illustrative studio caption sequences attained the speed and flow of film in spite of happening live before the audience's eyes on Heath Robinson equipment; to see that the speed and elasticity of the production team was not let down by a cumbersome, inflexible mind in the control room; and to catch whenever possible, in the way that only an inquiring studio camera can, the fleeting moment of tension between interviewer and interviewee, or of self-doubt or self-satisfaction on the face of a visitor. I do not subscribe to the view that television reveals character – of course it can on occasions; but the camera lies like the rest of us if its subject is sufficiently wily.

I always enjoyed looking for odd quirks of character in our subjects.

After interviews with Edith Sitwell had become a cliché, I filmed virtually an entire interview focused on her claw-like hands encrusted with enormous rings (and carried her in my arms from car to studio and back again). On another occasion, when the *Tonight* obsession with animals was well to the fore, a small pig got loose in the studio and we followed it for the rest of the programme through songs and interviews.

Then there were the moments of agonized waiting to see if film which had been delivered, edited and rushed to the projection room would be there in time for the last words of Michelmore or Hart or whoever was introducing it. The closest shave was a memorable despatch from Saigon. Trevor Philpott and Slim Hewitt, the cameraman, had sent home footage which showed them surprised by enemy crossfire in the middle of filming their report. It was a Friday night and by Monday the story would be interesting rather than exciting. Michelmore had a longish introduction and I decided to let him start it even though there was no sign on the preview monitor that the film had been loaded – a misty number, the cue, should have been visible. My act of faith had a happy outcome. I shouted 'Run telecine!' (equivalent of 'Roll film!') at the last possible moment and somehow it ran – the hail of gun-fire exploding on the screen exactly as a rock-steady Michelmore finished his last lingered-over syllable. At his best on *Tonight*, he was an unusually flexible rock in the programme's history of strong stone formations.

Individual memories jostle. The late Kenneth Allsop, a precise, elegant and concerned journalist, was always a joy to work with. He had an artificial leg and I became aware of a curious ritual through which he went on the odd occasion when a guest similarly disabled came on the programme. As one made for the other across the floor of the hospitality room or the studio, the stiffness of the legs became apparent and they would home in on one another and a formal Pinteresque exchange would occur.

'Leg?'

'Yes.... You too? ...'

'Yes.... War? ...'

'Yes.... Yours? ...'

'Yes.... Wood or tin? ...'

'Tin.... Yours? ...'

'Tin.... Above or below? ...'

'Above.... Yours? ...'

'Yes.... '

These seemed to be the qualities necessary for blue riband disablement

- war, tin and above the knee. I also loved his story of a time spent investigating the Chicago police force. Speeding on a freeway with his host and the host's small son, Kenneth became aware of a cop screaming up behind on his motorcycle. The car was flagged down and the host explained that he would demonstrate the nature of police morality in Illinois. He took out his licence and laid a twenty dollar bill in a visible but not too obvious position. The cop approached the window, looked down at the offering and said in an ugly voice, 'Get out of the car.' This alarmed Allsop because this was not the way a conveniently corruptible cop was supposed to react. His host obediently left the vehicle and on the further command, 'Come round the back', did as he was told, leaving Allsop and small child in the car. Some seconds later he returned grim-faced and did not relax his expression until he had put a few hundred yards between them and the patrolman. Then he began to laugh. When he had got to the back of the car the cop had pocketed the twenty dollar bill with alacrity, confining his strictures to one disgusted sentence, 'What'ya trying to do? Corrupt the child? . . .'

With very few exceptions – memorably one joyous day just before Christmas persuading a series of highly unphotogenic music publishers to sing their coy, quaint, cute or sentimental special Christmas songs to Trevor Philpott – I had little to do with the film side of *Tonight*, although I was once asked to an 'eligible bachelors' Valentine's Day party given by Heather Jenner's Marriage Bureau. I arrived after *Tonight* with Alan Whicker, who was mightily embarrassed when it became clear that the eligible ladies had mistakenly writen off the two of us as an item. My most useful contribution to filming on *Tonight* was a late one. I arranged for Julian Pettifer, whom I had seen doing good work for Southern Television, to join as a reporter. The original intention was for him to be studio-based but, although his journalistic flair and general brightness were undoubted, he was stilted and ill at ease in the antiseptic surround-ings of the studio. Moreover, he looked too handsome to be credible in the midst of the homely *Tonight* regulars. He was about to be 'let go' when a reporter was needed for some unglamorous film chore and Julian was sent off to fill in. Immediately he was seen against a slag-heap his golden good looks fell into unobtrusive context and audiences started to listen to him instead of worrying about what he was doing there.

Another favourite *Tonight* gambit was to provide an appropriately theatrical setting for some interviewees in order to add a little sense of occasion. There was a memorable bid by Lord Thomson to take over a rival group of newspapers and magazines; and we introduced him with an interminable camera trek across acres of the magazines in question, which were strewn over the studio floor, before panning up to the bemused mighty opposites. Dorothy Lamour was treated to an appalling tropical beach set, which did not amuse her a great deal – nor us when the projected film of a sleepy lagoon in the background ran out long before the interview was over. Harold Lloyd was quizzed high above the lights in the rafters of Studio G at Lime Grove; Bardot was interviewed before I arrived at *Tonight*, but I enjoyed photographing Mylene Demongeot curled up in a white fur, Lillian Gish, who helped a little with her lighting, and Jayne Mansfield on an old-fashioned love seat carrying all before her.

When Nubar Gulbenkian bought a London taxi, decorated with filigree gold basketwork, he bowled happily down to Shepherd's Bush in it and up in a lift to the studio, where he was interviewed through the window by Derek Hart and coined his famous explanation of why he bought it: 'Because I'm told it can turn on a sixpence, whatever that may be.'

An electricians' strike necessitated some odd improvised settings. One show was transmitted entirely from a fire escape outside Lime Grove overlooking the railway, with the sound often drowned by passing trains. The next night we used the roof at Television Centre and Marcel Marceau produced one of his snappiest pieces of mime when a gust of wind momentarily separated his toupée from his head, giving the viewer a brief glimpse of sky between skull and hair.

An interview with Mike Todd, the showman who was Elizabeth Taylor's third husband, was one of the better pieces of special staging on *Tonight*. Todd was opening his mammoth film *Around the World in Eighty Days* in grand style and before his gaudy Battersea Park launching party, which was a set piece of the period, he came to Lime Grove for an interview, dragging Miss Taylor in his wake. While Todd came up to the studio, she kicked her heels and narrowed her violet eyes impatiently in the hospitality room, plainly disenchanted at hanging around as an extra in her husband's star vehicle. Derek Hart was the interviewer and we used the slender resources of the studio to recreate the atmosphere of a tycoon's office. Todd, a small man in Cuban heels, was to sit at a large mogul-style desk surrounded by telephones, his large chair raised on blocks. Derek Hart, not tall either, was perched unimpressively on a stool, almost at his feet. Looking down at Hart and puffing on a large cigar, Todd dismissed Derek's early questions nonchalantly. The payoff was harder to weather.

'Have you ever done anything you've been ashamed of, Mr Todd?'

'Well, Derek, we've all done things we've been ashamed of.'

'Yes, Mr Todd, but you do things on a bigger scale than most people!'

Another vivid picture lingers which never got on screen: the Belgian statesman Paul-Henri Spaak, waiting to be interviewed, sitting on a chair beside a ten-year-old pop-singing prodigy, Little Laurie London, who was clutching his guitar before giving his 'He's Got the Whole World in His Hands'.

Occasionally we did auditions for straight singers or the more exotic rock 'n' rollers. My favourite of these was Wee Willie Harris who survives to this day. We auditioned him on the same morning as Tommy Steele's brother, Colin Hicks. Another firmly held *Tonight* tenet was 'never consider the real thing if you can have a near relation'. We had already examined Steele's mother; now here was a chance to observe his younger brother who, however, performed like a carbon copy of Tommy and paled beside the eccentricities of Wee Willie, whose shocking red hair would pass unnoticed these days. Wee Willie offered us three songs. His approach to the first was reasonably conservative: he stood at the piano and accompanied himself. For the next he played guitar. The third was obviously the climax of the act. With the first chorus his coat came off, with the second his waistcoat and with the third his shirt. (He was pasty and, apart from the violent hair, remarkably skinny and unprepossessing.) As he started the fourth, he began to fiddle with his belt and trousers, and as the song was as repetitive as most of its kind I stopped the audition and said, 'Thank you very much,' adding, 'I thought for a moment you were going to take off your trousers, Mr Harris?'

'Nah!' he dismissed the idea, looking more abject than ever, 'I just fiddle with me flies a bit – makes the girls go mad.'

In another encounter with the new music I shocked Larry Parnes by asking Billy Fury to wriggle a bit more provocatively for another *Tonight* perennial – 'Is Rock and Roll Finished?' 'They usually ask us to tone it down,' he said prudishly.

And I had a first sight of Ivor Cutler playing songs in the offices of Box & Cox, music publishers in seedy premises at the end of Denmark Street. 'Boxy' was a natural Charing Cross Road character. I arrived by appointment with Caryl Brahms one evening after transmission to find the office unattended except for Ivor Cutler, a fey, gnome-like figure idly tinkling on a harmonium. However, behind the door I could hear a steady stream of water hitting a wash basin. Boxy was relieving himself. Seeing Caryl, he buttoned up sharpish and explained in his defence that he had published many famous composers including 'Hermione Baddeley's brother, the Bishop of Australia' (sic), but never had he come upon a talent so original, so 'way-out' as Mr Cutler's. We both found Ivor's repertoire of Edward Learish, off-beat, blackish, folkish songs interesting, and the only disconcerting thing was Boxy's tendency to break up in giggles every time his artist started on a new number. Ivor was not the overnight sensation we had hoped on *Tonight* but he has built up a steady following since then.

Of all the music items we produced I should, perhaps, be most ashamed of an interview with Lionel Bart in his heyday. He was opening a new show and was to be interviewed by Derek Hart. For a new film he had written another song for Tommy Steele called 'It's All Happening'. It was virtually his latest hit and I said in the briefing room how much I admired it – perhaps the best song he had written, I murmured falsely. Lionel lapped it up and on the air Hart asked him about the difficulties of lyric writing.

'Easy,' said Lionel.

'Where do you do it?'

'Bath ... top of a bus ... wherever I get an idea. Some of my best songs I write in half an hour.'

'What do you consider your best song, Mr Bart?'

'Could be "It's All Happening",' said Lionel, plainly inspired by the praise that had so recently been lavished on it. 'Yes, definitely.'

'How does the lyric go, Mr Bart?'

'It's all happening,
It's all happening,
It's all happening to me!
It's all happening,
It's all happ ...' His voice trailed away as he realized just what he had claimed as his best lyric. Generous soul, he seems not to have harboured a grudge.

One of the interviews we recorded with Joan Sutherland had its farcical side. After the first question Richard Bonynge, her conductor husband, leapt forward displeased with the way the encounter was going. The problem was straightened out and the interview started again but unfortunately the tape-editing process went awry and when the programme was transmitted that evening, viewers were treated to Miss Sutherland's first answer complete with Bonynge's spirited entrance, arms waving, eyes flashing, vocabulary vivid, before the item limped into its conventional conclusion.

The most controversial *Tonight* incident pointed up dramatically the different approach of Baverstock's team and of the BBC old guard, frequently marched up to the top of the hill and then marched down again by the Director General, Sir Ian Jacob. After the particularly nasty murder of a small child, suspicion fell on the child's uncle, who was aged about twenty. After some days of police investigation the suspect was released and immediately snapped up by a national newspaper which wished to publish the story of his ordeal. It was a Friday and during the morning the paper offered the youth to *Tonight* for an interview before taking him off for the weekend to begin his literary collaboration with a couple of their journalists.

Baverstock and Milne agonized about the propriety of such an interview and found it impossible to confer with any highly placed BBC official because they were already leaving for the weekend. They decided to go ahead and Geoffrey Johnson Smith was assigned to the interview, which dwelt on the suspect's restatement of his innocence, the strain of several days of suspicion and an appeal to an acquaintance who could give him an alibi. On the night in question, he said sibilantly, he had been 'up the West End with a mate' whose name he did not know. He did know, however, that he was wearing a 'blue shirt, tight blue jeans and black shoes and he was with me all night and I wish I knew who he was'. With this compromising but not murderous account of the way he had spent the night the interview ended. The youth was given back to the reporters. One car blocked the exit from the cul-de-sac in St Mary Abbot's Place so that rival journalists could not follow, and the prize was spirited away to a country hideaway.

Little more was heard of the suspect, who was cleared in the end, but some protests got through to the BBC and Sir Ian Jacob apologized to viewers on Donald Baverstock's behalf. Baverstock hovered on the brink of angry resignation and most of his staff felt like going with him. Not long after – in 1959 – Sir Ian Jacob retired. As Mrs Wyndham Goldie reports, he had 'tended to treat television producers as subalterns who were there to carry out orders issued by their seniors at Broadcasting House'. His successor, Hugh Carleton Greene, brought a more sophisticated, sage and adventurous attitude into the Director General's suite at Broadcasting House, as well as a readiness to encourage experiment – without which the innovations of the sixties would not have been possible.

Light Entertainment

After about a year with *Tonight* it seemed a good idea to move on, so I applied for and got a producing job in BBC Light Entertainment. There is, or used to be, a stock joke by American television executives exposed to the BBC, on the lines, 'Light Entertainment – who the hell does the Heavy Entertainment?' However, there was more than a grain of truth to the title in the early 1960s. Most light entertainment programmes were mindless, escapist and anodyne. Commercial television had provided a salutary challenge to news and drama, but commercial variety shows were even less ambitious than those of the BBC. These consisted of naive, rudimentary situation comedy, variety compilations, quiz games and sing-alongs. Although the notorious BBC guide to acceptable humour – the Green Book – was no longer current, it cast a long shadow and the deputy head of the department, the late Tom Sloan, was not one to embarrass his programmes with ideas if he could see a way of keeping them out. In this respect he ran true to the form of many of the staff in his department. The traditional LE producer gloried in a successful series in which his star carried the burden of the show, but he was quick to dissociate himself from a flop and refused to accept the star's failure as anything to do with him.

An enlivening presence for a time was Eric Maschwitz, who had a more sophisticated and a broader-based attitude although he was able to do little to change things in his brief tenure. Maschwitz was also one of the most accomplished English lyricists, including 'A Nightingale Sang in Berkeley Square', 'Room 504' and 'These Foolish Things' among his songs. He had also worked on *Love From Judy*, *Carissima*, *Balalaika* and *Goodnight Vienna*. An engaging raconteur, *Goodnight Vienna* provided one of his favourite stories. On one occasion driving back from Brighton he passed the Lewisham Hippodrome. To his delight he saw that *Goodnight Vienna* was playing. He stopped the car and went in to ask the commissionaire how the show was doing. The commissionaire was dour: 'About as well as you'd expect *Goodnight Lewisham* to do in Vienna.'

Eric had done a stint at the BBC in sound radio before the war in the full glory of Reithian restraint, when the BBC predicated that programmes 'must at all costs be kept free of crudities, coarseness and innuendo. Humour must be clean and untainted directly or by association with vulgarity and suggestiveness. Music hall, stage and, to a lesser degree, screen standards are not suitable for broadcasting. . . . There can be no compromise with doubtful material. It must be cut.' Helpfully, the guide went on to give examples: 'Well-known vulgar jokes (e.g., the Brass Monkey) cleaned up are not normally admissible since the humour in such cases is almost invariably evident only if the vulgar version is known.'

There was an 'absolute ban' upon the following: lavatories; effeminacy in men; immorality of any kind; suggestive references to honeymoon couples, chambermaids, fig leaves, prostitution, ladies' underwear (e.g., winter draws on), animal habits (e.g., rabbits), lodgers, commercial travellers. 'Extreme care' was urged in dealing with references to or jokes about: pre-natal influences (e.g., his mother was frightened by a donkey); marital infidelity. '. . . The vulgar use of such words as "basket" must also be avoided.'

The guide had a confused approach to biblical jokes. 'Jokes built around Bible stories, e.g., Adam and Eve, Cain and Abel, David and Goliath, must be avoided or any sort of parody of them. References to a few biblical characters, e.g., Noah, are sometimes permissible [how did Noah get singled out?]; but since there is seldom anything to be gained by them and since they can engender such resentment they are best avoided altogether.' The BBC warned comics to keep off religion altogether, including 'jokes about AD or BC (e.g., before Crosby)', and spiritualism, christenings, weddings and funerals, '. . . parodies of Christmas carols and offensive references to Jews (or any other religious sect).'

Expletives could not be justified outside a 'serious dramatic setting' – they had no place at all in light entertainment – and 'all such words as God, Good God, My God, Blast, Hell, Damn, Bloody, Gorblimey, Ruddy, etc., etc., were to be deleted from scripts and innocuous expressions substituted'. Older viewers may remember the row that broke out when Peter Sellers used the word 'berk' in the early days of commercial television. As it raged I dimly perceived that its offence lay somewhere in the mysteries of rhyming slang and kept trying to work out why Burke and Hare could give offence – until I realized that Berkeley Hunt was the derivation.

Impersonations were also touchy ground. John Bird, who invented Wilson and Heath as vaudeville characters, and all the succeeding Mike Yarwoods, Faith Browns and Janet Browns would have had a terrible life. 'Artists' repertoires', the document proclaimed, 'are usually restricted to (a) leading public and political figures; (b) fellow artists.' As to (a) 'the Corporation's policy is against broadcasting impersonations of elder statesmen, e.g., Winston Churchill, and leading political figures.' As to (b) 'there is no objection but certain artists have notified the Corporation that no unauthorized impersonations may be broadcast: Gracie Fields, Vera Lynn, Ethel Revnell (with or without Gracie West), Renée Houston, Jeanne de Casalis (Mrs Feather), Nat Mills and Bobbie, Harry Hemsley.'

The guide had its social conscience too:

Avoid derogatory references to professions, trades and 'classes', e.g., solicitors, commercial travellers, miners, 'the working class', coloured races.

Avoid any jokes or references that might be taken to encourage: strikes or industrial disputes; the Black Market; spivs and drones.

Avoid any reference to 'the MacGillicuddy of the Reeks' or jokes about his name.

Do not refer to the Chinese as 'Chinamen', 'Chinks', 'Yellow Bellies', etc.

Do not refer to Negroes as 'Niggers' ('Nigger Minstrels' is allowed).

There were 'special considerations for overseas broadcasts, where humour was limited by different social, political and religious taboos from our own ...'. The guide warned: 'Chinese laundry jokes may be offensive. The term Boer War should not be used – South African War is correct. Jokes about "harems" are offensive in some parts of the world.' And the capper: 'Jokes like "enough to make a Maltese Cross" are of doubtful value.'

There was little in my first series which was likely to contravene these tenets. I was given the task of preparing a variety show around Henry Hall, the veteran band leader, a man of great sweetness and good manners who had survived as a trend-setting band leader on radio in the 1930s through innumerable broadcasts and television shows in the 1940s and 1950s. His signature tune was 'Here's to the Next Time', his distinctive introduction, 'This is Henry Hall – and tonight is my guest night.' I was to be his Waterloo.

From life in overcrowded Lime Grove I moved to share a caravan in the grounds of Television Centre, which was still confined to one corner of the present building (and which is now given over entirely to the design department). The caravan gave an appropriate feeling of impermanence to the whole exercise.

With magnificent optimism I decided that what Henry needed was a new look, that the guest night formula was outmoded and that the solution was to surround him with youth. Accordingly I collected together a team of young and largely untried singers, provided them with obscure and unfamiliar songs, and expected the old gentleman to introduce them with every sign of enthusiasm. This he managed to do with impeccable courtesy before a listless audience at the Television Theatre for the delight of a home audience which switched off in droves.

I was firmly and properly removed from the series and replaced by a more experienced director, who certainly improved the shows but failed to erase the full stop with which I had punctuated Henry's career as a television performer. He has remained kind and friendly and has never reproached me; but I have no illusions that I finished him off.

From Henry Hall I moved on to *Ask Me Another*, already a successful general knowledge quiz, hosted by Franklin Engelmann. The questions were set by John P. Wynn, who had a little corner in general knowledge quizzes along with his wife Joan Clark, a radio producer. He was an indefatigable setter of questions and liked to celebrate his successes in what his heavy accent declared to be 'chumpine!' Earlier he had contributed the 'Meet Dr Morell' mysteries on radio on *Monday Night at Eight* and enjoyed telling a story of a visit by a stranger to his house in Hampstead one Sunday morning.

'Are you Mr Wynn?' the caller inquired.

Putting aside his bubbling glass of 'chumpine', John P. admitted that he was.

'I am a policeman.'

John P. wondered what offence he had committed. None.

'It's like this, sir. Every Monday night my wife and I listen to your programme "Meet Dr Morell" – with all the clues. At the end of the mystery I can never work out the solution and my wife gives me a terrible time – "Call yourself a policeman" and all that. Now, if you could tell me what the clues are this week so I could come out with the right answer, that would shut her up for always. Just this week, sir.'

John P. gave the copper the clues and the correct answer for that week's riddle and never heard from him again.

He guarded the secrets and the standards of *Ask Me Another* very jealously. It was a very popular middle-of-the-road programme – viewed with much approval by my father, who shifted with embarrassment whenever I was involved with song and dance and more particularly with *That Was The Week That Was*. The programme introduced Reginald Webster and Olive Stephens, and above all Ted Moult, to television audiences, as well as a large roster of fledgling masterminds who lacked Moult's attractive, voluble, rustic eccentricity.

Other diversions during my Light Entertainment stint included a series with Semprini and the George Mitchell Singers, and a bizarre monstrosity, a summer replacement quiz called *Laugh Line*. I was shown an American pilot of the show, which the BBC had already acquired, compèred by Dick Van Dyke and with Mike Nichols, Elaine May and Dorothy Loudon, another American revue star, as panellists. I have enjoyed teasing all three about this early indiscretion in later years. Contestants were provided with cartoons which came to life, courtesy of posing actors, and which the contestants could reshuffle at will in order to create alternative 'laugh lines'. These they delivered on behalf of the miming actors.

Our panellists ran the gamut of English television personalities, and the most pleasant part of the series was the chance to give a lot of talented, amusing and out of work actor friends posing roles in the illustrative tableaux. As we were only a summer replacement, the show, which emerged as an asinine mistake, escaped almost unnoticed by the critics, but so pleasant for the upper echelon of Light Entertainment was the experience of starting a new, moronic quiz show without bringing down the wrath of the nation that it rather went to their heads. Winter came and they brought it back proudly in a prime evening spot. The wrath which had been suspended was now unleashed with a vengeance, and I was lucky enough to be doing other things by that time.

I only enjoyed one Light Entertainment venture without reservation, and that was a musical comedy. Under Eric Maschwitz's patronage some attempt was made to produce musical comedies for television. Caryl Brahms and I had enjoyed reading Schnitzler's *Anatol* dialogues – a series of one-act sketches for a man-about-Vienna, Anatol, his friend

Max and various girl friends. The sketches were sharp and funny, the atmosphere invited music, and Viennese snow scenes, restaurants and other interiors suggested an attractive traditional spectacle. It seemed an ideal choice and Maschwitz wanted a star composer for it and a star actor to play Anatol.

We were lucky from the first with our composer. *Anatol* is the only musical composed by Malcolm Arnold, whom Caryl knew well, and he provided a tuneful score to which I still like to listen. Casting *Anatol* was a harder problem. For a long time we thought we had persuaded Paul Scofield to play the leading part and planned on that understanding until he gently but firmly told us that he was not going to do it. We were quite near rehearsal time and a frantic search ensued – Keith Michell, Louis Jourdan, John Neville, Peter Wyngarde, Jean-Pierre Aumont, were all wooed and lost, as well as another Frenchman, Jean-Claude Pascal, to whom I had made a flying visit to Paris in a vain attempt to persuade him to accept. We also auditioned William Franklyn, who roared with laughter when told that he could not sing – in stark contrast to a distinguished actress, who made appalling noises in the audition, and looked upon our polite rejection as a personal insult.

We were due to start rehearsals on a Monday. On the Thursday before we had all the girls but no Anatol, and I was sitting in the Kenya Coffee Bar in the King's Road wondering who on earth could be rustled up at such short notice when a Canadian woman started to talk to me. We soon got round to the theatre and television and to my predicament. The Canadian lady explained that I was in luck: Canada's finest actor was between engagements and happened at that very moment to be in England. I was a little suspicious of 'Canada's finest actor' since the last Canadian actor to whom I had spoken, a good-looking and able but humourless man, had told me that he was going to throw up his English career to go home to play *Everyman* at the Vancouver Festival. I expressed some surprise. 'Ah, you see,' he said seriously, 'I can't let Canada down.'

The current candidate for Anatol turned out to be less solemn. William Hutt has since played Lear, *Long Day's Journey into Night* and even Lady Bracknell at Stratford, Ontario, but at that time he was a solid, well-set-up character actor who had done good work in Canada and was examining the possibilities of working regularly in England. Spurred on by his enthusiastic fan, I arranged to meet him next day, and by the weekend he was cast.

Modern television productions seem to be miracles of complexity, but

Parasol in 1959 was a ninety-minute musical, transmitted live, with a cast and chorus of over thirty and an orchestra of more than fifty, conducted by Marcus Dods in a different studio. There was a large church set, inside and out, several other interiors including an enormous restaurant to cope with, as well as a lot of filmed links of animated, whirling parasols. William Hutt battled splendidly, Peter Sallis supported him wittily as Max, and the girls – Moira Redmond, Pip Hinton, Irene Hamilton and Hy Hazell – were impeccable.

Parasol is the only television programme which has ever physically exhausted me. The enormity of the situation hit me as we started the live transmission. I had never before directed a professional cast in a play. Hours spent in studio control rooms had all had to do with current affairs immediacy or vaudeville splash, and suddenly the idea of getting away with ninety minutes of musical high comedy was daunting. I remember going down to congratulate William Hutt afterwards and finding tears forming in my eyes. I knew they were from tiredness and relief, but he, poor man, has nurtured for years the idea that I was tearfully disappointed by his performance.

That Was The Week That Was

If I had not been sacked from Light Entertainment, *That Was The Week That Was* would not have come to the screen – at least in the form it took and under that title – so in retrospect my visit to Tom Sloan's office to be told that my contract would not be renewed comes into focus as a happier meeting than it seemed at the time. Although I was not surprised, I had been continually in work since leaving Oxford and I was puzzled by the prospect of unemployment and wondered how to semaphore my availability. Fortunately, Talks and Current Affairs advertised for a new editor for *Monitor* to follow Huw Wheldon. Although I did not expect to get the job (it went to Humphrey Burton), applying for it was a more discreet way of letting the *Tonight* unit know I was on the market than going cap in hand to ask for my old job back. I went through one of those curious job interviews peculiar to the BBC in its discreet mixture of patronizing paternalism; but Mrs Wyndham Goldie was on the board and filtered the necessary information back to Baverstock.

Going back to *Tonight* was both seductive and stimulating. Going back is traditionally a barren prospect, but to return to that particular team was different. Nevertheless, it was important to use the programme as a taking-off point for something else.

Timing could not have been better. Baverstock and Milne, having happily filled the empty 6-7 pm slot, were now actively looking for fresh empires of time to conquer and suggested that nothing much happened late at night on a Saturday – surely a period which had a distinctive character. We started to talk about it and I arranged to go to America to have a look at the sort of late-night chat shows which were already established there, especially the Jack Parr Show. Parr – or his writers –

produced one of the craftiest first questions I have heard from one of these interviewers. Greeting the late Michael Dunn, a clever dwarf actor, he said quite simply after Dunn had hopped up to sit beside him on a stool, 'Tell me, Mickey, how do you put people at their ease?'

Over the years I managed to justify two or three trips to America on *Tonight*. On one ill-fated expedition I was due to make a comprehensive report on the new-wave American humour which was just beginning to surface in England through the gramophone records of Nichols and May, Mort Sahl, Shelley Berman, Bob Newhart, Jonathan Winters and the Smothers Brothers. I got to see Nichols and May in their after-dinner revue, and Mort Sahl at the Basin Street East, but never got within a mile of fixing an interview with any of them. Two particularly helpful and hopeless young Americans (they usually come as a team of two over there) offered film servicing facilities, and we finally managed to corral Jonathan Winters and the Smothers Brothers into a dismal Sheraton Hotel suite, where I asked innumerable earnest questions and they, much mystified by who was asking, why they were being asked and whether they were going to get paid, tried valiantly to turn each question into an excuse for working in another section of their acts. We shot miles of film and none of it ever appeared on the screen; but it made me into an unstoppable authority on the new American humour whenever I found half a chance to bore someone with my new knowledge. Ironically, the way Mort Sahl was subsequently mishandled by BBC Light Entertainment on his visit to Britain was a contributory reason for Hugh Greene to back the eventual Current Affairs offering, *That Was The Week That Was*.

As we talked and lunched and pondered on the problems of starting the show (as yet unnamed) certain conditioning arguments began to emerge. *TW3* started as a *Tonight* production and the influence of the parent programme was paramount in its conception. The *Tonight* brief was to be 'on the side of the audience'. As Mrs Goldie has written: 'It stood, so to speak, the accepted communicative process on its head. It looked at those in power from the point of view of the powerless.... Yet, though the appeal of *Tonight* was regard for the individual, it was never sentimental, doctrinaire or morally self-righteous. Realism prevailed.' Mrs Goldie goes on to suggest that 'from time to time, a broadcast programme embodies a change in the mood of a nation ... it is never easy to know to what extent a television programme creates a national mood and to what extent it merely reflects it....' In sound radio she points to *ITMA* as a programme embodying change. 'In television', she adds, 'it was true of *Tonight*.... *Tonight* ... was not rebellious, far less revolutionary, but it was sceptical, particularly of theorists and "experts". If *Panorama* with Richard Dimbleby had become the voice of authority, *Tonight* with Cliff Michelmore was rapidly becoming the voice of the people.'

That Was The Week That Was took the relationship between audience and programme a step further. From the beginning we were looking for a 'them' and 'us' polarization. Our 'us' constituted both the programme-makers (personified for the viewer by the actors) and the sympathetic part of the audience. 'Them' were represented by the public figures or establishment forces whom we investigated, challenged, mocked or pilloried. If *Tonight* was establishing a conversation with its audience, *TW3* was engaged with it in a conspiracy.

In the early stages of pondering the programme I felt an insecurity which I have since recognized as part of the process of starting any new venture. I look at the biggest successes of the last show and then quail at the improbability of finding equivalent peaks in the new package. As I considered the Saturday night show I was acutely conscious that the high points of *Tonight* had always been factual, unscripted and spontaneous. I had been responsible more for finding the scripted and performed inserts and I was well aware that their main virtue had been to ruffle the texture of the magazine and bring some quality of gloss, variety and surprise. They were very rarely show-stoppers.

On the other hand, we had decided to reject the American chat-show formula because it did not appeal to the *Tonight* mentality. *Tonight* production staff lived off the feeling of contribution, and the input of a production team on a talk show is of necessity limited. Book 'em, transport 'em, keep 'em fairly sober, congratulate 'em, and send 'em home is the function. The host and the circus of extroverts who regularly appear on chat shows carry a disproportionate part of the responsibility for the success of the programme. We were looking for a show which was considered, structured, edited and controlled.

At one point we toyed with the idea of using many of the best *Tonight* items each week – playing them back on a large projection screen in front of an audience. Donald Baverstock had recently done a lecture on the South Bank and had been excited by the audience's response to the film-clips he used to illustrate his talk. However, the more I thought about the peculiarities of the hour – which was to be around eleven o'clock – the more it seemed essential to invent something which had a life of its own.

Another of Donald's constant demands was that eloquence inform the programme, a laudable objective which led to our including in early editions some sections of quotation which placed an emphasis on the writing. In fact these did not fit the pace and presentation of the show as it had by then evolved, although they did spawn a purely 'quotation' show called *Dig This Rhubarb*, which Antony Jay was to pioneer; and they helped to increase the premium we put on the writers' work throughout the series.

Television shows are more often shaped in practice than on the drawing-board, and the distinctive features of *That Was The Week That Was* finally grew out of practical planning of the first pilot programme. The critical factor was the decision to engage a band and invite an audience. The moment the theatrical ambience was established certain items had to be included and others were bound to lose their place. The performed number began to be the one which was likely to grab the attention of the studio audience; the casual eavesdrop was likely to be less effective. We were keen to have a cast of new faces, and, throughout my *Tonight* and LE stints, I followed the usual peregrinations of dedicated BBC producers around the West End cabarets – Murray's, L'Hirondelle, The Blue Angel, The Embassy, Quaglino's etc. By now the new, fertile soil of The Establishment Club was ready to be tilled, and represented a second major influence on the programme.

If *Tonight* was the factual, documented, researched mother of *TW3*, the conception was completed by the rape of that responsible lady at the hands of the more rash, intruding, iconoclastic *Private Eye* and *Beyond The Fringe*. They called the baby 'satire'.

From 1956, when John Osborne's *Look Back in Anger* opened at the Royal Court, there was room for an alternative voice in the theatre, on television and in print. Clustering around *Look Back* in what seemed to the public to be a conscious movement were books like Kingsley Amis's *Lucky Jim*, Colin Wilson's *The Outsider* and John Braine's *Room at the Top*. At ABC Television Sydney Newman, a producer imported from Canadian television, was pioneering *Armchair Theatre*, a landmark in television drama, with writers like Alun Owen and directors of the order of Philip Saville, Ted Kotcheff, John Moxey, Dennis Vance and Wilfred Eades. Newman's principal influence had also been Osborne's play. As Peter Black wrote in *The Mirror in the Corner* in 1956, Newman 'had seen the new drama and it worked'.

Simultaneously, John Bassett, who later became a valuable production assistant on *That Was The Week That Was*, had paired two Cambridge graduates, Peter Cook and Jonathan Miller, with two from Oxford, Dudley Moore and Alan Bennett. At a café in Euston Road they united to make *Beyond The Fringe* for the Edinburgh Festival. Legend has it that the deployment of a fifth member of the cast – the unknown Julie Christie – as a running gag never got past the drawing-board.

While *Beyond The Fringe* was having its initial Edinburgh success and planning to come to London, Richard Ingrams and John Duncan (later another essential member of the *TW3* team) were running a touring theatrical company which included in its repertoire an early version of Spike Milligan's play *The Bed Sitting Room*. William Rushton was in the cast. Ingrams, with Rushton and Christopher Booker, had another iron in the fire – the magazine *Private Eye*, a direct descendant of *The Salopian*, to which Ingrams and Rushton had contributed as schoolboys at Shrewsbury, and of *Parson's Pleasure* and *Mesopotamia*, undergraduate magazines with which Ingrams, Paul Foot, John Wells and William Rushton (from outside the university) were involved at Oxford.

Beyond The Fringe had its problems getting to London. Its ultimate presenters were William Donaldson (later reincarnated as Henry Root, pimp, letter-writer and gossip columnist) and Anna Deere Wiman, an American whose father was a distinguished American impresario. I watched its vicissitudes from the touch-line.

News of mass protests in Brighton was encouraging. The Brighton audiences are notoriously conservative and any story of dissatisfaction in their ranks suggests to the experienced playgoer that the play on offer may be unusually interesting. The London critics loved *Beyond The Fringe* when it opened at the Fortune Theatre in May 1961 – so did audiences. Tynan and Levin in particular directed their attention to its satirical content – much minimized in retrospect by the four stars, but revolutionary to the audiences of the period. The old West End targets, inbred and cliquish, were replaced by politicians, royals and other public figures, and by public attitudes. The absence of relief in the form of traditional 'production numbers' concentrated the effect. Tynan's review was headed 'English satire advances into the Sixties' and Levin also used the word 'satire', which was to be bandied about as indiscriminately over the next few years as had been teddy boy, beatnik and angry young man by earlier generations of popularizers always eager to pin a label on a new phenomenon.

Part of my job as a producer on the *Tonight* programme was to be aware of these developments in the theatre and to make sure that they were reported on or reflected in our nightly magazine. As soon as *Private Eye* was published, Booker's writing and Rushton's cartoons came to notice; and with the opening of The Establishment Club in Greek Street in October 1961, John Bird, Eleanor Bron, John Fortune, as well as David Walsh and Jeremy Geidt, surfaced.

Attendance at The Establishment varied between the very full and the very empty but the nucleus resident cast always played to capacity when I was there in the early months. Often they were augmented by Peter Cook, who as co-owner made frequent guest appearances, usually performing scatalogical solos which were drastically amended when his parents paid visits from the West Country. On other occasions guests took the floor, and the club suddenly assumed the aspect of a deserted soup kitchen. Exceptions were Lenny Bruce and Frankie Howerd, who first signalled his intention of making a comeback with a triumphant season at 18 Greek Street. I saw Lenny Bruce there a couple of times, but I never caught the uncharming, unfunny side of his act which some people deplored. One night he provided one of the best put-downs for a drunken heckler I have ever heard and, examining it in retrospect, I am inclined to think it must have been new-minted for that particular drunk on that particular evening. On form he had enormous charm and he was battling sweetly, if scatalogically, to perform to a packed house in the face of one man's persistent maunderings and cat-calls. After twenty minutes or so, just when a note of irritation was beginning to creep into Bruce's patter, the joker stood up and, swaying, managed to enunciate clearly enough for all to hear, 'Why don't you tell an English joke?' There was a long, pitying pause before Lenny Bruce said – as kindly as he could – 'But you are an English joke.'

I spent deserted evenings there watching David Frost and Barry Humphries – whose Dame Edna in those days had none of her effrontery and plumage, but came over as a well-observed and slightly pathetic matron, clad in a homespun brown dress. She had not, as I remember, yet invented the gladiolus.

After Frankie Howerd's success, Michael Howard, who had been absent from the variety stage for some years, was also accorded a comeback platform. I went with a couple of friends because I remembered vividly from my childhood a radio joke of his which had got me into mild trouble. The burden of the tale was that he had gone to a fancy dress party at which one girl came clad only in gold paint, '... as a novelty; but the novelty soon wore off'. I retold this story proudly to my father in the forties and was soundly told off. I had hardly passed it on to my companions at The Establishment when Michael Howard bounced on stage and to our amazement opened his act with it.

By the time we started to recruit for the pilot of *That Was The Week That Was* – still unnamed – we also had the active support of the Director General and the late Kenneth Adam, the Controller of Programmes. Both had their own idea of the sort of show that might emerge. Greene's view was coloured by his experience of political cabaret when he was a correspondent in Germany, after the Weimar Republic but during the early Nazi regime. On the other hand, the memories which coloured Adam's vision were of Herbert Farjeon and the Gate Revues, small theatre shows in London in the late 1930s.

Lance Percival was one of the earliest recruits. I had seen him in cabaret at Quaglino's and at the Blue Angel – he had also appeared in a revue presented by Michael Codron which included a number of sketches by Peter Cook written when he was still an undergraduate – *One Over the Eight*. It starred Kenneth Williams. Lance's principal virtues for *TW3* were his ability to think quickly, especially when improvising topical calypsos which emphasized the fact of a live show and his facility with impersonations. Roy Kinnear had long been a favourite of audiences of Joan Littlewood's company at the Theatre Royal Stratford East. William Rushton I first saw in a revue devised by Stephen Vinaver at the Room at the Top, Ilford, an ill-fated cabaret venture above a furniture store. John Wells, Richard Ingrams and Barbara Windsor were also in the cast. Millicent Martin was an automatic choice because of the amount of 'instant performance' she had contributed to *Tonight*.

The main search was for a link man, and the first offer was made to John Bird. (The *Fringe* team were off to New York and by then hardly qualified as unknown.) John Bird had, I learnt when we met for lunch, already talked to 'the BBC' about a series based on the Establishment shows. Whatever conversations there may have been, they had nothing to do with my plans for shaping *TW3*. It was over lunch at Bertorelli's, a lamented BBC haunt on Shepherd's Bush Green, that the title finally arrived with the coffee. We had a long lunch and John, although guarded about committing himself to the show, was an invaluable new sounding-board for me as I tried to formulate my own ideas. In summing up I said that we were trying to construct a programme with a particular character for a particular time on a particular day of a week that was nearly over. We wanted to purge the memories of the week that had been, shrug and look forward to the next. John echoed and modified the

Shell advertising slogan in murmuring, 'That was the week that was.' It leapt at me as the perfect title.

When Caryl Brahms and I came to write the lyric for Ron Grainer's signature tune the second line supplied itself: 'That was the week that was/It's over, let it go ...!' The only moment of doubt about the title occurred when Stuart Hood, the new Controller of Programmes under Kenneth Adam, by then Director of Television, admitted at a press conference that although there would be a new late-night revue, whatever it was called it would not be given a cumbersome title like *That Was the Week That Was*.

Some time before my lunch with John Bird I saw an account in the *Stage* newspaper of a new young Cambridge comic, David Frost, who was conducting an improvised press conference as Harold Macmillan as the centrepiece of his act at the Blue Angel. I set off for the club which was to become a favourite talent-spotting ground and where on one occasion I heard a very drunk debs' delight dismiss a waiter who was offering a bill by drawling, 'Oh piss off and put it on Daddy's bill.' The waiter declined to move, saying severely, 'Daddy's over there.' Sobriety soon set in.

My account of the evening has been much disputed by David; however, it went like this. I arrived at the club at about 1.30. It was in a basement off Berkeley Square and was owned or managed by Max Setty, whose brother Stanley had come to an untimely end some years earlier, cropping up in several dismembered pieces strewn over the Essex marshes. Hovering in the lobby downstairs was a formidable old agent and booker, Beatrice Braham, who was always busy on the cabaret circuit. Some distance away sat a tousled young man who looked despondent. Welcomed by Mr Setty, I asked at what time David Frost was due to appear. Mr Setty looked sad and said that his act had not been going too well so he was unlikely to appear that night. I expressed disappointment at a wasted evening and began my retreat. Mr Setty pointed out that Hutch was top of the bill and would I not stay to enjoy him? I said that I had enjoyed Hutch enormously in the past and would doubtless do so again (I last saw him years later, just before his death, in the stand at Lords at a Benson & Hedges final); but I had stayed up on this particular occasion to witness the birth of a new star. Mr Setty was not wavering until Mrs Braham, a motherly soul, intervened. 'Give the boy a chance, Max,' she said, and Mr Setty relented.

This is the part of the story that does not ring true to David – he insists that since Mr Setty, a notable businessman, had paid him for the week there was no chance that he would have extracted less than his whole pound of performing flesh. David's evidence, though plausible, is, I suggest, circumstantial. Mine is what I heard and saw and remembered. As I have been telling the same story the same way for some twenty years I have to stick with it. Anyway, it had a happy ending.

The dishevelled young man in the lobby got on that night and conducted his improvised press conference in the persona of Harold Macmillan. His Macmillan lacked the charm of Peter Cook's interpretation, which had been created earlier, but he was adept at provoking questions from his audiences and at the improviser's knack of changing gear from an unpromising premise to a position which enabled him to bang home a prepared joke as an apparently spontaneous answer. At that time I was still hoping that there might be room in the programme for some improvised comedy in the American manner of Nichols and May and Mort Sahl, and in the way in which the Establishment group were experimenting in this country. At any rate it was quite clear that David was informed and enthusiastic and could think quickly on his feet. I arranged to lunch with him soon after, quite sure that I had found a valuable member of the supporting cast.

We met at Bertorelli's. Frost's enthusiastic biographer, the late Willi Frischauer, reports that he wore a turquoise floral plastic raincoat purchased from a corner store for three shillings to protect him against icy rain. I lunched him with Antony Jay of *Tonight* to get a second opinion; and, according to Frischauer, I sent Baverstock a memo, of which I have no more memory than of the turquoise plastic. Apparently it said, 'Ex-Footlights (Cambridge), looks promising. Have seen him conducting press conference as cabaret turn at a night club where he was limited by the stupidity of the customers.' It is probably accurate; but a sentence describing Frost on page three of Willi Frischauer's book – 'David rises, stretches his wiry, athletic body . . .' – has always made me suspicious of the accuracy and objectivity of the next 234 pages.

About two weeks before we were due to record the first pilot programme, John Bird decided not to appear. Plans to take the Establishment to America were firming up and we had to find another host.

From the moment that I switched David to the central position he was tirelessly inventive and energetic in helping to shape and colour the programme. His contribution was critical. He was closely in touch with many of the more recent graduates and undergraduates at Oxford and Cambridge, and was already looking for set pieces for himself by writers like John Cleese, Humphrey Barclay and Ian Davidson.

David was one of the first graduates to know no other job than
television. Having been a performer at Cambridge, he went straight to
Rediffusion as a trainee. His principal childhood influences, like those of
Peter Cook, John Cleese and so many of their generation, had been radio
comedy series and especially the Goons; to this David added what
amounted to an artistic crush on Cook while at Cambridge.

At Associated Rediffusion he was attached to *This Week* and gave
himself a performer's quick acquaintanceship with the technical set-up
of a studio. I missed his first programme, *Let's Twist*, but enjoyed a truly
awful sequel, *Let's Twist on the Riviera*. In this enterprise he was
working with Elkan Allan, now a television journalist but then an
important figure in the Rediffusion Light Entertainment hierarchy. He
sports a scrappy, dun-coloured pubic beard and was once massively put
down by a mousy Rediffusion secretary who had listened patiently for
several days while he speculated on what costume he should adopt for a
fancy dress party. Finally she lost her patience and muttered, 'Why don't
you spray yourself with talcum powder and go as an armpit?' She should
have gone on to stardom, but history does not tell us that she did.

Hearing rumours of a late-night BBC revue, Elkan and Rediffusion
decided to embark on their own. This put Frost on the spot, because his
discussions with me had not been revealed to his Associated Rediffusion
masters and they were beginning to think of him with his Footlights
background as a potential house funnyman. Hearing of the BBC's
interest, John Macmillan, AR's Controller of Programmes, offered him
a much better contract. *TW3* was still a highly speculative venture, but
Frost opted for it, leaving Rediffusion with some bad feelings, but no
regrets.

One of the programme-building principles to which I clung firmly
until the first pilot was the idea that the show should be open-ended – I
had been impressed by the casual nature in which some of David Susskind's early talk shows had hit an easy, interesting and unhurried stride
in America. Three items promised to be unpredictable in length. In the
first place we planned a series of improvised sketches for which, on the
pilot, we looked for contributions from John Bird, Eleanor Bron, John
Fortune and Peter Cook. (My memory may be playing me false, but I
recall some small drama during the recording as to whether Peter Cook
would turn up or not – in the end he decided against an appearance. The
telerecording has not survived.) Then there was to be a confrontation
between Bernard Levin and a group of opponents, which did happen.
The third open-ended item was to be an unchaired discussion between

three celebrated conversationalists, due to last no less than thirty minutes. For the rest of the programme we hoped to include sketches, songs, perhaps topical interviews, and to round it off with Lance Percival's improvised calypsos commenting on events which had happened during the course of the show.

The set and the camera plan fell quickly into place and stayed the same for the next pilot and the rest of the series. There were to be seats for an audience, no attempt to disguise the studio walls, space for a band, and cameras moving in and out in full view. The last-minute nature of the news content meant that cameras must at some time be seen inadvertently, so I decided that we might as well see them intentionally from the beginning. I had always found the clutter of a television studio an attractive background and enjoyed the ABC *Armchair Theatre* credits, which communicated something of the hectic atmosphere.

Our first pilot for *TW3* lasted two hours and forty minutes. Millicent Martin, who sang the opening number, had taken off from Heathrow for a Spanish holiday before we finished in the studio. Of the various ingredients we assembled, the opening number and its glancing blows at topical targets worked. So did the main sketch, which dealt with the first satellite transmissions from America and the Giant Dish through which they were channelled. Frost had a good time with the Giant Dish and shared the job of hosting with Brian Redhead, who had been working on *Tonight*. In the event there was hardly a role for Brian in *TW3*, and he opted out after the first pilot. Levin debated happily with thirty Conservative ladies. They wore their traditional hats and Levin his about-to-be traditional growl. He prompted two marvellous impromptus out of one of them. Several times she said, 'Mr Macmillan has always satisfied me,' and later, as the discussion moved on to law and order, 'Mr Levin, how would you like it if your daughter was out up a dark lane late at night and nothing done about it?'

The discussion section involved three nominees of Ken Tynan who, in the *Observer*, had called them the three best talkers in London. They were: Seth Holt, the film director, and Harold Lang, the actor – now both dead, and George Melly, who also sang. We looked for an amusing thirty minutes and in deciding on a subject convinced ourselves that a serious topic would give a less self-conscious opportunity for wit. In a moment of sublime solemnity we opted for 'human unhappiness', and the moment the discussion started a powerful gloom settled on the conversationalists and on the studio.

The reaction inside the BBC was curious. People came to view the recording when it was being played back in various preview theatres as though it were some sort of blue movie. I sat through one embarrassing afternoon at Television Centre, on a blazing hot summer day, watching it with Baverstock, Milne and Grace Wyndham Goldie. We enjoyed the opening songs and sketches, turned down the sound on 'human unhappiness', and finished the afternoon depressingly unsure of the programme's future prospects. My own feeling was that, though Alasdair and Donald were committed to further developments, Grace's fledgling sense of humour had not been sufficiently tickled to encourage her to fight for a slot. In *Facing The Nation* she writes that she found it, 'Long ... amateurish in its endeavours to seem casual, and politically both tendentious and dangerous ...'. Mrs Goldie is scrupulously accurate (and consistent over the years in her opinions) but she next picks up the story of *TW3* in November 1962, ten days before the first programme on 24 November.

In the meantime the Conservative ladies allowed their dislike of the nature of the whole programme to be known at the BBC and earnestly hoped that nothing like it would be offered for public consumption. As a result Kenneth Adam felt impelled to see the pilot and viewed it with Joanna Spicer, a more worldly and more easily amused viewer than Grace. Joanna jangled her usual large strings of beads happily and laughed unselfconsciously. I think we had chopped out human unhappiness by then. Anyone who has made a record, audio or visual, will know how unaccountably different it can sound on different occasions, played to a sympathetic or an unsympathetic audience.

As a result of this second screening, we ran a second pilot on 29 September 1962, at a length of just under an hour and a half. David Kernan and Roy Kinnear joined the show at this point and, Brian Redhead having retired to *Tonight*, Frost was the sole link man. Bernard Levin's spot remained, but that and Lance Percival's calypso were the only unscripted elements. The casual studio atmosphere contributed more to the tighter show and enabled the actors to slip easily in and out of political impersonations without heavy make-up and wigs. There was some room left for imagination, rather as in radio.

The shape of the programme was virtually that of the early transmissions in the series and most of the sketches in the pilot, which were not tied to the week's news, were used again during those weeks – notably a profile of a recording producer, Norrie Paramor, who had a habit of putting his own songs on the B side of potential hit singles. He was not alone in this, but he was notorious, and when we used the item on

the opening show he was furious. There was also a John Cleese monologue about a new star, 'Regella', which Frost delivered.

With the date of the second pilot only eight weeks before the first
transmission date, there was a tacit assumption that we were going to
get the show right. In any case it was late-night, ghetto television which
would probably only attract a fringe metropolitan audience – the sense
of importance which practitioners and commentators have felt in assess-
ing the programme after the event was not felt by the team in the weeks
of preparation. As Millicent Martin said later, 'If I'd known I was part
of an era, I'd have taken more notice.' There was a certain amount of
scepticism from Milly, who had a pantomime offer in Bromley and
feared she might be paid a salary similar to the pittance which *Tonight*
paid occasional singers – roughly twenty pounds. That problem was
ironed out; and two final cast members were engaged. They were Kenneth Cope, who had made a name for himself on *Coronation Street* and
who was John Bassett's suggestion and, at the last moment, the late
Timothy Birdsall, an inspired cartoonist, whom we thought might provide some drawings but who, almost by accident, pioneered his own
brand of illustrated monologue with a lightness and pertinence unique
among television illustrators. He came in the day before the first show to
make special sketches for an item, and as he worked on it with Frost
they evolved a simple illustrated interview which became a weekly event.

While I prepared *TW3* I continued to direct *Tonight* and the two jobs
worked well in tandem. There was also a brief distraction at the height
of the Cuba crisis. *Panorama* mounted a special programme at short
notice and found at the end of the afternoon that they lacked a director.
Paul Fox, the editor, asked me to do it and provided me with my only
opportunity to work with Richard Dimbleby. The 'special' lasted over
two hours. We took inserts on satellite from America on film and tape
and an outside broadcast from the Trocadero, where Alec Douglas-
Home, then Foreign Secretary, modulated an after-dinner speech into a
major policy statement. In the studio were complicated map and caption
sequences and Harold Wilson, the Shadow Foreign Secretary. Fox had
a fearsome reputation for shouting at his directors; but as I was similarly
supposed to impose silence on my producers in the control room we
reached an amicable compromise and he shut up.

Dimbleby was a revelation. There had been no time to write formal
introductions for many of the items. Nor was there any certainty that
various connections or film or tape inserts would be ready. We kept in
touch by telephone and, as he improvised his sedate, authoritative cues

into the recorded sections, he discreetly tapped his nose to give me the seven seconds warning needed to cue it. The nation was weighing the chances of war. In the studio, at close quarters, my concern paled before my admiration for Dimbleby's technique.

Soon after this we embarked on the first episode of *TW3*. We called on favourite moments from the second pilot, as much as we could find from the week's news – memorably a Hall and Waterhouse sketch for Roy Kinnear about private soldier candidates for Parliament, which was that week's wonder – and one of the lingering 'anthology' pieces so dear to Donald's heart, which was linked by that subtle, stylish actor Michael Gwynn. It was a form we only tried once more: on the second programme Peter Wyngarde narrated a short compilation designed to prove that we were not against everything; I decided on this occasion to be pro John Osborne. Neither item really looked like a genuine facet of the volatile, independent character which *TW3* was assuming.

We were lucky in that the programme hit its stride from the first. Hugh Greene, who had not seen the pilots, has been quoted as saying, 'I was delighted: the programme sprang fully armed into life – almost every item seemed to be absolutely on the ball, and I thought really we have achieved something.' One warning note was struck. I found David Kernan almost too tearful to go on just before the show. Asking him what the trouble was, I found that Donald had been explaining the political significance of one of his songs to him, as he might have done to a *Tonight* interviewer. The actor found it thoroughly confusing, and after that Donald made sure that he gave performers a wide berth until after the show.

David Frost's debut was extraordinary. A triumph, not over adversity, but of diversity. His curious classless accent, sloppy charcoal suit and over-ambitious haircut concealed a man who had come into his kingdom at a bound. As the programme became more successful he responded happily to the pressures and grew with notoriety. He rarely made errors except in sketches. I was often asked if success changed him and for a long time I could only find one instance: he was sometimes rude to waiters – but that was only a passing phase.

He could hardly be blamed for a technical error that occurred some months into the series. Frankie Howerd made a memorable appearance giving his view of the Budget (re-working the act he had tried out at the Establishment). His career had been in the doldrums, but together the chic of the Soho club and the vast audience who saw him on *TW3* turned the tide. Part of his uneasiness on previous shows, especially on commercial television, came from the uncongenial discipline of time. He found it inhibiting to know that at any moment the credits might roll. His script for *TW3* was impregnable, and I was fascinated by the thoroughness with which he rehearsed it into apparent spontaneity. He performed it for me privately behind a bit of scenery during a tea break, and only the 'oohs' and 'ahs' and 'ums' flowered in front of the camera. It was heartening to see him relax on transmission as he went on and on and no studio manager waved his arms to stop him. He over-ran by many minutes, unhampered, the time added by monosyllabic grunts and, more especially, by laughter. At the end the applause was deafening and prolonged.

David, quick to realize that goodwill accrues to the host when he presents a good act, led the clapping with enthusiasm. The ovation went on a lot longer than any of us had expected, and finally he glanced down at his notes to remind himself of the next item. Of course, it happened at the moment that I put the camera on him so that the audience could once again see David delighting in Frankie's triumph. All they saw was a bowed head and a frown (of concentration). An alarming number of viewers had no doubt that they had witnessed one of the 'young amateurs' showing signs of jealousy when confronted by the success of a 'real professional'.

David's other 'mistake' during the series was not a mistake at all, but an unfortunate stroke of irony which left us all with an uncomfortable feeling of guilt. Gerald Kaufman submitted a mind-boggling list of inaccuracies in the prophecies of 'Cross-Bencher', a political commentator on the *Sunday Express*. He found enough errors to get a lot of laughs, and when David came to wrap up the programme by quoting from the Sunday newspapers he turned immediately to Cross-Bencher. The prophet-journalist had blithely announced that Hugh Gaitskell had been ill (we did not know how ill) and was on the mend – it would not, he wrote with confidence, be long before Gaitskell was completely fit. David looked straight at the camera and said simply, 'Sorry, Hugh!' Within a week Gaitskell was dead.

The morning after the first night, I met David in the Kenya Coffee Bar in the King's Road at about eleven and we shared a feeling of anticlimax. Everything had gone as well or better than we expected. There had been calls of outrage and we had had congratulatory messages. However, what we wanted was notices. Suddenly and miraculously David came upon a review by Pat Williams in the place we least expected it – the back page of the *Sunday Telegraph*. It was an extraordinary editorial decision to find space and print it in that late edition. We had showed the headlines from the Sundays at the end of Saturday's programme – Clement Freud kindly used to do a freebooting drive around Fleet Street for us until it became accepted practice to have an official delivery – and the Sundays are not as prone to late editions as are the dailies. However, here was a long review bubbling with excitement and saying all that we would have wanted to say ourselves about the writers, the performers, the music and the attitude of the programme. I lost the cutting with all my other *TW3* cuttings some years later when a sympathetic American student of satire asked to borrow them with a promise to return them the next day and was never heard from again. The collection included my two favourite headlines – from the *Express*, 'These guilty men must go', and from the old *Herald Tribune* John Crosby's simple, 'The best television programme in the world'.

Other members of the cast confirmed the interest we had experienced. Willi Frischauer records the reaction in his breathless style, 'The wires criss-crossing London between the homes of the young writers and performers were humming with cheers and post mortems.' Only poor Roy Kinnear apparently sat in silence in Hampstead, wondering how it had gone. On Monday morning he plucked up courage and rang his agent, the late Freddie Joachim. Roy was treated as though recently bereaved. 'Don't worry – it was horrible, and they have a contract; but I have talked to people in very high places at Broadcasting House and I am assured it cannot last three weeks.' Shattered – like the rest of us he had thought he might be on to a success – Roy went out on to Hampstead Heath for a little air and bumped into Tom Bell, who clasped him warmly by the hand, treated him like a hero and banished any thoughts of suicide.

Assembling the programme very soon fell into a routine. After transmission on Saturdays we used to 'wind down' at the Casserole in the King's Road, and I would often get away to Brighton that night or the next morning and go to ground at the Royal Crescent Hotel. Sunday and Monday were free days. (According to Willi Frischauer, 'By Monday they were all at Lime Grove again ... the discussion was intense, the flow of ideas even richer than before.') On Tuesday the routine of collecting material began again. Occasionally sketches or songs could be commissioned ahead and stockpiled, but we used up most of our pre-pared ideas during the first six weeks. The programme was always at its best when the items sprang appropriately and as late as possible from the week's news. It was important not to make decisions early on Tuesday. The weekend and Monday papers have a habit of cleaning up the tail-end of the previous week, not finding the pulse of the week in question; but some stories do begin to emerge and Tuesday was a good day for making lists, knowing that they could be discarded.

Some regular writers were contracted to supply a sketch or a song: some trusted contributors rang in when they had an idea, with a fair certainty that it would be commissioned. Others took a chance, or, if the idea was particularly attractive, we took a chance. Obvious items attracted several candidates and had to be farmed out carefully. Many writers new to television submitted ideas. A peculiarity was the number of journalists who recognized the possibility of combining research and dramatization in the mock documentary style we applied to some exposé items. Keith Waterhouse and Willis Hall were hardly newcomers, but Peter Lewis (*Daily Mail*) and Peter Dobereiner (now golf correspondent of the *Observer*) soon became regulars; Quentin Crewe and Julian Holland were two more. David Nathan and Dennis Potter frequently submitted material and I used to try to assess, as with all two-handed teams, what each collaborator's contribution was. Nathan and Potter used different typewriters: but it was a dangerous simplification to assume that the typing of the final script was a clue to prime authorship. Although David Nobbs and Peter Tinniswood have gone on to successful separate careers, their first regular television exposure was on *TW3*. Herbert Kretzmer, at that time the drama critic of the *Daily Express*, wrote one lyric each week which was set to music by Dave Lee, who was music director for *TW3*.

I have mentioned Gerald Kaufman's 'Cross-Bencher' script, but it was not his first. About six weeks into the series a script arrived from him out of the blue – his name meant nothing to me at the time. He was working as a writer and researcher on the *Daily Mirror* and he had plainly watched the 'exposé' items on the programme carefully. The manner of presentation was idiosyncratic. The screen was split: Accurate quoted testimony appeared on one side and photographs of the public figures being quoted or members of the cast acting as spokesmen for them filled the other. With a pertinent text and an acid commentary the impact was often considerable.

Gerald's first exercise dealt with thirteen silent MPs, who had not spoken in Parliament for lengths of time up to ten or fifteen years. The research was bullet-proof and I found it irresistible – especially as he had scripted it so clearly and sharply that no changes in presentation were required for a four- to five-minute item which became one of our noisier *causes célèbres*. One of the silent M Ps suggested in the House of Commons that the item constituted a breach of privilege. Laughter greeted the suggestion and the Commons joined the unconscious publicists who were rallying to our cause. I was soon confirmed in my belief that good notices for a programme were pleasant to read, but that there is nothing like a national row to increase viewing figures. Front pages, M Ps, bishops and other less exalted pulpiteers freely gave a mass of valuable publicity to the programme. Gerald Kaufman went on to do more scripts – always relevant, neatly conceived and unassailable on facts.

Much later in the series I wanted to examine the career of Sir Reginald Manningham-Buller ('Bullying-Manner' in Bernard Levin's phrase for the *Spectator*), by now Lord Dilhorne, the Lord Chancellor, not a lawyer I admired. The first script which I commissioned was caustic, amusing and wild; and at about the same time I got a warning from Hugh Carleton Greene that it would be politically inadvisable to consider Dilhorne as a target. Disappointed, I filed the script and waited until another judge, Lord Devlin, came into prominence. On one of those wonderful weeks when everybody who knew of the BBC's unease about examining Dilhorne was going away for the weekend, I got Kaufman to check and reshape early material as a tribute to Devlin, who shone the brighter in the light of a comparison with Dilhorne. Mrs Wyndham Goldie, who was not privy to the Dilhorne ban, was chaperoning the programme that weekend and I deceitfully submitted the Devlin script for her approval without giving her the background. She found it strong but acceptable and we broadcast it. All hell broke loose over the Sunday, and my early call from Hugh Greene boiled down to three complaints of inaccuracy. Had I been foisted with the first script I would have had anxious moments; but Kaufman's record was too reassuring for alarm. His research turned out to be as impeccable as ever – even to the critical third accusation of a political link by marriage which the Lord Chancellor had apparently forgotten.

Apart from contributions by journalists, it was exciting to tempt scripts from celebrated writers in other fields. My routine began early in the morning and I was usually at the office around seven. There was a bonus in that the cleaners were making tea if I got in early enough and I could read scripts and write letters for two uninterrupted hours. The production staff began to arrive after 9.30, and from 10 am I had time to coax contributions by telephone or over luncheon without the feeling that there was a pile of desk work unattended.

Forays into central London usually meant the Grill Room at the Café Royal. Other lunches were pot-luck at Lime Grove. Roy Hattersley reminds me ruefully that we met at this time and he was not invited to appear. I do remember an uneasy lunch with Anthony Wedgwood Benn, inhibited by the solemn concentration with which he approached each topic – unleavened by those audience-pleasing techniques he uses as part of his public performances on programmes like *Any Questions?* Lunch with Cyril Connolly lingers in the mind because it produced an immensely scholarly Shakespearean sketch which would have played the length of an entire programme. Rejecting it was not easy.

One day when David Frost and I were to lunch Nigel Dennis, from whom we hoped to cajole a script, he was long overdue. Finally, searching the corridors of Lime Grove, I found him stumbling around, lost and distracted. He pulled himself together and told the story of his misadventure. Arriving at reception he had asked for me and been sent to one of the other hospitality rooms, where he was greeted by an effusive host whose face looked familiar, so he assumed it was me – we had never met though I knew his wife. 'Come in, my dear fellow,' said the other man, putting a reassuring hand on his shoulder, '. . . I think it's going to be very exciting.' Nigel Dennis was only expecting lunch and he doubted if BBC cuisine would justify 'exciting'; however, he took a drink and tried to share the enthusiasm. 'Orson's coming, you know. He's always good value . . . and so's O'Toole. . . . We've checked and he's left the house and he's on his way. . . .' The meal began to sound more improbable as the garrulous host switched the conversation to great Hamlets past and present, and Dennis struggled to keep up. Finally the mystery was unravelled. Another guest was announced – 'Mr Ernest Milton'. The host, Huw Wheldon, swung round to Nigel Dennis. 'Then who are you?'

Mr Milton, a distinguished Hamlet in his time but then about eighty, had come to appear in a *Monitor* special about Hamlet to celebrate O'Toole's appearance in Olivier's five-hour production which opened the National Theatre's first season at the Old Vic. Orson Welles completed the group. Nigel Dennis slipped away to us feeling vaguely that he had been accused of trying to gatecrash lunch with the witty and famous by masquerading as an eighty-year-old Hamlet. I never persuaded him to write for us and have always blamed Wheldon.

A pleasant diversion on *TW3* was the chance it provided to invite great theatrical stars to deliver special occasional pieces. Dame Edith Evans came to read a poem by Caryl Brahms. I called to pick her up for lunch one day in Albany. As I was ushering her down the stairs another visitor emerged from the chambers below. It was Lady Clark, Sir Kenneth's wife. She saw Edith and said, 'Hello'. Edith's face was a picture of puzzlement. Lady Clark came to her rescue. 'It's Lady Clark,' she identified herself. Edith switched to the attack. 'Why is she telling me that?' she said brazenly. 'I know perfectly well who she is.'

Michael Redgrave, Peter O'Toole, Paul Scofield, Ian Holm and Coral Browne all made appearances on one or other of the late night shows. Coral, apparently the most assured and elegant of actresses, rarely did television, certainly not live. She wrote her first line on her immaculately manicured nails and entered with her hand held up and her fingers stretched out. Her hand shook so much that she was quite unable to read the blur.

Dame Sybil Thorndike was twice a guest. She was always remarkable. The first time I had worked with her was in a radio play which Caryl Brahms and I wrote, with music by John Dankworth, called *The Sunday Market*. The *Daily Express* produced a memorable photograph captioned 'Thorndike sings Dankworth'. During the early weeks of *TW3*, Dame Sybil was playing St Teresa of Avila in the West End. The play did not have a long run and during the course of it she fell, leaping for a bus in the King's Road, an accident which triggered the arthritis from which she suffered so painfully in her last years. She made a rueful little joke about St Teresa's levitational powers and her own failure to stay airborne in this case. It was quite a surprise that she jumped for the bus in the first place. Almost invariably she walked. (On one occasion she and Sir Lewis Casson – even older – turned up for the first rehearsal of Noël Coward's *Waiting in the Wings* at a hall in Tottenham Court Road to find their producers, Michael Redgrave and Fred Sadoff, profoundly relieved to see them. The producers had learnt that morning that there was to be a transport strike and despaired of their cast arriving. When they showed concern for Dame Sybil and Sir Lewis the two senior citizens were uncomprehending. They had walked all the way across London from Swan Court in the King's Road, Chelsea, as they had always intended to do, oblivious to the strike except to notice that the streets were uncomfortably crowded with cars which made it hazardous for pedestrians.)

The week after Sybil closed as St Teresa I collected a sketch from Keith Waterhouse and Willis Hall. Like all their material it was funny, topical and delivered at the last moment. We used to discuss their contribution, which was a weekly commission, on Tuesdays and keep in touch during the rest of the week. On Thursday mornings they would sit down to write and as a result something quite different would emerge. Sometimes inspiration would fail Keith and Willis on Thursdays and we would have to wait until Friday. Their sketches were always beautifully crafted and eminently actable. Often they were for Roy Kinnear and Millicent Martin, but all the cast used to cherish a hope that they might get the 'Waterhall' contribution.

Their idea on this occasion was to parody a newspaper agony column by having current Tory Cabinet Ministers put problems to a super Marjorie Proops in the naive, inquiring style of 'Puzzled adolescent, Surbiton'. Casting the Cabinet letter-writers for this particular item was not difficult: Willy Rushton had already established himself as the Harold Macmillan figure, Lance Percival as Alec Douglas-Home, and so on. However, by now we were getting rather grand about casting our guests. Michael Redgrave had already done a couple of Caryl Brahms's scripts and, as I read the piece, I remembered that Dame Sybil had closed as St Teresa on the previous Saturday night, so I rang her agent and sent the text round in a taxi.

A few days later I was a little surprised and entirely delighted to hear that she was prepared to do it. When she arrived at Lime Grove she was surprised in her turn to find that we were broadcasting live the next day, in front of a studio audience; she had not done that before. Moreover, she was to read her piece from a teleprompter device. She had not done that either. She would have been quite prepared to commit the four- or five-minute script to memory at twenty-four hours' notice. She confessed that she had had no idea about the programme and was quite unaware of the furore it was creating. However, she read the sketch when it arrived and was about to tell her agent that it was perhaps too frivolous and too risqué to be worth her while, when Sir Lewis asked what it was. When she told him it was for a programme called *That Was The Week That Was* he was adamant that she should do it. 'You must,' he told her. 'The programme's practically Communist!'

She met the teleprompter for the first time in the studio the next day, the Saturday of transmission. I think she felt she was cheating; but she rehearsed happily, relished the studio guffaws and asked constantly to be warned if she was overdoing it – 'I always do, you know. You have to cut me down.' The Agony Aunt was required to dictate her replies into a dictaphone after each Cabinet Minister had stated his problem. Dame Sybil, grasping the dictaphone firmly in her right hand on the dress run, had no problems. The transmission produced one of those tiny, dramatic moments of television that are vividly etched in my memory. When we came to the sketch Rushton went through the first question to very reasonable laughter and I cut to Dame Sybil for her reply. There was a brief pause and I could see her right hand shaking slightly, betraying the nervousness that had overtaken her. It was riveting to watch her raise her left hand and smack it smartly across the right wrist to discipline it and launch into her performance with both hands under control. It was a lesson in mastering nerves delivered in a split second, and she went on to get her laughs and enjoy herself hugely.

Some months later we were all at the Dorchester to receive an award for the first series of *TW3* when the news of President Kennedy's assassination came through. Dame Sybil was presenting the prizes and when I went up to collect our award I hissed that I would have to hurry off to re-vamp the programme. We regretted that we had not met since the last *TW3* and speculated that it might be a long time before we met again. The next day Caryl Brahms produced an ode to Jackie Kennedy and once again Dame Sybil was back at Lime Grove giving a magisterial performance.

The last occasion on which I saw her was in a star-studded life of Dickens called *The Great Inimitable Mr Dickens*. Dame Sybil as Dickens's grandmother had a very short scene with a small child who played the infant Charles. She was in great pain during rehearsals, but entirely uncomplaining. I remember helping her into her car one day as she chafed about her disability. 'Oh,' she sighed, 'the spirit is willing, but the flesh is disgustingly weak!' When we recorded the programme the pain made it hard for her to concentrate and she fluffed one of her lines. She was furious with herself, especially as she knew we were short of time. We ran the scene again and she got it right. We had to press on with the rest of the recording and I sent my assistant, Nick Page, down to thank her, reassure her and make sure that she got off in her car as quickly and comfortably as possible. Nick, well briefed, thanked her and apologized for the retake. 'Sorry about having to do it twice,' he said airily, 'we had a little technical trouble. . . .' Dame Sybil looked at him beadily. 'You're a liar . . . but I like you,' she said. It was her last television performance.

Often it was attractive to writers who were used to filling a whole evening in the theatre with a large theme, and realized that an idea which had pleased them would not stand up to a two-hour play or even a one-acter, to recast it as a sketch. In such cases an item on *TW3* gave them a large audience and the satisfaction of a quick reaction. John

Mortimer, Frank Marcus, John Antrobus, Kenneth Tynan, John Braine and Peter Shaffer were among the writers who contributed occasional pieces.

Shaffer's first sketch was a classic rumination on the scandal surrounding the Vassal case. Much play had been made in court of Vassal's homosexuality, and wild and sinister implications had been read into the routine salutations and sign-offs of his correspondence with the late Thomas Galbraith, a junior minister. Lance Percival as a senior civil servant hauled David Kernan, a junior, over the coals, pouncing on potentially ambiguous phrases like 'my dear'; 'pursuant' ('It has an erotic penumbra'); 'favour' ('The Oxford Dictionary defines it as "to look kindly upon" '); 'thanking you in anticipation' . . . ('positively whinnies with suggestiveness'); 'yours faithfully' ('even "yours" is dangerous. . . . It suggests a willingness for surrender!'); 'your obedient servant' ('an *ipso facto* confession of sexual deviation. And that, as we all know, is an *ipso facto* confession of treason.').

Shaffer then broadened the argument: 'I think you secretly believe that the way to stop homosexuals being blackmailed is to change the law so that they can't be.' The junior agrees that the idea had occurred to him. 'Nonsense! . . . The only way to stop a homosexual being blackmailed is to stop him being a homosexual. And the only way you can do that is to lock him up in a building with five hundred other men. That way he can see how unattractive they are. . . .' Shaffer's pre-Wolfenden tract ended neatly in verbal slapstick:

'What is your name, by the way?'

'Fairy, sir.'

'Somehow, I don't think you are going to go very far in Her Majesty's Service.'

I wooed Noël Coward for a contribution and got a very quick 'No'. With Terence Rattigan there was a long correspondence, but in the end he decided that the technique was not his. John Osborne never wrote for us; but when, in its later stages, the programme was at its most beleaguered, he wrote a supportive thunderbolt for one of the Sunday papers, which was heartening.

David Frost and Christopher Booker wrote a lot together. I was rarely present at their sessions, which usually took place on Fridays or as late as Saturday morning so that the leading exchanges at the top of the show could be as topical as possible, or at least could reflect the topics likely to be uppermost in the viewer's mind. Booker has given his account of the process in *From Fringe to Flying Circus*: '. . . I would have some idea for a sketch and then we would talk it through for an hour or two. Most of the jokes came from me, but where Frostie's skill came was at a certain point he'd say, "Right – I think we've got enough now", and I would just go to a typewriter and sit down, and he would virtually dictate a script – he had an amazing gift for putting a sketch together in such a way that it would work on the air.' I like to compare this with Willi Frischauer's infectious prose: '... the thoughts were philosophical, sublime, esoteric. The material which emerged was down to earth, hard-hitting, rough. David was the one who barked most fiercely and showed his teeth – literally, with the greatest ferocity.'

Booker was at his best as a parodist, especially when inspired by an original's lofty prose. His *Private Eye* piece, 'The Decline and Fall of the Emperor Macmillianus', was wonderfully sustained; and a piece which he wrote at my suggestion on the occasion of Alec Douglas-Home's arrival at 10 Downing Street instead of Rab Butler used a measured Disraelian style. It was not best served on the air by David Frost's inelegant delivery, which went some way to sabotage the Disraelian panache and blunt its cutting-edge.

This item was the nearest I got to mounting a personal pulpit on *TW*3. The gesture of the piece was not anti-Conservative. It was a vigorous summary of a Butlerian – or Disraelian – reaction to a retro-grade elevation inside the Tory Party:

> My Lord: when I say that your acceptance of the Queen's commission to form an administration has proved, and will prove, an unmitigated catastrophe for the Conservative Party, for the Constitution, for the Nation, and for yourself, it must not be thought that I bear you any personal ill-will.... You are the dupe and unwitting tool of a conspiracy – the conspiracy of a tiny band of desperate men who have seen in you their last slippery chance of keeping the levers of power within their privileged circle. For the sake of that prize, which can at best be transitory, those men are prepared to dash all the hopes of the Party they profess to serve: or rather the two nations which by their actions they seek to perpetuate....

No such savage attack on a politician had previously been delivered on BBC Television and the monologue caused a storm of nearly six hundred phone calls and over three hundred letters – all in protest. The flames were fanned by David Frost's pay-off, reverting to his own persona and style: 'And so, there is the choice for the electorate; on one hand Lord Home – and on the other hand Mr Harold Wilson. Dull Alec versus Smart Alec.' It was rewarding to hear Lord Home (a pleasant man) say during a television interview twenty years later that it was the only thing that had hurt him in many years of public service – but then, he said, *T W 3* was an 'attack on the Establishment ... it wasn't satire'. I am surprised that he should have been so affected by one of the few pieces which got near to satire. Later Harold Wilson confessed admiration of the piece to David Frost and was presented with a copy.

Together Frost and Booker produced another piece of invective which had teeth. Again the form was a parody but, since the original was Eamonn Andrews's lugubrious style on *This Is Your Life*, the showbiz rather than literary source gave Frost more scope to contribute. Andrews was not, of course, the target – that was the then Home Secretary, Henry Brooke. Frost delivered the usual Andrews summing up after Brooke's 'victims' had given their testimony. '... Your policy, Mr Brooke, has been one of trial and error. Their trials. Your errors. On behalf of us all – THIS IS YOUR LIFE, HENRY BROOKE – and was theirs!' They gave Brooke (played by Rushton) the last word – 'Just shows. If you're Home Secretary you can get away with murder!'

When people ask what practical effect *T W 3* ever had on politics this is the only example to which I can point with some certainty. I am convinced that Henry Brooke's subsequent election defeat was materially affected by it. Certainly Edward Heath was of that opinion, inveighing against it for some ten or fifteen minutes at a rumbustious *Punch* luncheon.

On one occasion during our second series, David Frost and I were lunching at the Café Royal. It was after the series of scandals – Vassal, Profumo, etc. – which had shaken the Conservative administration. Across the Grill Room we could see Edward Heath lunching a guest who looked distinctly suspicious. What hair remained was carefully coiffed. Eyebrows appeared delicately plucked. Cheeks were perhaps touched with a pink smear of rouge. We speculated idly on who this mystery man could be, arriving eventually at a scenario which satisfied us. Plainly he was a senior civil servant on whom the current fashionable suspicions were falling. Heath had been told to warn him. He had therefore taken him to a sympathetic ambience – what better credentials than those of the Café Royal? – and was advising him to mend his ways and get the boy out of his life! Having cleared that up, we got on with our lunch and did not give it another thought until Mr Heath brought his guest past our table on the way out and introduced us: 'I don't think you know – this is the Balkan Ambassador.' Balkan must, I am afraid, hide the Iron Curtain diplomat's real nationality.

I also started a tradition of commissioned light music on the show – an area of activity much neglected by the BBC. John Bassett's contacts with jazz musicians produced some of these composers. John Dankworth, John Scott and Duncan Heath wrote many of the jazz improvisations to which words were set – in the manner of Annie Ross's 'Twisted' – by the late Stephen Vinaver and later by Caryl Brahms. Ron Grainer, who wrote the signature tunes for *TW3*, *Not So Much a Programme* and *BBC-3*, Carl Davis, Sandy Wilson and Dave Lee also wrote for the programme.

Millicent Martin's jazz solo was the most flamboyant musical contribution. She learnt these complicated pieces very quickly. When Vinaver was writing they often did not get to her before Thursday night, and yet she sang them two days later with great skill, in a succession of little black dresses. As the weeks went by it became more difficult to find a new way of shooting these moments, although putting a camera on Millie's face was always a rewarding experience for a director. My favourite variation was for a song which included a long break on the bongos, played by the virtuoso drummer Barry Morgan. I found in rehearsal that it was possible to superimpose Barry's fingers, fanatically beating the small round drums, on Miss Martin's breasts. We did not punch up the combined image in the studio until transmission. The effect on the audience was splendid, and when the artist caught sight of her picture on a monitor it was the nearest she ever came to losing her iron-clad, professional cool.

Herbert Kretzmer had an especially sharp ear for lyrics which were relevant to the attitude of the programme and the week's news. His 'Lullaby for an Illegitimate Child', broadcast in the early weeks of 1962, reflected on an announcement that one London baby in eight born during the previous year had been illegitimate. Sung with beautiful simplicity by Millicent Martin, it caused a great stir:

> Conceived you may have been in sordid passion;
> But, baby, you've arrived and you're in fashion!
>
> Don't you weep, my little baby,
> 'Cause you haven't got a dad.
> Go to sleep my little baby,
> Things aren't really quite so bad.

There's no reason any longer
Why you ought to feel so blue.
The world is full of bastards
Just like you. . . .

A musical parody, 'Song of Nostalgia for an American State', was distanced from protest because its objective was American prejudice:

I wanna go back to Mississippi,
Where the scent of blossoms
Kiss the evenin' breeze,
Where the Mississippi mud
Kinda mingles with the blood
Of the Niggers
Who are hangin'
From the branches of the trees. . . .
. . . Up above there's nuttin'
But a butter-coloured moon,
While down below
They're cuttin' up
A chocolate-coloured coon. . . .

Another song for David Kernan pastiched Noël Coward, expertly marrying current attitudes to teenage depravity to Coward's cautionary comments on flappers in his 1920s songs. Kretzmer called his 'Teenager':

Frivolous girl in frightful jeans,
Collecting scores of boys,
You'll add to your collection
All manner of infection.
In Soho
They sink so low
In their sad, erotic joys,
That if they're feeling seedy,
It's VD. . . .

. . . Before you rot
Cease your mad gavotte
Or your end must be despair!
Teenager, better take care,
Teenager, better beware!

Millicent Martin had a deeply ingrained mistrust of new material. Her constant cry was, 'Why can't I have a song as good as last week?' The next week, last week's 'no-no' became this week's measuring stick. A classic instance was a Kretzmer lyric, topically prompted, which started, 'I've been testing contraceptives all day long.' However, a suggestion that Lance Percival could perhaps perform it instead was enough to nudge the reluctant artist into activity; the laughter was loud and next week the plea for 'another song like last week' recurred.

The most controversial items covered a wide range. Apart from 'Thirteen Silent MPs', much fire was drawn by a tail-piece to the first series in which Keith Waterhouse and Willis Hall summed up through Roy Kinnear and Millicent Martin the lowest common denominator attitude to the show. A suburban couple stare at their television set after transmission:

She: Well, it was something different.
He: Well, it was satire, wasn't it? What we call satire.
She: All jokes and skits and that.
He: Yes! Mucky jokes. Obscenity - it's all the go nowadays. By law, you see. You're allowed to do it. You can say 'bum', you can say 'po', you can say anything.

For a time we were known as the 'bum and po' show. The scene was inspired by an early sketch of Vinaver's (usually thought to be by Hall and Waterhouse as well), which also involved Millicent Martin and Roy Kinnear. This time the couple were found in a café and the social embarrassment built speedily from the moment she leant across to him and whispered:

He: You don't have to whisper.
She: I don't want no one to hear.
He: Nobody's going to hear. Nobody's listening.
She: Well, I don't want to say it out loud.
He: Don't be daft.
She: Well, I don't want to.
He: Don't be daft.
She: Well, I don't want to.
He: Come on.
She: (giggling) Well, I don't want to.
He: Just say it out loud.
She: (loud) Your fly is open.

The word had an explosive effect. We had used the sketch in the second pilot and it had been very successful. Donald Baverstock had doubts about its propriety and we stockpiled it until the third programme. It is difficult to believe today that its acute observation of an embarrassing but credible social predicament caused alarm and some of our earliest accusations of smut-peddling.

On the religious front there was an old Cambridge sketch, 'The Bible Condensed', in *Reader's Digest* style: 'The Resurrection: "You can't keep a good man down".' It shocked David Frost's parents. 'I am thinking of David as an actor who just speaks the lines put into his mouth,' said the Reverend Paradine Frost loyally of his son's involvement in what was one of his favourite sketches.

The biggest religious row occurred over a lengthy piece of prose written and conceived by two actors, Charles Lewsen and Robert Gillespie. It was a 'Consumers' Guide to Religion' and it rigorously applied the language and standards of consumer guides to various religions. I tried unsuccessfully to defuse it by writing an introduction for William Rushton suggesting that if religions were seeking to make ever more worldly appeals to their flocks they must not be surprised if they found themselves judged by the standards of the world. In retrospect I am sure I knew the disclaimer would not stop the row; but I was well aware that it gave me an argument which, if not unassailable, would certainly be useful when the storm broke. (Millicent Martin had a more simplistic answer when questioned later by the press: 'It's just a send-up of those consumer guides.') One Catholic priest, whose religion had been tested and deplored along with the others, wrote, 'I'm sure you'll have a lot of trouble and a lot of protests about this. Don't take any notice. It was very good and the sort of people who complain will all be converts.'

The circumstances of that transmission were tense. I had discussed the item with Alasdair Milne and drawn his attention to the introduction. He was aware of the dangers, but agreed that we should broadcast it. On the Saturday, Kenneth Adam announced his intention of visiting the studio. Alasdair showed him the script since it was liable to make waves; but he prefaced his remarks by saying that he had made the decision to play it – he was only showing it to Kenneth for information. Kenneth would have preferred to have cut it: Alasdair's stance made that impossible. It is a good example of the protective umbrella which Milne and Baverstock held over the programme, making it much easier to operate with freedom underneath. 'The Consumers' Guide' is a long sketch which still holds up; but too long to quote usefully here. For those housewives keen to know the best buy it was:

> ... The Church of England.... It's a jolly friendly faith – if you are one there's no onus on you to make anyone else join – in fact no one need ever know. And it's pretty fair, on the whole, too. With some of these products we've mentioned ... you start guilty from the off. But the Church of England is English. On the whole you start pretty well innocent, and they've got to prove you guilty....

Sex, politics, religion; and royalty – the programme's attitude to royalty was that it was not outside our scope, although none of our items dealing with the Royal Family had the cutting-edge that those with political or religious content sported. They usually concentrated on the cap-in-hand way royal occasions were reported. The biggest row was over a monologue by Humphry Berkeley – now Head of Light Entertainment at London Weekend Television. David Frost had seen it in a revue at Cambridge – just as we had collected from Oxford another setpiece, Ian Davidson's mime for a conductor conducting orchestrated battle noises. Barclay's premise was a Dimbleby figure confronted by the spectacle of a royal barge disappearing beneath the waters of the Thames. 'The royal barge is sinking in the Pool of London. The Queen wearing a radiant smile is swimming for her life ... and now the Royal Marine Band has struck up "God Save the Queen".'

Controversy advertised the show and the reasonably high standard enabled us to hold on to the audience.

A minor irritation was the automatic assumption that anything the least unlikely or unusual was rigged. For example, when a man stepped into the studio and hit Bernard Levin one night, there was an immediate suggestion that the incident had been staged. (Levin had given the man's wife a bad notice for a theatrical performance.) But to have set it up would have been entirely foreign to the whole idea of the programme. John Bassett had found the man a guest ticket, without having any idea of his intention to make the attack.

The *Daily Express* rang the musical director, Dave Lee, trying to get a story proving the incident was fixed. Lee encouraged him, 'Well, I certainly know what the director of the show said when Levin got punched because I was wearing headphones at the time and I could hear every word he said.'

'Tell us, *please*.'

'Have you got your pencil?'

My mother and father on their
wedding day

My older brother, Alfred, and me –
both extremely young

Our home: Lower Farm, Kingweston

Going out to bat for Kingweston Cricket
Club with Ken Birch (*right*), late 1940s

Undergraduate poses for *Isis*

(*Left*) Miss Smith's first solo lines on the London stage: 'It's my première tonight,' at the Watergate Theatre Club. (*Right*) Maggie Smith and Pamela Harrington in the same show

Early days at ATV

(*Back row, left to right*) Kenneth Cope, me, Willie Rushton; (*front row*) Al Mancini, Millicent Martin, Lance Percival and David Kernan reading *TW3* fan/hate letters

With David Frost, watching a *TW3* playback

Eating oysters with Caryl Brahms in Whitstable

With Eleanor Bron in *Not So Much A Programme*, 1964

Discussing the Donald Wolfit obituary programme with (*left to right*) Brian Rix, Michael Elliott and Harold Pinter

With *Zsa Zsa Gabor* on the set of *Up The Front*, a first World War film

Virgin Soldiers on location in Singapore: (*left to right*) Leslie Gilliat (co-producer), me and Ken Higgins (lighting cameraman)

At-the-end-of-filming party for *The National Health*

The Mitford Girls: (left to right) Patricia Michael (Diana), Patricia Hodge (Nancy), Collette Gleeson (Unity), Julia Sutton (Pamela), Lucy Fenwick (Jessica) and Gay Soper (Deborah).

Cindy-Ella or I Gotta Shoe: (left to right) George Browne, Cleo Laine, Cy Grant and Elisabeth Welch

Side by Side by Sondheim with
Millicent Martin, David Kernan and
Julia McKenzie

Researching for my television news quiz,
We Interrupt This Week, in Central Park

'Yes, yes.'
'And paper?'
'Yes! Yes. What did he say?'
'He said, "Who the fuck is that?"'
No story.

Towards the end of the first season of *TW3* early rumours of the Profumo affair began to filter through. (Ironically, *TW3* is often remembered as playing a large part in the scandal, but in fact the heat was not really on by the time we had broken for the summer.) We hinted at dirty work in one of Millicent Martin's opening numbers, interjecting a spurious anniversary for the Victorian song as a peg:

> ... See him in the House of Commons
> Making Laws to put the blame
> While the object of his passion
> Walks the streets to hide her shame. ...

Tension was already building and we were very self-conscious about the risk on that Saturday night. Twenty years on it hardly looks like a brave gesture. When Miss Keeler disappeared to Spain we allowed ourselves a short item in which court ushers called 'Christine Keeler' *ad infinitum* around the studio and down the corridors – in vain. The only substantial item was a beautifully animated collage of headlines and photographs to the tune of 'I Could Write a Book', which the late Geoffrey Martin edited to greet the Denning Report on the whole affair. It coincided with the programme's return to the air in the autumn.

I spent the break going to America and touring the south coast of England with Robin Phillips to call on Millicent Martin and Lance Percival, who were in different summer shows at Bournemouth, and on David Frost, who was co-starring with Al Read in, of all places, Weston-super-Mare. David's love affair with live performance and stand-up comedy is a permanent puzzle. Properly briefed and fully concerned, he is a fascinating television interviewer. I once said of him that he is the only person I know who learns from his own mistakes without having admitted that he has made them. Watching his hopeful clowning alongside Al Read's contained, confident, immaculate act was a powerful reminder of an older school of professionalism coming after the euphoria which at that time surrounded the studio performances of *That Was The Week That Was.*

My visit to America was clouded by the news of Timothy Birdsall's death, which I had to carry to John Bird and Eleanor Bron, both close Cambridge friends. They were having a great success at the New York 'Establishment' – not sharing, it seemed, the momentary fury which Peter Cook, playing on Broadway in *Beyond The Fringe*, felt at David Frost's success back home. 'England ... giggling into the sea', was his verdict.

Timothy had been ill for some time, but Jocelyn, his wife, had kept the news from him that his illness was leukemia. She had made the decision that he would not want to know that he would not see their sons, Adam and Toby, grow up. She came to ask me if the BBC would offer a contract for the next season at a much inflated fee so that Timothy's mind would be relieved of financial worries over the last few weeks. Touchingly, she guaranteed that he would not be able to fulfil it. It says something to counter the bureaucratic image of the BBC that it proved human and flexible enough to work out a way of doing what she had asked. Unhappily its imaginative gesture was not tested.

One of Timothy's last cartoons had been a giant dragon, Rumour, rising above the Houses of Parliament in the apocalyptic style he employed in some of his later drawings. We produced a compilation programme in his memory, narrated by his friend Michael Frayn. Sadly it has not survived; but I had occasion to see a number of telerecordings of *That Was The Week That Was* again some years ago and was struck and saddened to feel a different response when I watched him and his colleagues. His contributions had lost none of their wit, warmth and individuality. His approach was as fresh, incisive and personal as ever. It was simply that the others have survived and my view of what they were then and my knowledge of what has happened to each of them since gave them all an extra dimension, whereas Timothy was as I had known and loved him – no more, no less; no further access of happiness or sadness had been allowed to round out my perception of him, and it was an uncanny and melancholy experience to be reminded so vividly that his life had stopped and ours had gone on.

The fellow feeling on the *TW3* team was always warm and companionable. In revues, performers tend to jockey for position, but on *TW3* there was always enough material for every performer to get a chance to shine, and a light load one week was usually compensated for by a flurry of activity the next. Even in such a friendly atmosphere the universal affection for Timothy was unique, the sense of loss deeply felt.

By now the 'satire' label was firmly fixed on the show. There was a court case where a witness said, 'Oh, he got in with some of them satirists, your honour'; and I had a letter from one forward-thinking, muddled mum who wrote, 'What is the best way to educate my son so that he can be a satirist when he grows up?'

We were careful not to use the word satire ourselves. I had a sixth sense that it would rebound, and it did. It is not an easy word to define and I was chary of using a label which I knew we could not, and frequently would not want to, live up to, except in the sense that the original Latin, *satura*, means hotchpotch. Laughs crop up in ordinary life that can only loosely be considered satirical. In Switzerland at the Montreux Festival a Swiss television producer said to us, 'You should not make fun of war. We Swiss have lived through two world wars!' – and that seemed fairly satirical. Then there was a taxi driver on Fifth Avenue, New York, who got the whole Profumo business wrong. The news of the War Minister's statement came over on the radio as we sat in a traffic jam. He said, 'I don't see why this Macmillan guy shouldn't sleep around. At his age, it's to his credit!'

In *The Anatomy of Satire* Gilbert Highet writes:

The type of subject preferred by satire is always concrete, usually topical, often personal. It deals with actual cases, mentions real people by name or describes them unmistakably and often unflatteringly, talks of this moment and this city and this recent fresh deposit of corruption whose stench is still in the satirists' curling nostrils.... Most satiric writing contains cruel and dirty words. Nearly all satirical writing contains trivial and comic words, all satirical writing contains colloquial and anti-literary words.... The satirist tries always to produce the unexpected to keep his viewers and readers gazing and gasping.... Any author therefore who often powerfully uses a number of typical weapons of satire, irony, emotion, antithesis, parody, colloquialism, anticlimax, topicality, invective, violence, vividness or exaggeration, is likely to be writing satire.... He intends to shock his readers. Brutally direct phrases, taboo expressions, nauseating imagery, callous and crude slang, these are parts of the vocabulary of every satirist.... A typical emotion which the author feels and wishes to evoke in his readers must be a blend of amusement and contempt.... Some villainies are too awful for us to despise. We can only shudder at them and in horror turn away – or try to write tragedy. Against all lesser crimes and against all 'follies', it is a powerful weapon.

In some cases our work was satirical in Highet's sense, but it was not our whole brief. We were gathered together on Saturday nights in order to have a conversation with the audience but not in a conversational form. It was carried on in performance, in songs and in sketches, and in argument; we tried to convey an attitude and some information which might not otherwise have got through.

Unlike the great satirists, we had a mass audience. It was a sobering thought that on one Saturday night we 'played to' more people than Bion, Juvenal, Lucian, Petronius, Pope, Dryden and Voltaire, not to mention Abraham a' Sancta Clara. George S. Kauffman said, 'Satire is what closes on Saturday nights'; Harold Macmillan was nearer to it in our case when he came down to Television Centre one day and murmured to Hugh Greene, 'I hear that you have some sort of saturnalia out here on Saturdays.'

We had a lot of visitors once we became fashionable. Edward Heath dropped into rehearsals when he was down to record a party political broadcast; George Brown turned up in the audience with Cliff Michelmore one night, and the next week the Chancellor of the Exchequer, Reginald Maudling, arrived with the Director General. I had a message to say that he was on no account to be photographed so we carefully kept the cameras off him. Afterwards I said what a pity this was: it would have been pleasant to have taken a shot of him – laughing, we hoped. This was plainly the coverage he had hoped for too. He was annoyed that the effect of an image-building exposure had been countermanded by over-zealous officials.

TW3 ended for a variety of reasons. One was the initial success of the programme. In the first weeks there were some three million viewers, and at its peak the figure rose to between twelve and thirteen million – an unprecedented number in those days at that hour. The love affair was too hot not to cool down.

There were contributory factors. During the summer break when we were off the air political suspicions grew stronger. To attack *TW3* was an unpopular move as long as it delighted the nation, and most of our opponents realized that it would be maladroit to attack us simply on political grounds. However, they were given a lead by a BBC executive who made a speech at Blackpool saying, 'Yes, the programme will certainly be coming back in the autumn: but the element of "smut" will be omitted.' We had never really worried about 'smut'; it was not a very important feature of the programme. We were not particularly conscious of it nor, I think, were most of our viewers. However, once the spokesman had lit the blue touch-paper political opponents realized that they could stand well away and watch. A wave of reaction gained momentum.

When we came back on the air after the summer to start the second series, we did four dull shows. There is a self-consciousness about a second series. Diaghilev, returning to London for a second season, said, 'Paint the colours twice as bright. That's how they will remember them.' Our efforts to be bright produced stilted and self-conscious programmes. People said that the show had lost its magic. The anti-brigade had more ammunition at their disposal – it is much easier to knock a show which looks in trouble.

The second season began on Saturday 28 September. On 13 November the BBC made a formal announcement that 'The present run of *That Was The Week That Was* will end on 28 December 1963 and not continue, as had originally been intended, until the spring.' The explanation given was that 1964 would be an election year and rather than 'dilute [the] content and so alter the nature of the programme ...' it should stop. 'Election year? Tell that to the Marines,' one viewer wrote. In those days, whenever I had a programme taken off it always seemed to be Barry Norman, a showbiz reporter on the *Daily Mail*, who was first up the stairs of my Dover Street flat to ask if I knew we had been taken off and had I any comment to make.

Mrs Wyndham Goldie gives a detailed account of the strain *TW3* placed on senior executives. Describing one occasion on which she was asked to exercise control, she allowed herself a rare foray into the clichés of melodrama. 'I was dismayed. I felt I was being asked to ride a tiger.' During this undoubtedly uncomfortable period she was also on the horns of a dilemma:

There was never any disagreement about what the general approach should be. The problem came later: when the general consensus had to be translated on Saturday into a script for the next edition of the programme ... this was very much a hit and miss procedure ... overtly there were never any difficulties. Ned Sherrin, if told that a particular item must not be included, did not argue. He was too cool a character as well as too concerned with getting the programme effectively on the air....

Mrs Goldie mentions one other sketch in October 1963 which she found 'humanly offensive' and laments the 'loss of the experienced *Tonight* approach'. She does not identify the sketch and I cannot remember the incident, though I apparently said, 'Oh, don't you like it? Then of course we'll take it out.'

My own feeling about the period is that I could not have navigated the rocks and storms of *TW3* without having imbibed a good deal of the *Tonight* approach. Our brief was always more dangerous and provocative than *Tonight*'s and we survived for most of four seasons playing a rather risky game. A programme's running order was never sacrosanct until we came on the air, and in cases where Mrs Goldie reports surprise that I would drop an item without protest it may well have been in my mind to drop it in the first place – the way the script played or the texture of the whole programme was often a conditioning consideration at the last moment. On other occasions what seemed like a harmless list of items could develop a life of its own during the course of live transmission. One close-up leer, one dirty laugh, one missed cue, and suddenly the flavour of the programme could change and go sour just as easily as, on some occasions, an apparently limp script would come together with the pace and attack of the performers and the warm rapport of a studio audience. Mrs Goldie quotes Donald Baverstock again on the 'humanly offensive' item: 'I told him what was in the sketch. He said, "Oh my God!" There was a pause, then he added slowly, "It's important to understand that if a group of people are expected to go to the limits of what is permissible, they must have it within them to go beyond those limits." '

Mrs Goldie's final verdict is that '*TW3* died not so much from excessive censorship as from confusion of purpose'. My own feeling is that it was self-destructing in that what we had conceived as a service attracted undue attention. It was as though we had set out to build an aeroplane and come up with a rocket. When the rocket had run its course it fizzled out. This was one fault which we attempted to rectify when we started to plan *TW3*'s successor, *Not So Much a Programme, More a Way of Life*. But first we had to do six more programmes.

By now we had hit our stride again. Mrs Goldie records that, 'Strangely enough it [*TW3*] disappeared in a blaze of conformist glory.' She refers to the Kennedy memorial programme on 23 November 1963 – after which we put out four or five of our best programmes. However, the Kennedy show was unique, occurring in the middle of a series which was associated, in Bernard Levin's phrase, with 'filth, sedition and blasphemy'. It was ironic that at the time when the news of President Kennedy's death came through, most people in television were at the Dorchester, or on their way to the Dorchester, for the Annual Television

Ball at which producers and artists receive awards for the work that they have done during the past year. They are now called the BAFTA awards and provide a substitute for an entire evening of real television. All of us in the *TW3* team were there to receive an award. If there had been any doubt that we would get one, taking the programme off had made it inevitable.

Within a few minutes the ball became rather like the ball before the battle of Waterloo. The news came through soon after 7 pm. Television programmes were interrupted. *Tonight* stopped and after the announcement Peter Batty, the producer, was asked to continue. All he had was a typical *Tonight* story about the biggest pie in Leicestershire, which he and Michelmore thought, quite rightly, was not appropriate. Batty declined to carry on, so the BBC screen went blank for some ten minutes before they inserted their next comedy programme, bringing down just as much criticism as the ITV Controller, who went blank for even longer. It is as hard for a television executive to do the right thing in the case of an emergency as it is for a local council after a heavy fall of snow on the roads.

At the Dorchester the full news took some time to seep through. First, the rumour was of wounding, only later of death. We trouped into dinner wondering whether we should all be sent home or whether somebody would think of calling for two minutes' silence, which is what happened. I was beginning to consider Saturday. Since our brief was to sum up a widely held feeling at the end of a seven-day period and perform the function of a national sigh before embarking on the next week, here was an event which would surely change everything that we had been scripting over the previous five days.

Before setting off to the ball I had left behind the script of the planned programme to be typed up for the prompting machine. I always finished the camera script on Friday nights, leaving spaces for last-minute contributions, usually by Frost and Booker, next day. There were fifty or sixty minutes of songs and sketches written between Tuesday and Friday, some not yet finished but still giving a picture of what we felt about a week which so far had, from our point of view, little to do with President Kennedy.

Obviously, there would have to be changes and, pondering an international disaster from a purely personal and professional point of view, I spent the meal wondering what they would be. David Frost and I were in and out of the ballroom using small change to telephone writers who worked with us regularly to see what they thought, testing and feeling for the correct approach. In the development of *That Was The Week That Was* all the new ideas which made the programmes memorable came from writers and, on this occasion, my first reaction was to talk to them and see what they could offer and then, using these conversations as a briefing, make up my own mind at the last possible moment.

As soon as I had collected the *TW3* award I went to Television Centre, where Kenneth Adam, Rex Moorfoot, the Head of Presentation, Mrs Wyndham Goldie and, for some reason, the Assistant Head of Light Entertainment, Bill Cotton Jr, were all sitting around watching the mass of news coverage. Nothing but news and more news about one event. It was the only thing that people wanted to hear. As I watched commentator after commentator trying to gild the gruesome pictures with words and failing miserably, and saw politicians racing to microphones to make their quickly studied obituary speeches, it became difficult to see how we could add anything to the mass of verbiage the next day. The atmosphere in the central control room was stunned and maudlin; words were slurred, public grief was being drowned in private glasses and the despairing chorus 'News has failed us again' could be heard every so often in the faintly hysterical climate.

I tried to assess what the mood of the audience would be in twenty-four hours time. Would they be able to take any more? Would they want a change? Would they want to be reminded? Would they want to forget? Would they want to escape or would they want to wallow? Checking also with Baverstock and Milne, I changed my mind at least three times during dinner and a few more at Television Centre.

I continued to phone the writers. I remember tracking down Ken Tynan at about eleven o'clock to get hold of the number of the American writer Gore Vidal – I knew that Vidal was in Rome and it seemed appropriate that we should try to persuade him to write a special piece. I rang Vidal three or four times and got no reply. I then went back to Quaglino's to watch the end of David Frost's cabaret act and to talk to him. I seem to remember that he cut a monologue about Hilton hotels, out of respect for the dead President of the country which gave them birth. He came back to my flat and we talked inconclusively. I kept ringing Rome without success until finally, at 4 am, I got hold of Vidal – only to find that he was already packing his bags to fly back to Washington. Then I went to bed and got up at six. I awoke to feel that too much fuss had been made of the whole business the night before. In the goldfish bowl of television, events often loom larger than they are. Because you are focusing on them or commenting on them·

they have a greater significance for the practitioner than they do for the public.

The cast of *TW3* was called for rehearsal as usual at 11 am. My assistants, John Bassett and John Duncan, started to rehearse the script and I went down to Christopher Booker's house on the river in Chelsea where he was working on a piece which might preface the programme we had originally intended to put on. He was writing it as a long monologue, and he and David Frost agreed to split it up between the various members of the cast so that it would be an impersonal statement coming not from one member of the cast but from the team.

Back at Television Centre we saw more of the news films which were coming in from America. At last it became obvious that it was no good thinking of doing anything but a Kennedy programme and that we might as well forget the idea of combining it with the other sketches we had been rehearsing from eleven to one o'clock. Alasdair Milne and Donald Baverstock agreed.

At one o'clock I sent the cast home. There was nothing yet written for them to rehearse except the song Herbert Kretzmer and Dave Lee had half-finished for Millicent Martin, 'In the Summer of his Years'. Millie was able to start learning the tune of the first eight bars of that.

By now I was expecting two pieces from Bernard Levin: his own contribution on Lyndon Johnson and a second for which we hoped to harness Levin's ability to let his prose soar when the occasion demanded. Words were always important on *TW3* and Donald Baverstock urged us to strike somewhere the note of a funeral oration. He felt that no one had yet found an appropriate eloquence and that this was what we should feel for. We checked that Robert Lang, who had often been with us in the second season and who was appearing in the first production at the National Theatre (*Hamlet*), could get away in time to deliver the piece if Levin could get it written. David Frost was polishing up linking dialogue of his own, and in the early part of the afternoon we remembered that we had planned no mention of the widowed Jacqueline Kennedy, so I suggested to Caryl Brahms that she should write this. She was in the middle of a rehearsal for a radio play at Broadcasting House and spent the afternoon sitting on the steps outside the studio trying to write some verses for Sybil Thorndike, whom I called during the afternoon. Dame Sybil said she had an evening engagement but that if we could get the script to her in a taxi she would be there by 10 pm and would deliver it. 'Nothing funny,' she said sternly.

By 8 pm the script was assembled, typed and put on to the prompting device. The cast got back to the studio. Also in attendance was that redoubtable old cockney character actress, the late Rita Webb, who was to have been in the show but for whom there was now no place. She gave moral support and occasionally complained that she should have been speaking for cockney London, 'like I always bleeding do'.

We had one run-through. It was a curious and quiet occasion. Donald Baverstock then made a decision which had far-reaching consequences. He could see that this programme which might be effective at home would be even more moving in America, and he decided to record it on both the English and American systems. That way it could be flown immediately to America and shown on American television within twenty-four hours. In the event they repeated it many times during the ensuing days. The long-playing gramophone record won a 'Grammy' and eventually we restaged the whole thing at a charity show in the old Madison Square Gardens.

Usually before *That Was The Week That Was* I did a warm-up in order to cheer up the audience and get them into a party mood. They were also plied with mulled claret. On this occasion all we could do was to tell them that we were sorry but there was to be no party; that we were doing a twenty-minute show and that those who wanted to stay were welcome.

We went on the air.

There were some thirty protests on the telephone, some from people who felt we should not have been allowed to broadcast at all; some who felt that it was our job to be amusing and we should have continued to be amusing; some who felt, though goodness knows why, that we were trying to be funny at the expense of the late President.

Since the programme went out reactions to it have been a miniature of the response to *That Was The Week That Was* in general. At first people said that it was especially memorable. Then a sprinkling of people found it sentimental and not worthwhile. In Malcolm Muggeridge's words, 'They are probably now all thoroughly ashamed of it.' I think not. It is difficult to assess how valuable our comments were, conceived and delivered in the haste and emotion of the moment, but I tried to be consistent with our brief for the series in general. We were not trying, any more than on other nights, to provide a lasting document. The week that had just gone by had been obliterated by one event. All we could do was to try to gauge the feeling of that evening and distill it in a way which we felt appropriate.

The reaction from America was enormous. It is the only time that I have been rung at my home by half a dozen people calling from Texas, San Francisco, Oregon and all over the USA, who had simply rung the BBC and insisted on being put through. Many Americans became aware of the existence of the BBC for the first time and it served to sell an American version of *TW3*, which they proceeded to botch with whole-hearted American thoroughness, enthusiasm and showbiz know-how – not least by putting it out at peak time on Tuesday nights which made it hard to sing with any conviction 'That Was The Week That Was'. Ironically, it was not until *Saturday Night Live* that NBC realized the virtue of the original time slot – more than ten years on.

The last *That Was The Week That Was* went out on 28 December 1963. It was an emotional occasion for participants and audience. Almost entirely retrospective, it was a trip through some of the best-remembered items. Viewed again some years later, it is so full of plums that some of them do not taste as juicy when juxtaposed as they did when they were highlights in a routine show. I miss the ballast of minor stories and interesting detail which crops up in the weekly programmes. Donald Baverstock led cries of 'More!' after the opening song, and the mood of nostalgic euphoria continued throughout the hour and a half. And why not?

Not So Much A Sequel

During the summer of 1964 our main concern at Lime Grove was to find a successor to *TW3*. The election was over, that alibi exploded, the cover blown. In any case, the combined blaze of glory from the single Kennedy programme and the sum of the last editions strengthened the movement to 'bring back satire'. Donald Baverstock, Alasdair Milne, David Frost, Antony Jay and I had a round of conversations. Or, as Willi Frischauer wrote, 'At the BBC the future of David Frost was a major subject of discussion, the planners deliberating how best to harness his tremendous drawing power....' Plans were also forming for David to commute between New York and London in order to make regular appearances on *TW3* in the American version.

This would not have fitted into our original plans, which were to do five nights a week. While I was in America, Donald and Alasdair suggested that we should only do three shows. Unlike American audiences, long conditioned to late-night television, their weekday British counterparts went earlier to bed. On the other hand, Friday, Saturday and Sunday – a whole weekend – had character, continuity and a fair chance that some viewers outside London might be awake.

We started to consider how we might fill them. We welcomed the challenge because we thought it would give us an opportunity to defuse the hysteria which the weekly editions of *TW3* inspired. We hoped that over three nights we might at last devise that elusive 'service' programme. We knew we would have to broaden the scope of the shows. We would not be able to provide enough sketch material to fill three nights; but Frost was anxious to extend his role as a talk-show host – a profession with which he had fallen in love in America. We spent a deal of time arguing how to blend conversation, sketches and songs. We decided, wrongly as it turned out, that the answer was to use our sketches as premises for conversation. Once or twice it worked smoothly, but as a rule it was cumbersome and all the audience heard was a noisy gear change.

Our next mistake stemmed directly from the size of the undertaking; and from our reluctance to throw the whole weight of the show on Frost. We experimented with a triumvirate of hosts, each taking a larger role on different occasions. Willy Rushton and P.J. Kavanagh, the actor, essayist and poet, completed the trio. Neither of them turned out to have much of a taste for a role which Frost coveted. As Rushton has remembered, 'Frost was determined in his heart of hearts that it should be his: and Kavanagh and I really didn't mind. Neither of us wanted to be on the programme. So we got elbowed to one side a bit; and in the end we were being paid £80 a show for doing nothing – it was the best job I ever had, except that it was driving me absolutely up the spout.'

We did six pilots, which contained some interesting features. Denis Norden summed it up a year later, when Frost introduced him jokily after a similar long-haul in preparation for a Rediffusion series: 'And that', said Norden, 'is David Frost, who's had more pilots than the average BOAC air hostess.' One feature worked beautifully on the pilot but disastrously on air: an attempt to stage a particular sort of controlled conversation. We were self-consciously looking for ways to avoid the basic chat-show simplicity of a host and one or two guests by creating dramatic situations. The first shot was a simple mock trial. Gerald Kaufman agreed to assume the persona of an historical monster and to defend his record against a couple of cross-examiners. As a closet film buff, he chose to be Louis B. Mayer. In looking for Hollywood experts who could do the interrogatory hatchet job I was lucky enough to stumble, through an introduction from the late Burt Shevelove, a witty, much missed, expatriate American, on Harvey Orkin, an American agent working in London. Harvey crossed swords so wittily with Kaufman that it looked as though we had hit on a winning formula. With a different subject on the first weekend the idea sank like a lead balloon, but at least we had found one new potential talker in Kaufman and a star in Harvey.

On another pilot we experimented with a slice of drama played on our bare cabaret stage. There had been a particularly long sentence for murder that week and we used it as a premise to play a long scene from Genet's *Deathwatch*, directed by John Gorrie, with Robin Phillips and David Weston. Again it was included to test how much we could extend and vary the form of the programme and to see how many elements it could contain. In fact it overbalanced the pilot and we did not include its equivalent when we went on the air. Nor were we lucky enough to lure Mike Nichols on to the show, although he did a couple of improvised sketches with Eleanor Bron on the pilot. Another experiment tried to capitalize on Tommy Trinder's unique ability to talk back to an audience. Once again we failed to find the right atmosphere in which he could dazzle as he does in live performance.

Assembling the nucleus of regular performers was easier. John Bird, Eleanor Bron and John Fortune were back from America. John Wells was around, as was Doug Fisher whose appearances in cabaret and review I had enjoyed. They were all author-improvisers, which promised a different sort of sketch from those on *TW3*. In addition I recruited Roy Hudd whom, on the recommendation of a friend who had toured with him in a farce, I went to see in an Old Time Music Hall at Richmond, supporting Clarkson Rose. His broad vaudeville style complemented the 'university comedians' remarkably well, and his ability to provide a string of show-business impersonations extended the range of our sketches, alongside the George Browns, Harold Wilsons and Jomo Kenyattas of John Bird, the Conservative ladies of Eleanor Bron, and the de Gaulles and Selwyn Lloyds of John Wells. Leonard Rossiter was also originally a member of the team.

Looking for more new faces, I consulted Kenneth Tynan again. This time he suggested the late Lord Glenavy – Patrick Campbell – who was to become famous and popular with 'the General', but who at that time was still tucked away with the caviar. We had lunch at the Café Royal Grill and the two celebrated stutterers competed in hesitation. Paddy had an irresistible setpiece – how he had been on only one television programme in his life and what an unmitigated disaster it had been. John Irwin tried him out from the New Cross Empire studio in the early days of ITV. It was all very glamorous: limousines purred Paddy to the place; champagne was poured and placed in front of him; beautiful women were on hand to minister to his needs. Never had he felt more cosseted. He hardly realized that the programme had begun. Others talked earnestly and confidently. Early on someone had turned to him and put a question. No words came. He had been abandoned and, apart from one half-hearted attempt at the end of the programme, remained silent throughout.

He was anxious to know if this encouraged me to engage him. He went on to particularize the vowel sounds which would inevitably lead to failure. 'S' was the Waterloo, illustrated by a story of trying to spit out a telephone number compounded of sixes and sevens. If there was one subject on which Patrick Campbell could talk with authority it was stuttering, and so we arranged that Frost's first question to him on the air would get him off to the flying s..s..s..start he needed.

Much later Kenneth moaned mildly that in view of the Patrick Campbell industry which had sprung up he did think Paddy might have bought him lunch. However, when I was starting a talk show in America Ken was the first person I called in the search for new faces. (It was the last time I spoke to him.) No Paddy Campbell emerged on that occasion.

Engaging Roy Hudd and, as a researcher, Esther Rantzen created problems in the long run. As a direct result I had to give up the vanity trip of monitoring my progress via the newspapers. This exercise in self-denial has nothing to do with a thin skin. I have always enjoyed reading about myself and never subscribed to that much touted attitude, 'I never read my notices.' (The best permutation on that was Robert Helpmann's; he launched into Caryl Brahms at the bar of the Lyric Theatre, Hammersmith, the night after she had adversely criticized a ballet of his in the *Evening Standard*: 'Caryl,' he said, 'I never read my notices; but my mother who is sensitive to criticism. . . .')

I had to cancel my subscription to a press-cutting agency because Esther (an enterprising researcher, though already prone to puns) and Roy have always gone well over the top when it comes to gratitude. They are always being interviewed, and most of these interviews are syndicated in dozens of provincial newspapers. Every article starts off with a brief but dutiful description of how I gave them their break, followed by columns about their dazzling progress since then. Dearly as I love them, there is a limit to how much I am prepared to pay to read the same things about these two. No more press cuttings.

Leonard Rossiter was prevented from settling into the team by various complications, and he left after the fifth show. During our first weeks he was still filming *Hotel Paradiso* in Paris because the schedule had over-run. Leonard would fly in on Friday and leave on Monday, so he never had the chance to feel fully part of the team. Moreover, in those early weeks much of the material was being provided by Bron, Bird, Fortune and Wells, for themselves. I was trying to assess Leonard's range and to encourage the contributing writers to find opportunities for him. I had discovered on *That Was The Week That Was* that it is not until an actor has been seen to do something funny that the scriptwriters start to write for him. After a funny Rushton, Kinnear or Percival sketch, a batch of scripts would arrive designed for Willy, Roy and Lance. Indifferent writers sent in scripts which simply identified their favourite performer and assumed that he would supply the idiosyncratic behaviour which alone might make the material funny. Better writers extended the actor's range and managed something more than stereotyped cameos.

However, Leonard soon became impatient at the lack of sketches for him and asked to be released. It was ironic that by the time he was due to leave scripts had just started to arrive for him. On his last appearance he did a subtle impersonation of Groucho Marx, written by Dick Vosbrugh, which was a five-minute hint at the sure-footed, sustained pastiche Vosbrugh wrote some fifteen years later in *A Night in the Ukraine*. Leonard had by now committed himself to a theatre role, but of course after his superb Groucho the usual batch of scripts poured in, all too late.

Michael Crawford's debut on *Not So Much a Programme* was an interesting precursor of his later successes. I had seen him first – as far as I knew – in *Come Blow Your Horn*, Neil Simon's first London comedy, at the Prince of Wales, but in fact as Michael Ingram, a child actor, he had appeared in *The Little Beggars*, a radio play and the first produced work which Caryl Brahms and I wrote together. Years later he told me ruefully that he envied David Hemmings, then still a boy soprano, who played the child lead. Michael was livid that Hemmings, in the cloakrooms, seemed to be getting all the way with one of the girls while Crawford/Ingram was off in a corner with another girl – 'simply practising how long we could kiss'. Both were about twelve at the time – and those were the innocent fifties. Caryl Brahms tells a sad story of remonstrating with Grace Cone, Hemmings's headmistress at the Arts Educational School, on hearing of Hemmings's expulsion. 'But he was kissing a girl in a bus queue,' said the shocked headmistress. 'You should be grateful it was a girl,' snapped Miss Brahms.

After *Come Blow Your Horn* I saw Michael as Feste in Colin Graham's production of *Twelfth Night* at one of the Inns of Court, and meanwhile he began filming for Dick Lester in his screen version of Ann Jellicoe's *The Knack*. I was living in Dover Street by now in a four-floor walk-up which I had taken over from a friend during the second season of *TW3*. It had previously been a Piccadilly ladies' pad and occasionally colonial administrators arrived on the doorstep looking for the delights of long ago and left sadly disappointed. I moved in on the night of another Television Awards Ball at the Dorchester. Apart from collecting a second award, I won an electrically-illuminated plastic water fountain in the raffle. This came as no surprise. In my time I have won half a

dozen eggs, a hundredweight of coal, a chicken and a Christmas cake in
various raffles. After the ball I got home to find that my predecessor had
left no other bulbs in the flat and the weird water fountain was the only
illumination until the next morning. However, by the time Michael came
for an interview the lights were in working order.

It is usual for young, little-known actors to grasp at chances of solo
exposure on a probably fashionable, potentially long-running television
series. Michael showed no instinct to conform. The idea – worked out
by Peter Lewis and Peter Dobereiner – was that we should channel the
views of the teenage generation through an actor who would approxi-
mate to an English version of J.D. Salinger's Holden Caulfield in *The
Catcher in the Rye*. They named him Byron and gave him his own point
of view and his own vivid vocabulary. I felt that he would fit best into
the developing shape of the Sunday night programme. This should have
made it even more attractive for Michael, because he could at the same
time play in the theatre, in movies or in other television shows, and had
simply to study his text for a couple of days, turn up on Sunday, and
read it from the teleprompter – which he ultimately did, with the skill,
charm and aplomb that are some of the qualities that make him an
outstanding performer.

However, at our first interview he grilled me severely about the
attitude and background of the character, the place he would occupy in
the programme, his point of view, and innumerable other aspects of
Byron which I had not yet thought about. Downstairs he had left an
actor friend, Cavan Kendall, the late Kay Kendall's younger brother,
who occasionally shouted up for Michael to get a move on. Nothing
moved Michael until he had satisfied himself on all points. I agreed to
send him a script as soon as we had one for the programme, and indeed
Lewis and Dobereiner completed several in their search for the character
before we went on the air. Byron was an immediate success and did a lot
to launch Michael.

In becoming a star Michael has developed a reputation for being
demanding, but in our period of working together I only had two
problem moments. Of course, actors are notoriously easier to manage if
they have good scripts, no one else on the screen with them, if they get
laughs and are, for extra measure, in a medium tight close-up. The first
hiccup came during a week when I considered that Lewis and Dobereiner
had, unusually for them, not come up to scratch. They submitted a
strained and unfunny monologue and I phoned Michael on the Friday to
tell him that it was not good enough and that, although he would be

paid, he would not be appearing unless they provided a better script. They failed to do so and Michael fretted and fumed and explained that his immense following of fans would be mortified and he would be shamed. Finally he had to be sent home in a tantrum. However, since then he has been over-generous about the decision and insists that it taught him a most important lesson of not going on unless the material is absolutely right.

Our second misunderstanding occurred a year after *Not So Much a Programme* when I was doing *BBC-3* and Sir Winston Churchill died. All through the day of the funeral the solemnity, the pomp and the processing poured out of the television and Michael, who was sitting at home watching it all, was inspired to address the nation through the character of Byron and to explain the impact on his generation of discovering the greatness of the dead ex-Prime Minister. It was difficult enough to find an appropriate way of treating Churchill's funeral without having to cope with an actor who felt moved to speak about it on behalf of the youth of Britain. I was a bit short with him, and this incident finds no place in Michael's lexicon of great lessons learned early.

The first weekend of *Not So Much a Programme* was a fair disaster. Fans of *That Was The Week That Was* found little which was familiar; enemies found too much which revived old grievances. We strengthened the resolve of our opponents and divided our friends. The Friday night programme produced a mass of attacking phone calls and a telegram from the drama producer Tony Garnett to Donald Baverstock (with whom he was arguing about cut-backs in drama production) congratulating him on 'having fallen flat on his face tonight'. It was a far cry from the euphoria after the first *TW3*.

One undoubted success that first weekend was Patrick Campbell, whose stutter and wit kept the viewers somewhere between the edge of the chair and the aisles. Eleanor Bron was also an instant hit. She introduced her Conservative Party supporter, Lady Pamela Stitty: '... It's never easy to choose a leader. You see, leaders are not made in a day – of course, Alec was, he's rather the exception, that's why we're trying to find another method of choosing....' John Bird's Jomo Kenyatta, developed from his Establishment monologue, was liked by all except the Kenya High Commission. '... I myself will temporarily assume the office of Queen until a reliable native replacement can be found....' Byron clicked and the three new singers – Barbara Evans on Fridays, Josephine Blake on Saturdays and Cleo Laine on Sundays – all found supporters, Cleo singing a wide range of songs, many specially written for her. On the first Friday Barbara Evans introduced a rarely sung Stephen Sondheim song, 'The Girls of Summer', which I had found on Burt Shevelove's music stand in New York. I am not aware that it was sung again until we used a snatch of it in the final medley of songs in *Side By Side with Sondheim* in 1975-7.

The main body of speakers were another matter. The number of strange talking heads whom we flourished in front of the public during the early weeks confused and irritated them. However, during this beleaguered period we found a nucleus of speakers who got the measure of the programme. Patrick Campbell became a Friday regular, Denis Norden usually took Saturdays, and Harvey Orkin was Sunday's man. An intense rivalry grew up between Campbell and Orkin, but both were invaluable side men for David Frost, who very soon showed an easy mastery in leading conversation and shaping that part of the programme. The conversational sequences also took some pressure off the search for sketch material: if a sketch was not up to standard for one of the three forty-five-minute programmes I was able to reject it and expand a conversational sequence. David's keenness to chair discussions sapped some of his enthusiasm for performing in sketches and doing the stand-up comedy in which he was less at home than his colleagues. Besides, he was also appearing on the American *TW3* every Tuesday, which provided an outlet for any frustrated acting ambitions. By now his affair with Janette Scott was well under way and he had an awe-inspiring schedule doing three BBC shows on Friday, Saturday and Sunday, flying to America first thing on Monday morning, performing on Tuesday and returning to London on Thursday, or even Friday, morning to pick up the threads here.

Although the American version of *TW3* is still remembered fondly as a breakthrough in the USA it was a limp, lack-lustre affair. It was produced by a charming senior man-of-the-theatre, agent, film producer and husband of Randolph Churchill's ex-wife, Leland Heyward. A dignified legend, Leland was probably the only producer who could have put on *TW3* in America in that nervous era. In retrospect the tactic appears similar to that of Hollywood in bravely allowing Warren Beatty to attack a potentially explosive subject like *Reds* and then safely to congratulate itself on its courage while watching the anodyne outcome. Leland acted as a Trojan horse to transport the wild young men in through the gates of the NBC establishment. However, once let loose they found that most of their swords had been blunted *en route*.

I watched the first programme. Admirable performers and writers had been assembled including Elliot Reid, Tom Lehrer, Robert Morse and Buck Henry. With the usual instinct of Americans who invest in success, Leland wanted to preserve everything he had bought. That included our studio, and his set-designer recreated the grotty old BBC bare-walls setting, pipes, air vents and all. However, since this was colour television they painted everything in delicately shaded pastels. The script was buttoned up days before transmission and so were the intrusive cameras as they dutifully manoeuvred in and out of shot. Leland made sure that the content was defused, and Nancy Holmes, cast in Millicent Martin's role, lacked both her striking singing voice and comic punch, importing instead one more antiseptic ingredient. Frost had to fight harder for his spots in America, and on the first rehearsal I was saddened to see him have to resort to shouts, stamps and a suggestion of a tear to preserve his second featured moment. He had earned an easier passage. However, he won easily in the end and the programme became generally identified with him. He used it brilliantly as a bridgehead for his campaign to gain a commanding place in the American television system.

David's shuttling to and fro across the Atlantic was an awesome spectacle. 'Sorry, Mr Frost, caviar again,' was the BOAC air staff's standing joke. On one occasion I rode with him from New York to Kennedy, long behind the normal check-in time. His car telephone was called into service to see the plane was held. We staggered through a baggage door attended by eager uniformed steward fans who seemed to regard getting young Mr Frost on at the last moment as a matter of pride. As we reached our seats David lolled into grey somnolence and then deep sleep, which lasted until touchdown by which time, I suppose, the effects of the sleeping pill, slipped down on leaving the office, had worn off.

The double life made it hard for him to keep a perspective about the impact of American news on an English audience. Our only serious studio disagreement happened at this time. John Bird had written a particularly sharp sketch dealing with the ironies of a white, liberal television producer patronizing a cultivated black newsreader, played by Kenny Lynch. Over the weekend the news of Malcolm X's assassination came through and David reacted to it with the awareness of how much it would mean in America and with the impresario instinct of a man who had played a part in the success *TW3* had scored in the aftermath of the Kennedy killing. I did not judge the mood of shock in England to be comparable with the feeling for the previous tragedy: I turned down David's idea of a special show and insisted on playing the sketch. David, of course, had to accept the decision, but it was clear that our careers were ready to go in different directions. American experience confirmed David in his realization that in American television the face in front of the cameras controls the show and the role of the producer is to service the star who is frequently the head of the controlling company. This is not a role that any BBC producer trained for the responsibility of current affairs programmes finds attractive.

I have only worked with, or rather for, David twice since then. On one occasion he forgot to book a director for a gaudy variety show he was selling to America and I got out of bed in response to an emergency call to tape segments with Danny La Rue, Lulu and other talented vaudevillians; the rest of the show, with which I was also involved, was a George Devine tribute at the National Theatre. It meant taping, virtually 'on the wing', a vast mêlée of distinguished actors in many brief excerpts. The climax was a performance of parts of Wesker's *Kitchen*, littered with stars, including Olivier, Coward and Thorndike, milling around in tiny overlapping cameos. Mercifully it was also being covered on film at the same time and I can only hope that the film coverage was what was mainly used. It was a hectic day with just time to notice out of one eye a growing romance between John Osborne and Jill Bennett, who were playing a scene from *A Patriot For Me*.

Our last joint effort was a nightmare born out of David's generosity. A film which I produced, *The Virgin Soldiers*, opened in a blaze of silence in New York and he generously booked me for his Westinghouse talk show to plug the film. He assembled a curious group – Harvey Orkin, Tsai Chin, who was in the movie, and Helen Shapiro. I had ample time to assess the stories which ran around that series of David's late starts and casual preparations. When I was introduced he provided a warm welcome, a sympathetic face, and leant forward for his first question: 'Tell me, Ned, how did *That Was The Week That Was* start?'

I have never felt more at a loss for a word. In the first place the convention of telling millions of Americans how we started the show by recounting it to the person who had done most to help develop it boggled my mind. The only amusing way around it would have been to tell the story of discovering David, which I knew he hated. That seemed rude from a grateful guest. The result was dithering incoherence from which I was only rescued when Harvey Orkin came on and David's look of disappointed sympathy could go away.

A few years later I was interviewing Gore Vidal for a television show and he said, 'You're rather good – I don't know why David Frost says you can't do it on camera.' I tried to mix modesty with curiosity. 'Yes,' Gore said, '. . . we were on a plane together the other day and your name cropped up and David said, "Pity about Ned, so amusing, such a good producer, pity he can't talk on television."'

David's juggling with girl-friends is famous and was awe-inspiring to watch. Willy Rushton has recorded his encounter with one who was in tears because David would not give her the number of his car telephone. It was also Rushton who, when David started international commuting, came gleefully on a file marked 'Airport Quips'. Two of the prettiest in his regular cast were Janette Scott and Carol Lynley, both of whom produced at least one memorable line to augment their more obvious charms. Janette, on the set of a film about beauty queens, came upon a star whose career was in ignominious decline berating an inoffensive make-up girl. 'Be careful,' she said, 'always be nice to them on the way down. You never know when you may meet them again on the way back up!' Carol Lynley's crack was even sharper. 'Lord Goodman is', she said one day, apropos of very little, 'the only man to be flattered by a Gerald Scarfe cartoon.'

One of my cherished Frostisms occurred on his first appearance on the Johnny Carson Show. It was still being broadcast from the NBC studios in New York in those days and David was excited about his début. I arranged to go with a friend to join him and Janette in their suite at the Shoreham to see the transmission which had been recorded earlier in the evening. Just before his entrance David became concerned and interested. 'Oh,' he said, 'I wonder how they announced me? It was so hectic and noisy backstage I didn't hear.'

We very soon did. 'Would you welcome the star, producer, writer and originator of *That Was The Week That Was*, David Frost!' said the genial voice over.

'Oh,' said David superfluously, 'I hadn't heard that.'

'I thought *you* produced *TW3*,' said my guest suspiciously on the way home.

In February – well into the run of *NSMAPMAWOL* – we found ourselves in one of the biggest rows of the series. During *TW3* I had commissioned a sketch from Donald Webster prompted by a topical row about birth control. The moment passed before I could use the script, but I kept it on file. In mid-February there were two headlined reports of Catholic priests who said they would have to leave the Church if it did not change its attitude to birth control. In Webster's sketch the priest, played by Brian Murphy, calls on an Irish mother, played by Patricia

Routledge, in a Liverpool slum. Miss Routledge's casting was an added irony. She had turned down a John Mortimer sketch the week before on grounds of bad taste (Beryl Reid had a success with it). However, Patricia accepted the mother's role without a query, only to find a gigantic storm of controversy breaking around her head. The priest solicits a donation for his church and asks how the woman's children are. It transpires that she has twenty-five. The priest notices that at this moment she is not pregnant and asks gravely if she has sinned in the use of contraceptives. She tells him her husband is not doing his nightly duty because he can no longer afford to get drunk. Mortified, the priest gives back her ten shillings so that the husband can buy his beer and start performing again. I was reminded of an interview on the same subject by Douglas Warth on *Paper Talk*. He asked a father of nine if he practised birth control and got the answer, 'No, but I'm thinking of starting.'

The simplistic, overstated plot and the offensive stridency of the argument were different in texture from the subtler Bird, Bron, Fortune style: with cartoon clarity it summed up most of the pro-birth control charges against the Church. It is one of the sketches that can make a claim for genuine coarse satirical status in Highet's definition. Moreover, it provoked a passionate debate between Norman St John Stevas, who did not like the sketch and refuted its premise, and Dee Wells, who accused the Catholic Church of refusing to allow the United Nations to distribute contraceptives in the Third World, so contributing to population problems.

It was the most dramatic discussion on the series – so intense that the late Al Capp, the American humorist who was the third guest, did not say a word for twelve minutes, for him an unaccustomed silence. The aftermath was hysterical and prolonged. Hugh Greene made some sort of apology to MPs but we were not asked for an official retraction. The show contained the potential offence of the sketch in the context of the argument which followed, even though some people felt that the discussion was the cause of more annoyance than the sketch.

On the last weekend of *Not So Much a Programme* there was more trouble. It was the end of March and on the Friday night show Eleanor Bron discussed Sir Alec's leadership again, in her Lady Pamela Stitty character. In the ensuing discussion (chaired by David Frost) between Ian Macleod, Patrick Campbell and Bernard Levin, Levin dropped the word 'cretin' into his assessment of Douglas-Home. It became a famous red herring. Campbell first picked up the word and belaboured Levin with it. Macleod took him up on the more serious side of his argument.

Campbell persisted in making Levin look foolish and Frost drew from him first a modification, then a withdrawal and then an apology. Frost controlled the incident impeccably and it was irritating to find a habitually responsible critic like Peter Black accepting a commission to condemn in print an incident which he admitted not having seen on a programme and of which, plainly, he had heard an inaccurate report. There was a lull on Saturday the twenty-seventh; but Sunday 28 March 1964 was the final programme in the series and the one that broke this particular camel's back.

I have no doubt that on this occasion the error of judgment was mine. For some time we had been preparing an elaborate piece of animation – an amusing mock operatic treatment of the Duke of Windsor's abdication crisis by B.A. Young. Mild almost to a fault, its stance, if anything, was sympathetic to the Duke; but just as it was completed the Duke was admitted to hospital for an operation on his eyes. Plainly we could not put out such an item in our programme until he was better and out of hospital. I shelved it, conscious that it had cost some four or five thousand pounds of the licence-payers' money. Eventually the Duke went home and I heaved a sigh of relief. We had just time to put out the highly polished piece of film on the last Sunday night of the series.

Early on the Sunday morning the Princess Royal died. Neither Frost nor Alasdair Milne appeared to have any idea of the closeness of the family relationship between Princess Mary and the Duke – brother and sister. I knew; but wrongly I decided to justify the expenditure and include the number in the running order. It was a major miscalculation. No sympathetic attitude to the Duke was perceived. The timing was interpreted as a deliberate and tasteless lampoon on the Royal Family in their moment of grief. Compounded by the 'cretin incident', it provoked a decision, sudden and irrevocable, that *Not So Much a Programme* would not return in the autumn. Barry Norman's foot was back on the staircase at Dover Street.

Two series having been taken off, it was important to the BBC that, in contemplating a third one, they had better get it right. There was still a large public demand and most of the summer was spent trying to agree the format. The cast this time was different. In the last weeks of *Not So Much a Programme* a palace revolution ousted Baverstock, and Alasdair Milne soon followed him into exile. Michael Peacock took some responsibility for the programme, and Huw Wheldon moved into Baverstock's office. The *coup* was announced on a Friday. I remember two small, irrelevant incidents that weekend. A bemused Al Capp pointed to a copy of the *Evening Standard* headline which trumpeted the story and remarked that a network reshuffle would never make such large headlines in America. He did not live for the Silverman crises.

An extraordinary character, Capp made great play of his wooden artificial leg. On one occasion a very attractive girl who worked for the BBC invited him to her flat. Coming back into the room, she found him ready and waiting, leg unscrewed on the floor and her cat sharpening its claws against it. The next time she visited his hotel room. He sat limbless on the bed when it was time for her to go, suggesting she should find her own taxi and saying plaintively, 'You wouldn't want me to put this on again tonight, would you?'

The second vignette of that weekend is of a similarly bemused, virtually unknown Bob Dylan, mouth-organ hanging from his neck, trotting from BBC studio to BBC canteen between rehearsing and recording a small part in a BBC drama by Ian Dallas. Dallas, a witty conversationalist whose plays have never quite captured his original style, did produce one line which I have cherished – I think alone. A film producer enters his ultra-modern, eccentric apartment and says conspiratorially, 'I tell you, between these four, six, eight, ten walls . . .!'

On Monday morning I had to present myself in Huw Wheldon's office to discuss the final weeks of the series. The change was dramatic. All Donald's effects had been removed, none of Huw's was yet installed. Floor, desk and walls were bare. I took in the room at a glance and said spitefully, 'Ah, Huw, put the stamp of your personality on the office already!' He laughed and we went on to discuss the situation. I felt inordinately pleased with myself on account of a put-down which, had I stopped to think, I should have realized lacked the essential element of one grain of truth. Whatever one says about Wheldon, he does not lack personality. The incident rebounded immediately. I related it proudly to Frost, who thought it funny and told a friend on the *Daily Mirror* gossip column where it duly appeared the next day. In cold print the ghastly inaccuracy looked wilder, and I was aware that since there were only two people in the room when I made the remark it must be clear to Wheldon that he was not the source of the leak. He never mentioned it – if he noticed – but I have been a fraction more careful of what I am recorded as having said. A fraction is not always enough.

The Chairman of the Governors, Lord Normanbrook, the Director General, Sir Hugh Greene, the Director of Television, Kenneth Adam, and Huw Wheldon as Controller of Programmes were all involved in the last throw. Indeed I had to fly back from a holiday in the south of

France to meet Huw and Normanbrook at Television Centre. There was one point on which all were agreed: Frost must go. Officials in broadcasting always identify the screen face with the success of a programme – their wives want to meet it, they themselves want to hobnob with it. Unfortunately in this case custom was working the other way. They polarized their fear of the late-night monster around a determination to behead it by sacking David. It was unfair, but I was excited by the challenge of being without him. I had done three winters with David, and now facing a third series without his support was both daunting and attractive.

Huw Wheldon's attitude was very like Grace Wyndham Goldie's over the devolution of responsibility. He felt that there was a mystical BBC way of defusing awkward situations which David had not yet acquired. We needed someone with a sixth sense of what was right and proper for the Corporation, someone who would instinctively intervene at the right moment in any discussion to rob outrage of offence, magisterially guiding argument on impeccably acceptable lines. We searched and searched and emerged with Robert Robinson, an admirable broadcaster who gave loyal service, especially when he was called upon to introduce and lend his apparent approval to sketches which he disliked or thought unfunny. A particular cross which he bore politely was Bill Oddie, whom I had wrongly booked in an attempt to broaden the scope of the songs on the programme. Mercifully Oddie has found his own audience since then, but he failed to respond to the political and social content of *BBC-3* and seemed obsessed with becoming a popular singer purveying a powerful sexuality. It was not pleasant to let him go half-way through the series, but it was the only answer.

David reacted with magnificent resilience to his non-engagement. If the Muggeridges were suggesting that he had 'risen without trace', Bernard Levin was already beginning to polish up his vignette of Frost as Britain's 'man of the Sixties'. And the potential man of the Sixties set about rehabilitation. We had a tacit agreement that I would let him say that he had opted out of a third show, and I kept to that until the truth became public knowledge. Willi Frischauer records it in more sober prose than usual.

If David had two enemies, or two pockets of resistance, in television at that time they were the jealous head of BBC Light Entertainment, Tom Sloan, who always resented *TW3*; and the establishment at Rediffusion. Boldly David attacked these two sources for work. Over dinner in New York he charmed Sloan and sold him a revue series, *The Frost Report*, in which he starred. He introduced Barker and Corbett as a comedy team as well as John Cleese and Julie Felix, and many new writers. At Rediffusion he developed *The Frost Programme* behind the doors from which he had been sent packing three years earlier. Both established him firmly in their respective fields.

In many ways *BBC-3* (Saturday nights only) contained the best material of all three shows in the series. John Bird, sometimes working with Alan Watkins, sometimes alone, perfected his Wilson, George Brown and Ted Heath impersonations, aided by Sandra Shepherd who, as we moved towards visual as well as vocal impersonations, brought a specialist make-up skill.

People commented on 'lack of bite'. This was to a great extent because 'attacking' sketches had become the norm rather than the six-day wonder they had been on *TW3*. However, several of John Bird's Harold Wilson pieces made waves:

> Now I imagine you'll think it a bit peculiar for me to appear on such a gay and light-hearted programme as this. But, you know, I don't have to go on being a prime minister for a living – I could always go back to being a socialist. . . . I'll be frank with you. I'll admit, in the privacy of this television studio, that all is not well within the government. Some of my colleagues have not performed as well as I expected them to. Even worse, some of them have. But there are better prospects to come. This morning, for example, George Brown told me he had seen the Queen. Well, there it is – some people see snakes, some people see elephants. George sees the Queen.

John Bird has quoted Lady Falkender to suggest that he and Watkins were sufficiently successful at thinking Bird into Wilson's mind to provoke some paranoia at No. 10. (Not, in the light of later information, that that was the hardest thing in the world to do.)

Alan Bennett's contracts were whimsical. He would meet Bird or Fortune towards the end of the week and see if the spirit moved him. If it did not, he went home, and the other two, perhaps with Doug Fisher, improvised without him.

BBC-3 was certainly the wrong title. We nearly called it *It's All Been Done Before*, in an attempt to pre-empt criticism, and I wish we had, instead of saving the phrase for the title song. The title *BBC-3* was intended to indicate our continued independence. There existed BBC-1 and BBC-2. We were to be a separate entity, *BBC-3*. We very nearly were: Grace's feeling of 'riding a tiger' was now shared by most heads of department, who were reluctant to have us in their fiefdoms, and my direct responsibility was not to a department, but vaguely to Peacock or Wheldon. Early viewing figures were disappointing. If quizzed people were inclined to say, 'BBC-3? I can't even get BBC-2!'

The Tynan incident solved that. Robert Robinson had been handling the interview side of the programme as well as Wheldon had hoped. He was brisk and purposeful, bringing his own rather bland authority and highly idiosyncratic prose style to his introductions. When he did not approve an item which appeared under his apparent patronage he strove manfully to conceal his lack of enthusiasm. (He had frequent doubts about a group of dancers whom we called the 'Vietcong' dancers until David Toguri, the leader, went off to *Charlie Girl* at the Adelphi Theatre, and subsequently the 'Pompidou' dancers because René Sartoris, a Swiss who had come to us via Paris, was featured.)

Robert's handling of the discussions was skilful though it lacked some of the sense of danger, of balancing on a knife-edge which Frost had brought. On one occasion Peregrine Worsthorne had advanced a theory that there was indisputably a ruling class, a proposition which Gore Vidal was anxious to demolish. On the air Gore was dazzling and eventually he cornered Perry in a position from which there was no escape. Sadistically, I was enjoying sending the cameras in for the kill – that rare television moment when the talking head has no more to say and defeat shines clearly from the victim's eyes. Robert unfortunately filled the awkward silence which was hanging so eloquently over the studio and got Perry off the hook with a new line of questioning.

The Tynan incident was quite different. It has been reported and reinterpreted by a number of people, so I might as well recall it accurately for the record. I was aware of the long 'feud' between Tynan and Mary McCarthy which had been fought over the years in the letter columns of various literary magazines. I remembered vividly a fine, disdainful per-formance McCarthy had given on *Monitor*, ably interviewed by Huw Wheldon, when he had asked her about Hemingway's ideas and she had looked down her long nose – I connect the remark in my memory with a profile shot – and said, 'Oh, I don't think he was ever troubled much by an idea. . . .'

Since she was to be in London, some sort of public combat looked a good idea to Robinson and to me. Experience of famous feuds sounded a note of caution. Tynan and McCarthy had never met and celebrated enemies are frequently charmed by meeting their opponents, especially when they are as intelligent as Tynan and McCarthy. I lunched with them and with Robert at the Café Royal and we set about finding a premise for the debate. Sure enough, they agreed about almost everything and most especially about their major source of disagreement in the correspondence. (Letter writing as a prime source of misunderstanding is a subject in itself.) We discussed various topics. We nearly settled on a critical analysis of Truman Capote's documentary novel, *In Cold Blood*. Had we done so, 'that word' would never have been uttered. In the end the only area on which they could agree to disagree was censorship. Tynan was against it absolutely. McCarthy could visualize a case for censorship in some circumstances. This was Thursday, the engagement was for Saturday and we settled for censorship.

Ken said nothing about his intentions in the hospitality room before the transmission (B.O.15 was its curious name). He had decided that he could not properly argue the case against censorship and at the same time censor himself. On the other hand, he felt that to tell Robert or me beforehand that he was going to use the word 'fuck' would embarrass us into forbidding him. So he said nothing. In the discussion he introduced the word in as quiet and low-key a manner as possible. I hardly heard it – I was saying 'cut to two' or something like that at the time. Neither Robinson nor McCarthy looked surprised or lingered on the moment.

The furore seems the more incredible in retrospect. At the switchboard all hell was let loose. Asked to comment after the programme, I could only say, 'It's a better word than "super",' which was being enthused to death at the time; I left for Brighton for the weekend. It did everything for our viewing figures. The following week several millions found *BBC-3* on BBC-1 with no difficulty – presumably hoping to hear another blow struck for freedom.

My favourite postscript came from a woman who taught a class of infants in London. All Monday morning they pestered her coyly to find out what 'that word' was. 'What was it now, miss?' She hedged all morning but by lunchtime her patience gave out and she submitted to the latest tease. 'What was that word, miss, on telly on Saturday? … What did he say?' She braced herself. 'He said "fuck".' There was an audible groan of disappointment and one little boy muttered, 'Is that all? We thought he said "cunt"!'

It was sad to see the disproportionate space given to Tynan's word in Ken's obituaries. Apart from his critical brilliance, I liked especially his enthusiasms, his impresario instincts, his keenness to find new talents and to give them an outlet.

Apart from the television début of an unacceptable word, *BBC-3*

provided the only clear and unequivocal example of a censorship decision by Hugh Greene with which I found myself in complete disagreement. The subject was Vietnam and in particular Harold Wilson's
keenness to accept Lyndon Johnson's package. Peter Lewis and Peter
Dobereiner came up with a nicely judged monologue in the manner of
Hiawatha, and at the same time I got a directive that we were not to
touch the subject. I telephoned, memoed and wired and made a great
nuisance of myself to no avail. We had always been able to reach a
compromise before and I was unprepared for frustration. I am sure that
in the political context of Wilson's relations with the BBC the sketch was
not worth the trouble from Hugh's point of view. I reproduce it with the
authors' permission partly because it is unique in that series of shows in
having been censored, and also because it holds up remarkably well and
still deserves an airing.

The Song of Lyndon
by Peter Lewis and Peter Dobereiner

Once across the deep blue water
There arose a mighty chieftain
Came in triumph to the White House
Six-foot Texan, Lyndon Johnson
And the little Harold Wilson
Sent his warm congratulations.
Soon the President's advisers
Brought a map and sadly pointed
To the troubled land of Vietnam
Whither he had sent advisers.
Mighty was the wrath of Lyndon
At the legends they recounted,
'If we are not quick to action
There is patently a danger
That this ancient land of Mekong
Will be ruled by favoured Mekongs
Chosen by the Mekong people.
We must act before this sickness
Spreads to other lesser peoples.
Liberty is all men's birthright
We must kill a few to prove it.'

And the little Harold Wilson
Said that he was right behind him.

Should you ask me if the Army
Swiftly crushed the peasant rabble
I would have to answer sadly
That it was a different story.
Now the noble Lyndon Johnson
Trembled for the cause of freedom.
'Peace', he cried, 'is our objective
We must send in more battalions.'

And the little Harold Wilson
Sent a note of understanding.

So the supersonic Phantoms
Roared above the jungle tree-tops
And two thousand plucky GIs
Found themselves rubbed out in error.
Then the giant brain of Lyndon
Stumbled on a new conception:
'If we want to end the killing
All we have to do is stop it.'
How the watching world applauded
At this statesmanlike decision
And the emissaries scuttled
Round the world with peace proposals
Which to put them at their simplest
Were that each would stop the fighting
If the other side surrendered.

And the little Harold Wilson
Sent a note of firm agreement.

Thirty-seven days of talking
Were enough for Lyndon Johnson
And he went on television
To announce a new decision.
'Friends we have but one objective:
Human life must be safeguarded
So today I have directed
We at once resume the bombing
And because our aims are peaceful
We will bomb them twice as often.'

From across the deep blue water
Came a note from Harold Wilson
Warmly backing this decision.

Once again the Supersabres
With their phosphorus and napalm
With their Mighty Mouse and Bullpup
With their Sidewinder and Zany
With their Puff the Magic Dragon
And its hundred rounds a second
Sent the people of the Mekong
Diving once again for cover.
And the ones who did not make it
Sighed, 'Farewell, O Lyndon Johnson.'
Victims of the peace offensive
Sobbed, 'Farewell, O Lyndon Johnson.'

And the little Harold Wilson's
Note of most sincere condolence
Was most promptly re-directed
From the kingdom of the Mekong
To the land of the Hereafter.

The last moments of the show were emotional. I knew that I was ending my loose arrangement with the BBC in order to do other things. The four years of the late-night shows had been very special. Music quickly evokes nostalgia and the potency was strong on that occasion. Peter Greenwell arranged Ron Grainer's three themes, which were sung by Lynda Baron, the resident singer on *BBC-3*, by Cleo Laine, representing *Not So Much a Programme*, and finally – the link back to the first pilot, the musical corn-crake sound with which it all began – by Millicent Martin hitting in with 'That was the week that was/It's over, let it go....'

I have produced or directed other television shows since *BBC-3*: a couple of series with Eleanor Bron and John Fortune; a set of parodies of current affairs reporting by N. F. Simpson, *World in Ferment*; three shows by Caryl Brahms – *Steam, Sanctity and Song, The Long Garden Party* and *The Long Cocktail Party*, essays which counterpointed the events of the Victorian Era, the Edwardian Age and the 1930s with evocative popular songs of the period; and a few shows which gave me treasured opportunities to work fleetingly with some extraordinary actors.

Sir Donald Wolfit was one. Wolfit stories are legion. In theatrical memory Sir Donald is perceived as the last of a line, the epitome of overacting, a definition of ham, and selfish and mean to his inadequate companies. Towards the end of his life he was inclined to encourage these reports: he was well aware that he had become a character and fed the legend. Ronald Harwood's biography, one of the best theatre lives ever written, tells the famous Wolfit stories and evaluates him more accurately than most. He was the Shakespearean actor to whose performances I would hasten with keenest anticipation. No exceptions.

My own encounters with him were after the great days when his Lear was generally accepted as the best this century and when his unfashionable tours of Shakespeare, without subsidy, made him a one-man Arts Council.

He could easily be encouraged to talk of those days. He had a set piece in which he described how to clothe a stage army with knitted chain mail and two suits of armour picked up at an auction and cunningly redistributed. He would proudly flourish the correct name for each piece and divide it in his memory among his actors – a breastplate for one, a kneeplate for another – evoking a stage picture which may have been thin and unconvincing for his more sophisticated audiences but which remained vivid in his own imagination and well inside his budget. The unsophisticated audiences had no reservations. Watching his dagger scene in *Macbeth*, Caryl Brahms heard a galleryite at the Old Bedford breathe excitedly, 'Cor, 'e's seein' things.' Going round to Wolfit to tell him, she found him more impressed than amused. 'Ah, Miss Brahms,' he said sagely and seriously, 'the illusion of the Theatre.'

On one occasion Rosalind Iden, Lady Wolfit, was not available to play Juliet. Joan Greenwood, a young actress with Wolfit at that time, was offered promotion at short notice. Wolfit recalled lovingly how he gave her the chance. 'Could she have a new dress for the role?' she asked. Magnanimously he let her have the run of his dressing baskets. She found the perfect dress, ransacked his supply of stage jewellery and painstakingly sewed a mass of beads and bits of glass all over the costume to her satisfaction. Happily gowned she played the role and after her success he was generous with his praise. Encouraged, she made a request. It had been a wonderful experience, one that she would treasure; might she, as a memento, keep the dress she had made? In retelling the story I could see Wolfit's awareness of his reputation for closeness fuelling the enthusiasm with which he built to his pay-off. ' "No," I said, "no, you may not keep the dress ... but you may always wear it when you play the role in my company." '

His 'ham' reputation tends to make imitators who never saw him thunder and bark when they tell Wolfit stories. In fact his voice was very flexible; its more characteristic notes were light and high and, when he was suggesting shocked surprise, as he frequently did, it approached a whine.

I went round to see him once after a performance of *Ghosts*, which had moved to the West End following an initial production at the Old Vic; Sir Donald had replaced Michael Hordern as Pastor Manders. I had enjoyed Michael's performance, but the farce during the announcement of the fire went a little too far and I told Wolfit how much better the scene was playing. Characteristically, he agreed. 'Hordern was playing it at the Vic,' he said. There was a long pause and the voice became quiet and conspiratorial. 'I know Hordern ... had him as Macduff to my Macbeth on the wireless....' A long intake of breath and a sad shake of the head, '... very dangerous!'

We went on to discuss the rest of the production, especially Dame Flora Robson's Mrs Alving, which had improved a good deal since the Waterloo Road. Again Sir Donald agreed emphatically. 'I'm glad you thought that. She is better, isn't she? ... much lighter.... I had quite a battle achieving that.... You see, what Flora didn't realize was that Ibsen didn't write for tragediennes ... there weren't any in Scandinavia at the time. All he had were comediennes with a gift for pathos....'

No one should embark on an Ibsen play without considering Wolfit's theory, and it probably explains why Joan Greenwood's savagely funny Hedda Gabler is easily the best I have seen.

On the same evening Sir Donald went on to discuss future plans. The BBC had asked him to give his *Volpone* on television. He viewed the suggestion with a mixture of proper pride and extreme pain. 'My old friend Stephen Harrison is doing it ... shan't have to worry about the cam-e-ra angles ... but do you know? ... do you know what they, the BBC, have had the effrontery to ask? I am to give my Volpone to the television ... a lifetime of study ... shan't be able to play it again in the theatre for ten years ... giving my Volpone for a paltry few hundred pounds....' The voice was rising: '... and they said ... they actually said ...' (higher!) 'we must have a *name* for Mosca!' (It went through the ceiling.) 'A *name* for *Mosca* ... I want me old John Wynyard. Best Mosca I ever had ... but they want a *name*! I know what'll happen ...

stop every two lines while the fellow says, "What does that mean?" Well, you haven't got time for that in television. . . .' More head shaking and a dying fall, '. . . a *name* for *Mosca*!'

He got his 'old John Wynyard'; and for posterity the unforgettable moments when Wolfit opens the play and bids good morning to the sun and ends it with the exhalation of breath which signifies the end of the fox are murkily but magnificently preserved in a grey telerecording.

The occasion of my one working experience with Wolfit was a television production of a play, *Benbow Was His Name*, which Caryl Brahms and I had written for him for radio under the title *Those Cowardly Captains*. He was not available for the radio production and the part was beautifully played by Michael Hordern ('I know Hordern. . . !'). It was a naval drama set in the early years of the eighteenth century, based on an actual mutiny in the West Indies and on the literature of the sea. Our starting point had been Caryl's love of sea shanties and our wish to find a narrative which could be carried along by them, sung by the folksingers, Robin Hall and Jimmy MacGregor, with whom I had worked on *Tonight*.

The mainspring of the mutiny was the clash of personality between Admiral Benbow, a sea-dog of the old school, and Captain Kirkby, a gentleman officer, much given to foppery. Shadwell's play *The Fair Quaker of Deal* concerned two such characters and we stole our establishing scenes from it. Opposite Sir Donald we cast John Wood, most elegant of a new breed of actors. John has now become one of the most sought-after stage stars, but in 1963, his career at the Old Vic having failed to prosper, he was beginning to carve out a reputation as a television star. He has a demanding temperament and a reputation for it. (There is a more recent story of an agent calling him in New York and telling him that a director had asked for him. 'That can't be true,' John said. 'Yes it is, I just put the phone down,' said the agent, 'he definitely wants you.' John was not to be persuaded: 'He can't. I've worked for him before.')

The parallel between the old salt and the elegant fop in the story was echoed in the contrast between the styles of the stars. We wondered how they would get along. On the first day of rehearsals Donald arrived knowing every word. 'I've got a lot on my mind,' he said touchingly. 'I don't want these young sparks to see me struggling for the words.' John Wood's approach was the opposite. He learnt his lines effortlessly during rehearsal. However, they deferred continually to one another, enjoyed and admired one another, and provided a bumpless passage. The nearest we got to a flash of anger was one day when we were going from the outside rehearsal room to the BBC for lunch. An actor playing a small part was getting into his car. Donald was looking his most Wolfittian, eyebrows beetling, face flushed, the astrakhan collar on his coat spiritually, if not actually, there. The taxi I had ordered had not arrived so we rode with Peter, the nervous actor. Donald crammed himself into the small front seat. As the driver got more nervous his hand slipped from the gear lever onto Wolfit's knee. Peter's voice shot up a few octaves as he apologized. Wolfit was reassuring: 'That's all right, lad. We get used to that sort of thing in the theatre.'

Wolfit was working in the theatre at the same time as we did *Benbow*, playing John Gabriel Borkman at the Duchess Theatre. The television play was scheduled to run sixty minutes and to be recorded over two days at the BBC's Riverside Studios. During those two days we were to see Sir Donald only for Saturday morning and Sunday; on Saturday afternoon he was giving two Borkmans. It was a heavy chore for a man of his age, especially as he never felt as much at home in studios as he did in the theatre. A complicated production included film sequences cut in, simultaneous back projection and Hall and MacGregor singing their sea songs against it. Michael Byrne, then a young actor just out of RADA, stood in for Wolfit when he was absent, marked his positions and ferried him into place when he rejoined the company on the Sunday.

I do not think Donald knew much about the actual recording. Michael put him on his marks and he gave a fine performance; but the bustle of the studios, the strain of playing Borkman at the same time and the length of the role meant that he had to conserve all his energy to say the lines correctly in alien surroundings. His death scene took place on board ship at the height of a particularly dirty, smoky battle. He had one obsessive concern. He took me aside. 'Lad,' he said, 'I don't have to die with my face dirty, do I? . . .'

Caryl and I went to stay with the Wolfits on the night the play was transmitted. They were always warm and welcoming hosts at Swift Cottage in Hampshire. He seemed very nervous. After a while we realized why: there was an unnatural concentration of admirals in the district. Donald, playing an admiral, was worrying what sort of figure his neighbours thought he would cut. It took a couple of calls from them before he felt off the hook. He had watched the transmission with a mixture of surprise and pleasure. He had not been aware of the projections and film sequences in the studio. They had all been taken from old feature film footage – tall ships banging away at one another in the heat of battle. Donald appeared to have got it into his head that this was special film that I had run up ingeniously with a Box Brownie and a tank full of models. As classic cinema sequence succeeded classic sequence, I became more embarrassed. 'Splendid shot, lad!' he kept repeating. As the sequences became more ambitious his admiration became more fulsome. My embarrassment reached a climax with the biggest and best battle lifted straight from *Lady Hamilton*. I decided that I had to confess, before I could be handed credit for that as well. 'That's from *Lady Hamilton*,' I whispered. His reply was immediate – 'Not as good as yours, lad.'

I was glad that the notices were good. It was impossible not to be aware that somehow at the back of his mind Donald was counting up the performances he had left to give. Some were sacrificed to cash. He played many films simply to leave as much as he could when he died. He had supported touring classical theatre single-handed for so long that he was entitled to take the sort of role that made people arch their eyebrows. Not all the film roles were negligible. He scored a great success as Mr Brown in *Room at the Top* – though this rebounded.

He told the story rather ruefully. He was proud of his Shakespearean readings which he toured with Rosalind. (Somewhere in the repertoire was their two-man *Othello*: 'We've cut out Iago – do it all with lights!') On one occasion they arrived in San Francisco. 'I went down to the Theatre to check the Arrangements, as I always did; so that Rosalind could rest a little at the Hotel. I had Expressly Asked for a Tudor chair – of course they gave us a Victorian one. But we are used to that. Then I went to Inspect the Front of House.' The great tragic actor's mask registered shock with no trace of humour. 'They had billed me as DONALD WOLFIT,' he paused to consider the ignorance which had obliterated five decades of distinguished service to the classics with one billboard, 'DONALD WOLFIT, MR BROWN, of ROOM AT THE TOP FAME!'

When Wolfit died, Caryl and I mounted his obituary programme at the BBC. She wrote a linking commentary, spoken by Michael Elliott, who had directed his last television performance (Pastor Manders again, not at full strength; with Celia Johnson as Mrs Alving and Tom Courtenay as Oswald). I started to search for people to talk about Wolfit. It was important that it should be considered, but not solemn. Caryl called the programme *The Knight Has Been Unruly*. First I looked for other knights who would speak of their peer. I did not approach Sir Ralph Richardson, understanding that there had been some friction long ago when they had both learned their business in a touring company run by an old actor–manager called Charles Doran. (Wolfit was an encyclopaedic rememberer of stage business. Once when I said I had been to see Richardson's Shylock, he hissed, 'Did he drop his dagger on the way out of the trial scene?' 'Yes,' I said. 'Ah! Ah! Doran's business!' he cried.) I tried Sir Laurence Olivier. But he was to read the lesson at the memorial service and thought that was enough. Sir Michael Redgrave was ill. Sir Alec Guinness's refusal was subtly judged: 'I thought he was a wonderful film actor,' he said, 'I never really saw him much in the theatre.' Finally I went down to the Old Vic to see Sir John Gielgud between performances – without much confidence. He was disarmingly frank as usual. 'I couldn't do it,' he said. 'It would be so hypocritical. We used to think he was a joke.'

And so, of course, the West End had always thought, and I was reminded of another of Wolfit's long-held grudges going back to a forgotten Old Vic season when he had played Macduff to Gielgud's Macbeth. He said that they had quarrelled on the first night, and I became vividly aware of the naked animosity that can be kindled between ambitious young actors as Wolfit dwelt in secret tones on his revenge – 'Got him by the eye with me sword in the fight on the second night.'

Finally it was Sir Donald's most famous adversary who buried the hatchet on his behalf – Sir Tyrone Guthrie. Guthrie had directed his legendary *Tamburlaine*, then quarrelled over a revival of *King Lear* at the Old Vic and Wolfit had left the company. Yet Guthrie's epilogue was just and generous, and recalled the distinction with which Wolfit spoke Shakespeare's verse and his awareness of the need to keep his voice, 'his instrument, honed and bright'; and the devotion with which he had done so.

Richard Burton remembered Wolfit in the storm scene in *Lear* on a night when the hovel collapsed on his back and he had to play the whole scene carrying a house around the stage. Sybil Thorndike still saw him as an actor of great promise joining her and her husband in a Sunday night try-out in Swiss Cottage; apparently most concerned about the tragic waste of this man who in her perspective was dying so young. Members of his company – Harold Pinter, Brian Rix, Eric Porter and Ronald Fraser – told their stories. Film clips, television recordings and the L.P. of *Lear* filled out the programme. But most moving was a simple roll-call of all the Shakespearean parts that he had played in all the plays. It was an incredible roster – the best epitaph on a unique career – and I was dismayed when the programme was repeated that it had to be cut for time.

Wolfit's obituary also gave me my second chance to observe Elizabeth Taylor in her role of lady-in-waiting. When Donald died Burton was shooting *Where Eagles Dare* at Elstree and I went over to the studio to ask him to record a piece. He was warm and welcoming to the idea, but it was impossible to ignore the feeling of a circus surrounding him at the peak of his fame. The large suite of dressing-rooms was full of odd extras, chauffeurs, hairdressers and secretaries, the feeling very much that of Prince Hal's hangers-on with the Prince doubling as Falstaff. One quiet presence saying little and sipping from a beer can in a corner was Clint Eastwood, who was making his change of career from spaghetti westerns to international movies, and observing the hoop-la with one raised eyebrow.

At Lime Grove Burton smartly cut through Miss Taylor's reluctance to wait downstairs by asking if she might sit in the control room. She spent an hour or so either fascinated, or behaving with scrupulous good manners, watching the process of television – as opposed to film – from a new vantage point, and professing amazement at its complexity.

Donald's memorial service was held at St Martin-in-the-Fields. It ran much after the pattern of those occasions. I like a good theatrical service, the mixture of stars and fans, fellow workers and fellow sufferers; the determination that this is a 'celebration', a 'commemoration', a 'party' – anything but a funeral. I came in behind a little old woman, I think a member of the public, of Wolfit's public, not an actress. She was bent and she moved slowly and finally arrived at an usher. He showed her courteously to her place and gave her a form of service with some concern. As she took it to move past him she unwound to look up and thank him: she had to unwind quite a long way as he was very tall. When her eyes at last met the usher's she gave a little start. 'Oh,' she said, 'you're Paul Scofield.'

'Yes,' he said gently, 'but we're not here for that, are we?'

One bane of modern television is that vast numbers of valuable pro-grammes are lost because there is no space in which to store the tapes on which they are recorded. No trace remains of an extravagant musical I wrote with Caryl and Ron Grainer, *Take A Sapphire*, with a cast including Georgia Brown, John Wood, Max Adrian and Elisabeth Welch, and the last public appearance of the ballerina Lydia Sokolova, a name unknown to the chorus dancers until she electrified them by a stunning entrance in the rehearsal room.

Again in 1970 Caryl and I wrote a biography of Dickens for the centenary of his death. It was culled almost entirely from autobiographical scenes from his novels. Gordon Jackson was the narrator, and the cast included Anthony Hopkins as Dickens, with Joan Greenwood, Vivian Pickles, Arthur Lowe, Patrick Cargill, Mona Washbourne, Dandy Nichols, Jenny Agutter, Michael Wilding, Nora Nicholson, and, in virtually their last television performances, Stanley Holloway, Dame Gladys Cooper and Dame Sybil Thorndike. Dame Gladys flew in just in time to rehearse, and spent most of the first day telephoning British Airways to argue about some articles of jewellery missing after her flight from the West Indies. She had five lines in her cameo scene with Jenny Agutter and was not going to be rattled about remembering them. By the time we got to the studio some days later for the first run-through she had mastered two out of five and retained them for the dress-rehearsal. At the end of that she loomed up in front of the biggest camera wearing street clothes and a headscarf. 'Boy,' she called sweetly, 'I'm going to dine at the Ritz with my agent; I'll be back in plenty of time for the show.' The next thing we heard was a call from a coin box. 'It's Gladys Cooper. I'm getting into a taxi now. Please have the money ready when I arrive. I haven't any on me.'

She got one of her two lines right when we recorded her, and patiently allowed us to record the other four in single takes as though she was humouring us. I had always admired the story of her courage when, presenting herself in a new play on Broadway, she made her entrance on the first night to find that a man in the front row had placed his hat on the stage. Walking straight down to it she booted it coolly into the fifth row and carried on with the play. It was pleasant to find that the composure survived.

Sadder circumstances attended my attempt to enlist Dame Margaret Rutherford to play Miss La Creevy, the miniaturist. She had been ill and had not acted for some time, but Stringer Davis, her husband, felt that coming out to work in a small but charming role might be therapeutic. We sent her the script for her scene some weeks ahead and Stringer heard her lines daily. Just before we went into rehearsal, I took Anthony Hopkins, who was to play opposite her, out to meet her. They read the scene and then her husband encouraged her to do it without referring to the book. It was not a good idea. Time after time she forgot the lines; and each mistake added to her distress. We were as encouraging and admiring as we could be. Tony especially struck up a rapport with her; but it became agonizing to watch.

She was a wonderful actress with a much greater range than is usually appreciated, but she was very ill and very tired and very old. The more she failed the more determined to try again she became and the more tearfully disappointed. Our difficulty was to release her without allowing her to feel that she had let us down. We left at last with heavy hearts on Stringer's optimistic prophecy that her return to acting would perhaps be best judged in a large role in the theatre. It was not to be. She died soon after.

The Great Inimitable Mr Dickens was a success – in spite of a *Sunday Times* prophecy that although the idea sounded good 'the word around the BBC is that it doesn't work'. When the film was repeated I asked if we could repeat that sentence among the other raves which were added to the *Radio Times* billing – unfortunately it was not considered politic. Some years later Yorkshire Television produced a series of programmes telling the story of Dickens's life, written by Wolf Mankowitz. They announced proudly that they had found a new approach: they were going to illustrate important moments in the novelist's life by scenes from his books. I suggested to the BBC that we repeat *The Great Inimitable* the week before and the response was enthusiastic. As the time drew nearer I heard no more and rang to find out when we were scheduled for transmission. There was an embarrassed pause. They had wiped the tape. None of those fine performances – in some cases last appearances by great actors – existed.

It is a fortunate coincidence that most *TW3s* and some of the other shows, particularly those telerecorded before tape was widely used, have been kept – in many instances because they were held initially in case there was a query for libel. For the rest storage is the problem and as a result, to paraphrase Shakespeare, 'These our actors ... are melted into air, into thin air ... and, like some insubstantial pageant wiped ... leaving not a wrack behind.'

Virgin Producer

In the late 1960s and early 1970s I produced or co-produced nine full-length feature films and one short. It was a career into which I fell almost by accident, and not one to which I was well suited, in spite of several early successes.

The initial invitation came from Columbia Pictures and more especially from Max Setton, who was in charge of their European operation, and John Van Eyssen who had, if not then very soon after, one of those wonderful movie executive titles like 'Vice President in charge of Artistic Endeavor (Europe)'. As an agent, Van Eyssen had represented the *Evening Standard* critic Milton Shulman.

Herbert Kretzmer and Shulman wrote an outline screenplay about sex and advertising which they called *Goldilocks*. As a motor for their plot they invented an advertising campaign intended to give porridge a more sexy image, and they explored the strain this effort of creation might bring to bear on the home life of the impressionable advertising man responsible for the campaign. The material could loosely be described as satirical, which was why Kretzmer and Shulman suggested that I should be asked to produce it. The storyline, though worked out in considerable detail, was not yet a screenplay and they felt perhaps that a team of writers might be needed to get the mixture of parody, fantasy and satire which they envisaged on to the screen.

My choice was simple. I could leave the BBC on a two-year contract in order to do something new in a medium which I imperfectly understood, or I could embark on yet another round of the Saturday night trouser-dropping from which my BBC type-casting made it hard to escape. I was delighted to say yes to the former. There was a period of overlap and as

I was leaving the BBC I also started to plan the direction of a musical called *Come Spy With Me*, which was Danny La Rue's first West End vehicle.

It was an odd time to choose to break into films. The British film industry had already embarked on its slide into penury and money was getting scarce – though not as scarce as it was to be ten years later. In my innocence I thought I should make as many films as possible as quickly as possible – hoping to achieve a crash apprenticeship in much the same way as I had learned to produce television programmes in my early days at ATV. It took me a long time to adjust to the worldly ways of the cinema jungle after the game reserve which is the BBC.

When I joined the BBC – the Corporation as it is known inside – people were still paid in guineas rather than pounds or, if they were not, they had been until very recently. Producers were not allowed to negotiate fees. They were protected by a community of genteel but tight bookers and negotiators, and were encouraged to concentrate all their energies on preparing the programmes. Communication inside the BBC was usually by reams of memoranda. This could sometimes be a double-edged weapon. On one occasion I produced a programme which ran enormously over budget – about double the estimated cost. It was the musical *Take A Sapphire*. When the full extent of the damage was known a sharp memo descended on me. It was incautiously worded: 'Would you care', it said, 'to explain this overspending?' My reply was 'No', and I heard no more.

No one wrote memos in the cinema, with the exception of John Trevelyan, the Secretary of the Board of Film Censors – whose manner was much more BBC – and for some months I suffered severe withdrawal symptoms with no memos to send. I trailed around from office to sound stage to editing room trying to learn to be a film producer by osmosis. Of course I made some practical moves. I talked to writers. I wooed directors. I listened to the wisdom of experienced producers whom I met at cocktail parties or screenings or premières. I learned how to schedule and budget my film once I had a screenplay from Marty Feldman and Barry Took. (All this was before Marty Feldman's great celebrity, although he and Barry were already successful radio and television writers and Marty was beginning to emerge as a television performer on *At Last the 1948 Show*.) However, even with writers, scripts, schedule, budget and, in theory, Columbia's backing, there was still an unreal air about the exercise.

Nothing excited the front offices of film companies in the 1960s more

than a casting orgy. If they did not know that George Segal was determined to make a film in England, they were sure that Albert Finney was
keen to have a go at comedy. A part written for Alec Guinness could
surely be rejigged for Richard Chamberlain with very little rewriting. If
an actor did show an interest in a role, the front office had immediate
information that, although he may have been box office last week, this
week you could not finance a trailer on him, let alone a movie – at least
not at the price his agent was asking. The agent never seemed to have
heard that his client was box office poison.

The months slipped by and after two years I had still not assembled
what Columbia considered an attractive package. I was told that they
were not going to pick up their option on my contract.

At that moment, with impeccable timing, Carl Foreman made his
entrance. A senior screenwriter and a producer with a near impregnable
position as an independent working through Columbia, Foreman had
encouraged them to acquire a novel by Leslie Thomas, *The Virgin
Soldiers*. It was a best-seller which generously mixed slapstick, melodrama, wry humour and touchingly accurate observation as raw recruits
tried to lose their virginity before they lost their lives in Malaya back in
the 1950s. Leslie Thomas held an artful balance between autobiographical reminiscence and optimistic fantasy. Carl had had this property for
some time, but he had been involved in weightier matters. His speciality
was the literate action epic and he had not pushed his *Virgins* on to the
screen. He was getting impatient. Leslie Thomas and his diminutive but
dynamic agent were getting impatient. I was only too available, so
Carl enlisted me to give the project a nudge.

To watch him handle Columbia politics was a revelation after two
years of stumbling in the wilderness, and it was a magical translation to
move from contract producer with no film to independent producer with
a subject handed on a plate and on better terms. My co-producer was
Leslie Gilliat, who produced innumerable English movies and who, with
great tact and kindness, saw me through the teething troubles and growing pains of this first experience. Carl had already chosen the director,
John Dexter, a friend of his family, with a superb theatrical record at
the National Theatre and the Royal Court. However, John had never
directed a movie before and we started developing the script somewhat
warily as acquaintances rather than friends. (As part of his deal, Leslie
Thomas had written a script, but it did not do justice to his novel.)

First we appoached John McGrath, who loved the premise and settled
down to produce a first treatment some hundred pages long. Unfortu-

nately the treatment which he delivered sprang far more from his interest in the subject than from Leslie Thomas's book. A lot of it excited Dexter and me, but it dismayed Foreman and Thomas. We examined the possibility of encouraging McGrath to go back to the original book but in the end the best solution seemed to be to find a new screenwriter. This time we chose John Hopkins, who solved most of the problems of adaptation with great speed. Low comedy is not his speciality, but there was enough of that and to spare in the original, and he was able to clarify the storyline and extract from Thomas's novel the tender story of young people struggling tentatively towards some knowledge of their sexual potential. At the same time he preserved the infectious sense of fun with which Thomas remembered many essentially autobiographical incidents. Now we had enough to go on, we could start thinking about casting and testing. However, there were as usual some delays, and when the time came for rewrites John Hopkins was not available. We needed more jokes, so Ian La Fresnais, who with Dick Clement had written *The Likely Lads*, came in and supplied them.

Dexter, Gilliat and I set off to do a reconnaissance in Singapore and Malaya, where part of the film was to be shot. We were based in Raffles Hotel, which was everything Maugham and Coward had led me to expect: imperial furniture, wickerwork and leather, punkahs whirling and purring in the evening, a courtyard with tables laid for dinner illuminated by pink-shaded, moth-beckoning lights, insects buzzing and Mulligatawny soup and lamb chops and trifle. From there we explored, and found, within a space of five or six days, all the locations we needed. It was my first view of the Far East.

Casting the film seemed an interminable process beginning with an endless parade of young actors interviewed at my house in Bywater Street. We needed at least a dozen new faces who would carry conviction as the motley crew of raw recruits which Leslie Thomas remembered. Dexter was looking for a definitive army 'shower' and many of the actors we saw were, of necessity, very new to the game. In order to perk them into some sort of animation, to engage their minds sufficiently to make them forget the nervousness which attends an audition-interview, he devised a series of short staccato questions – 'Can you shoot?', 'Do you ride?', 'Can you swim?', 'What games do you play?' – and then, when it was least expected, 'Are you a virgin?' In many cases this relaxed the interviewees into a joky, confidential mood and they opened up easily. But there was one disastrous come-uppance. A young man from Leigh-on-Sea who had sent a photograph of himself looking like a Home

Counties Tarzan duly took a day off work and came up to audition. He got the normal list of quick questions climaxing in 'Are you a virgin?', at which he burst into tears, said, 'Yer, that's the whole problem of my life,' and had to be led sobbing from the house.

Another intriguing interviewee was David Bowie, who was at that time an aspiring singer and mime. He stayed for lunch, weaving a fascinating story about his false eye. According to Bowie, he lost his eye in a fight with another man over a girl. After the eye had come out, the two men forgot about the object of their mutual affection and became close friends. Dexter and I could not decide whether he was inventing the story to rouse our curiosity about him. In any case, we gave him a screen test, but decided against giving him a leading part – in 1967 his strange quality was too elusive to capture on the screen. However, we did give him a small part in a NAAFI dance sequence and he had his hair cropped to a severe military length and did five days of filming. Bowie fans are always asking which is their hero. Unfortunately I have never been able to identify him in the finished cut although each time I see the movie I check again.

We also talked to Mick Jagger about an important cameo late in the film, but Mr Jagger was not convinced that this was the right vehicle for his movie début. For me to have introduced him on both small and large screen would perhaps have been greedy.

Eventually we set off for the Far East with a motley crew of actors and technicians filling a chartered aeroplane. In those days the various unions required that everyone should fly first class and so champagne and caviar were anticipated within seconds of take-off. Unfortunately the charterer had forgotten to put the champagne on board and there was a good deal of friction until the oversight was made good in Tehran. We flew into Kuala Lumpur because we were going to do the jungle sequences up country in Malaya first, and we arrived in the late evening, proceeding in convoy to a beach hotel which overlooked the Indian Ocean. There we settled in, ready to start shooting the next morning.

The first day of filming stays vividly in my mind. Damp, sweaty jungle. A scatter of warm rain, and little Wayne Sleep, the Royal Ballet dancer, too short to stand up in the river which our recruits were fording. Stones had to be laid so that he could be seen above the water.

For lunch, the Asian caterers, reckoning that the British would be homesick, thoughtfully provided fish and chips, to everyone's delight except Hywel Bennett, the leading virgin. Hywel, who has a tendency towards podginess, was on a strict diet and did not intend to break it for fish and chips. I did not take his complaint as seriously as he did and, without thinking, I said, 'Just up that driveway there, through the jungle, there's this Belgian couple who run a little bistro. You can get awfully good onion soup, and they do rather amusing things with veal.' Before I knew what had happened, Hywel had called his driver and set off up the jungle track, heading for the little Belgian bistro which did amusing things with veal. Half an hour later he came back not at all amused and by that time it was too late to get him any fish and chips either. Not perhaps the right way to deal with your star on the first day, but at least he had kept to his diet.

That night we opened some appalling champagne which, to say the best for it, had not travelled, and drank a great deal sitting on the verandah of the hotel, thinking how pleasant location shooting was as we watched the Indian Ocean stretching away in the moonlight, which flecked it and made a halo over the rim of the world. In these beguiling circumstances Nigel Davenport suggested that we should all have a little Drambuie on the rocks before going to bed. Drambuie on the rocks is never my idea of a great celebration, but on this occasion at that time in the evening I was absurdly open to suggestion. I had forgotten that Drambuie is whisky-based, and whisky and champagne is a mixture my system cannot accept. By two o'clock in the morning I awoke with a whacking headache. I was violently ill until six. Desperately I pretended that I had caught Asian flu, and stayed in my room for the rest of the day. I could not reconcile my new-found producer's dignity with an incapacitating hangover on only the second day of filming. Luckily Asian flu was fashionable at the time and there were no sceptics.

One of the Columbia executives wanted badly to visit us on location. It is a trick of film executives, when they want to go on expensive location trips, to invent a reason. These jaunts are eventually written off against the budget of the film, directly or indirectly charged; but the executive needs an excuse in the first place. The ploy is simple: to create trouble in order to find an excuse to come out and stop it. The producer's part in this elaborate game is to keep the VIP away.

Just before we flew, our man started to discover all sorts of objections to the language used in the script, in spite of the fact that it had been on his desk for some months. In one sequence an RSM (Nigel Patrick) accuses his daughter (Lynn Redgrave) of frigidity and lesbianism. The use of the word 'lesbian' was built up by our would-be visitor into an enormous crisis. A regular clean-up scare was going on in Hollywood, particularly with regard to the words which were acceptable in the eventual television versions of the movie. Cables started to fly saying, 'p. 103 delete "lesbian" '.

On the eve of flying to Singapore it seemed certain that our VIP would have to fly out to join us for vital script conferences. Leslie Gilliat and I began to enjoy the manœuvre. I sent back an immediate telex saying that we would be delighted to see him and that indeed we had reserved the Dragon Emperor suite (or some such name) at the Goodwood Hotel for him. Fortunately I remembered that he was a monster hypochondriac. I added a friendly tip that he should be very careful to have all the possible vaccinations against Asian flu and tropical diseases before he set off because the town was in the grip of innumerable epidemics. By providential timing the message arrived in Los Angeles while he was in conference with the Columbia top brass. It was passed ritually from the head of the company down through the assembled vice presidents until it got to our man at the end of the table. By the time it reached him the consensus was that he would not need to go to Singapore after all.

After this flurry of excitement we were able to carry on quietly. There were occasional irritating messages from executives. Front office film men speak very much their own language. One senior Columbia man had told me over a lunch at the Café Royal, 'Before I can make a decision on this I shall have to make a hemisphere to hemisphere telephone conversation,' by which he meant he had to call New York.

Columbia bombarded Dexter and me with telexes and telegrams as evidence that the spectre of lesbianism had not disappeared altogether. Dexter found this attempt at remote string-pulling disconcerting. He went into production nervously and after a batch of these instructions he asked me to keep them away from him. It was not an easy time for him. He had accepted the film under the wing of Carl Foreman, whose work and international reputation he admired. Now here he was on location in Singapore with two quite different producers. He could appreciate Leslie Gilliat's great experience and efficiency, but they found communication difficult. Looking at me, on my first film, he reckoned that I knew no more than he did, and it created unease between us.

When we had completed the jungle sequences in Malaya, we moved down to Singapore for the parade ground locations. Every morning we passed Changhi Jail. It is an agonizing box of a building, now a civil prison, and no more attractive for that. It is also an awful reminder of conditions of imprisonment in Singapore during the Japanese occupation. We filmed our parade ground sequences on a beautiful tarmac square surrounded by lofty imperial barracks, imposing palms and tropical flowers, haunted by the memory of other wartime atrocities. In the officers' mess hangs a panoramic picture taken surreptitiously during the war when the Japanese filled the whole parade ground with English servicemen who were kept there for days in the baking sun, suffering and dying.

In our case it was the British Army who were uncooperative. Unfortunately for us Dick Lester brought out a movie called *How I Won the War*, an anti-war picture for which he managed to get Army cooperation without revealing the final stance of the film to the War Office. When the lampoon emerged, stern questions were asked about why the Army had cooperated in sending itself up. Some time elapsed between our modest proposal that we should be allowed to use parade ground sites and our final request for full cooperation, during which Lester's film opened. Luckily, as we already had the Army's word that we could use the sites for the parade grounds, which were essential for the authentic look of our film, we held them to that. However, they banned the employment of British soldiers as extras – Portia offering Shylock his pound of flesh but denying him a single jot of blood. It was disappointing for the soldiers because a lot of them liked the idea of being movie stars, and indeed some did a little moonlighting. Instead, the parade ground was filled with short Singapore soldiers, who were kept in the rear ranks because they were not only too short but also the wrong shade. The foreground was stocked with schoolboys, sons of serving soldiers who were not bound by the regulations which stopped their fathers from earning pocket money.

Off the set, Singapore offered a rich harvest of anticipated delights in much the same way that first views of the New York skyline flesh out the postcard views which are already familiar and in no way contradict them. For one thing the Far East yielded all the expected funny Chinese names and pronunciations which I was naively unable to take in my stride: Lai Kee Fun, and Mr Wee, the sanitary engineer; 'flied lice' (heard for real); a camp and flustered SAS counter clerk for whom the job of re-routing a Russian to Moscow from Singapore via Delhi proved so daunting that he flung all his travel documents in front of his supervisor screaming, 'It's all Gleek to me!'; a little Chinaman of great sweetness whom we cast for the role of F. Yew; a Chinese tailor, whom we found in an old people's home run by nuns, whose name was Hallelujah – he was seventy, had lived in Singapore for forty years, and his favourite film star was still Norma Shearer.

The list of entertainments available was eclectic: the Great Royal

Circus of India; the Greatest Show of Culture and Geste from China; countless touring Chinese operas running five hours and performed on the roadside; '*2001, A Space Odyssey* – 19th Big Day! Season Ending Soon!'; *At Last the 1948 Show* and *The Forsyte Saga* on television with the nagging Ileenee the toast of Singapore; *Show of Swords*, a Shaw Brothers production in Shawscope, in Mandarin with English and Chinese subtitles (a screenful), starring Wang Yu and Li Chin; the première of *The Tragedy of a King Poet* at which both Yam Kim Fei and Pak Suet Sin, two ladies who took the leading male and female roles, were mobbed. *Up The Junction* was doing a few days with the additional subtitle *Don't get caught was what she wasn't taught!* Across in Indonesia an attempt to revive gladiatorial contests in the presence of the Foreign Minister failed when the imported Javanese gladiator, Bandot Lahargo, was confronted by an unusually sophisticated lion who sensibly declined to put up a fight.

Singapore was well supplied with traditional seaport facilities. Cabaret restaurants like the Car Park, featuring 'Five Korean Lovelies' and conversations with not very chatty hostesses at $12 an hour, represented it at its most respectable. Down the road drag queens patrolled Bugis Street after midnight like strange giant kewpie dolls, painted and fantastical, saving up for their sex change operations in Tokyo. But when Trixie and Edna and Lulu had to cross the causeway into Malaya and show their passports, official photographs required short hair and a brief reversion to Jim or Fred or Omar.

One lotus-eyed Edna or Trixie captivated Hywel Bennett to such an extent that he did not identify her as Jim or Fred until it was almost too late and they had returned to his suite at the Goodwood Hotel. She became his devoted admirer, visiting him very formally on the set, to John Dexter's considerable irritation and embarrassment. When we left she invested in the Singapore custom of airmailing orchids, which were waiting for him when he got back to England. A few days later and Edna herself was waiting – she telephoned from a girls' home in Windsor. Cathy MacGowan, Hywel's girl friend put her foot down and Edna was last heard of entertaining the patrons at a drag club in Birmingham.

There is an imitative quality about film crews, and once the star had considered the bent attractions of Bugis Street it became acceptable for others down the pecking order to try. To some degree it may have been a wise precaution. On leaving, when we offered a free medical check, especially against VD, to the crew before flying home, the only casualty was the crew member who had poured most scorn on the Bugis Street 'girls' and plumped for legitimate ladies.

There were other attractions. Discreet pleasure parlours offered terms of three Singapore dollars a drink and three dollars more for treatment in the sawdust-floored back rooms. One was known as the Winky-Wanky bar with the alluring slogan 'One on the Rocks and One off the Wrist'. Round the corner men with gold teeth offered blue movies, exhibitions, girls or boys or boy-girls. The traditional girl meets donkey film evoked the traditional cameraman's put-down – 'Not a very good print.'

The political climate was set by Lee Kuan Yew's strong arm. As I left he was starting the last phase of his 'Keep Singapore Clean' campaign, giving Singaporeans one final voluntary month before 'enforcing discipline on those who do not yield to social suasion'. It was not easy to imagine discipline or social suasion having a lightning effect on Singapore, which featured a rubbish tip around most corners, a tumble-down kampong under each towering new block, the smell of rubbish surging up from open drains, and the pong of pigs alternating with clouds of frangipane scent in more open country. And yet Mr Lee's Singapore had the air of a place where things were happening to a plan, and I am assured that the rubbish has now disappeared.

Social suasion and discipline have a sinister ring; and it was easy to see a dark side to Mr Lee's control of the radio and television networks – a point of view which seemed to be shared by some younger staff members at TV Singapura. Television documentaries told the audience that it was all happening in Singapore. The radio reminded them that it was 'the Swinging City'. Both media had to do it in English, Chinese, Malay and Tamil. The two television channels were permuted so that if there was an English-language programme with Malay subtitles on one waveband a Tamil film with Chinese subtitles would be on the other. The problem of staggering the languages made the jobs of Controllers BBC-1 and BBC-2 seem like playing with children's blocks.

Singapore was four nations, violently different from one another. However, unlike the situation across the causeway in Malaya, merit was at a premium in Singapore – it appears that this is a very Chinese trait. If there is a chance to select by examination, there is an examination. This is hard on the Malays, for while the Chinese love examinations and are good at them, it is widely rumoured that no Malay has ever passed one. Waiting in hotels used to be an unfashionable job, second only to joining the Army. National Service removed the stigma from the services, and schools of waiting were opened to service the boom in hotel building: fledgling hotel employees emerged with a relentless smile, a knowledge of knives and forks, and a diploma.

More traditional dining centred on a group of happily discovered Chinese restaurants. There was Faty's, where Faty cooked exquisitely on the open pavement and was reputed to have a Rolls at the back and a son at Eton. There were meals at the Hong Kong Bowl, one in the middle of a Chinese wedding so noisy as not to be believed, putting away baked crab claws, turtle, suckling pig, 'fresh fried milk' and all those vegetables that taste so much nicer in the East. And there was entertainment at the Hollywood-style home of Run Me Shaw, the head of the Singapore branch of a family of tycoons who straddle the entertainment world in the Far East.

Two censorship remarks remain in my memory. A Malayan censor had just viewed John Wayne's hawkish *The Green Berets*. I asked him how he liked it. 'I pass it clean,' he said happily. And there was a legendary girl censor who had a test I can recommend to anyone joining that dying breed – official censors – 'If a film gives me a funny feeling I know it is dirty; but if I feel nothing I know it is culture.'

We finished on schedule in Singapore and returned to England to shoot a jungle ambush near Saffron Walden. We transported an old steam engine to a disused British Rail siding and converted it to look like an authentic period piece. The small copse which lined the track was filled out with bamboos and palm trees, and made a fairly convincing jungle setting. However, by now October was giving way to November and spots of tell-tale yellow were appearing in the trees. It was a night ambush and in the cold English night air we had to be careful that the breath which came steaming from shivering soldiers did not give the game away. We spent a week in Cambridgeshire and then moved on to shoot the interiors of the ambush in another abandoned camp near Crowthorne in Berkshire.

The subsequent history of *The Virgin Soldiers*, once shooting was over, completed the first stages of my apprenticeship as a film producer. There was the long editing process, cutting, rejigging, and finding the right music. Ray Davies of The Kinks wrote a memorable march theme and Peter Greenwell arranged the rest of the score. The movie was a great success in England, getting good notices and making more money at home than any other film that year except the current Bond offering. However, Columbia were in no haste to show it in America. For a long time they considered it too inflammatory to offer laughs alongside death in the jungle at a time when the Vietnam War was being fought. Suddenly, albeit a year later, I began to sense a change in their attitude. In fact Columbia were beginning to hear good things about 20th Century-Fox's *MASH*; and at the same time American public opinion was beginning to swing against the war. It was comic to watch the speed and thoroughness with which a large company can change its face.

I was flown to New York for a sneak preview only to find that the print had been impounded in customs at Kennedy Airport on the suspicion that it was pornographic. (At least I was able to get to the second night of *O Calcutta!* in the time available. Kenneth Tynan had earlier asked me to direct it, a job which conflicted with my commitment to *The Virgin Soldiers*, and it is always interesting to see how shows turn out.)

The crowning irony in the sudden saga was the engagement of a pair of elderly protest writers to write a lyric to Ray Davies's march expressing the universal antipathy to war felt by 'young people the world over'. The enthusiasm with which the company suggested that this 'moving testament' would be 'plugged' on peace marches on Washington was not shared by youthful protesters. Eventually we opened in New York almost unnoticed. *MASH* had long stolen a march on us, buttonholing its audience in more vivid and immediate American accents. Ten other films were premièred that week and, among the ten, *Patton* said most of what the United States wanted to hear about war that week. *The Virgin Soldiers* sank without trace.

Virgin Films

After we had completed the principal photography on *The Virgin Soldiers*, I had occasion to take stock. During two years as an apprentice film producer, I had produced nothing. My one film so far was set up as a result of Carl Foreman's acumen in acquiring the property and then because he needed an instrument to push it through. In the day-to-day administration of the movie, Leslie Gilliat was the guiding force. I could hardly look on *The Virgin Soldiers* as mine. By now I had no 'property' which I could turn into a film, and the starting point for a film producer is a 'property' – a play, a novel, an original story. If necessary you spend your own money on acquiring one; if you are more clever and canny, you get a film company to do this for you.

There are rules in the game played between producer and distributor. The distributor encourages the producer to take as many risks as possible – to deck out the 'property' as attractively as he can; to commission writers to make an adaptation; to hawk it to directors, hoping to land an exciting, bankable fellow, get him involved, perhaps pay him something and use him to attract stars. After this the producer brings the whole package to the distributor. The distributor's game has been to do as little and spend as little as possible while sounding as encouraging as he can so that the producer will give him an unofficial first refusal. The odds are heavily stacked in favour of the distributor as long as he can keep encouraging the producer to put enough into his package to allow an easy assessment of success or failure.

I had no resources to buy or commission a property, but I began to see that this might be the time to do something with *Every Home Should Have One*. Columbia, particularly the Hollywood and New York offices, had no interest in it, but by a stroke of luck Marty Feldman had become an attractive risk in the English cinema. The Boulting brothers, Roy and John, had just had a huge success with a movie version of *Till Death Us Do Part* and British Lion had made a fortune out of it. I approached the Boultings and they were happy to go with Marty. Marty was nervous but intrigued and, considering the other actors we had thought of – Alan Bates, George Segal, Tom Courtenay, Albert Finney – it was hardly type-casting. However, it made some sense – there were fantasy sequences and extravagant parodies – and Barry Took and Marty did a new draft for the Boultings. The two brothers were fascinating to deal with. If you went into John's office Roy always materialized beside him like ectoplasm, apparently without a door having opened. They were very tight negotiators, but they were enthusiastic and encouraging.

To direct *Every Home Should Have One* we chose Jim Clark, a distinguished film editor who had worked on many of John Schlesinger's movies. Some years earlier for our first episode of *BBC-3* he had made a funny film about a nudist camp, in which Beryl Reid played the leading nudist. I had first asked John Schlesinger, who had just finished *Darling* and was doing nothing, to direct this, and we were all set to go when John got an attack of nervous jitters. He was heavily tipped for an Oscar for *Darling* and suddenly the idea of a ten-minute nudie short looked as though it might prejudice his chances – so he pulled out a few days before we were due to shoot. By now I had committed quite a lot of BBC money. John suggested that Jim Clark, who was keen to break into movies, would be the right person to direct it, and at that notice it seemed easiest to follow his advice. It was good advice, and as directors with an instinct for comedy are not thick on the ground he was a natural choice for *Every Home*.

He established an immediate rapport with Marty Feldman. Marty was switching from television to the cinema, and although he was excited about the change he was also nervous. Everyone born in the 1930s and 1940s starts with this curiously reverent attitude towards movies. As small children we sat in the stalls and looked up at enormous cinema screens, believed what we saw and invested it with disproportionate glamour and importance. Early professional lives spent in radio or television do little to exorcise the romantic aura which surrounds the big screen. For Marty this was very much a first chance to get at the 'real thing' and he did not want to go wrong.

We were due to film at Shepperton (the British Lion studios) with a certain amount of work on location around Shepperton. The rest of the cast included a gallery of clever young English comedians many of whom have since been brilliantly successful. Judy Cornwell played Marty's wife and Frances de la Tour and Penelope Keith were both in small parts. Frances played a Mrs Whitehouse figure and Penelope a massive German lesbian au pair girl.

We had a daunting search for another Scandinavian au pair. Having done an exhaustive search in England we tried Sweden, but found no one whom we could attract on our modest budget. Returning in despair with no idea who would play this important role, we were visited the very next day by Julie Ege, just delivered of a baby, who was apparently the reason we had not been shown her mother before. It was the start of a short but lively career in movies. She had appeared in the background of one of the Bond films, *On Her Majesty's Secret Service*, and having played for us in *Every Home Should Have One* and in *Up Pompeii*, made a few more films and then returned to her native Norway, where she has married an offshore oil man, become an immensely serious actress, and is inclined to give her Hedda Gabler to the citizens of Stavanger in those long light nights.

The other leading actor was the American comic Shelley Berman, who played a Mephisophelean character who pushed and shoved Marty's innocent-at-large on to further excesses and indiscretions. I had always admired Berman's work but was not quite prepared for his nervousness, which is apparently also legendary. He is a wonderfully able actor-comedian with a tremendous sense of character and a king-size sense of self-persecution. It did not make it easier for him to come to England and find that his co-star, a comic he had never heard of, was enormously popular here and was receiving columns of coverage in the press. The first manifestation of insecurity was his insistence that his character should be called by name five or six times at the beginning of the film to promote immediate identification. Then again, with Marty's comic star riding high and his remarkable face demanding to be photographed, the publicity department had an impossible task trying to get newspapers to write stories about Shelley at all.

Two other unfortunate accidents did not help his morale. In a crowd scene set in a trendy Chelsea restaurant an extra encouraged one of his girl colleagues to go across to Shelley and ask him for an autograph. This pleased Shelley mightily. So far, so good. Unfortunately the girl had been briefed to say, 'I loved your driving instructor record.' The instigator knew perfectly well that 'the driving instructor' is Bob Newhart's record and that Shelley Berman's classic routines are telephone conversations. The reverberations of the row lasted for days.

Towards the end of the movie my housekeeper Miss Godfrey, who sports a fine line in stylish hats, came down to lunch with us. She took very good care of me and looked forward to visiting the studio, a day on the set and lunch with Marty and Jim – both of whom she knew well. Half-way through a happy lunch I could see Shelley across the room getting more and more agitated. Finally he came over and hissed in my ear: 'This', he said, 'is the final insult.' I was nonplussed. 'What do you mean?' His whisper swelled to a whine, 'You have this important lady journalist down here and you have not brought her anywhere near my table. You have flourished her and Feldman under my nose and it's not good enough.'

Miss Godfrey's hats were in the best tradition of Hedda Hopper and Louella Parsons, so I had a hard time convincing him that she was not England's most powerful columnist but simply a very nice woman, who made my life go smoothly, having a day out. He was pacified, but only just.

Every Home Should Have One was another of those films which cost just too much. It was budgeted at something over £300,000. If it had cost £200,000 we would have been in immediate and substantial profit, and if we had made it a year later we would probably have brought it in for something near the lower figure, but the film industry reacted slowly to the idea of cutting its celluloid according to its income. However, like *The Virgin Soldiers*, *Every Home* was one of the top ten grossing British films of the year.

During the production of *Every Home Should Have One* I formed a partnership with Terry Glinwood, who was associate producer of the film, and we formed a company, which we decided to call Virgin Films. Continuing my policy of doing as much as possible and getting as much experience as I could, we contracted to do a number of films over the next few years. For EMI we produced three spin-offs from Frankie Howerd's *Up Pompeii* series on television. For Rank we made *Rentadick* from an original screenplay by John Cleese and Graham Chapman. For Hemdale we did *Girl Stroke Boy*, a comedy based on a West End play called *The Girl Friend*; and for Columbia we did a sequel to *The Garnett Saga*, and a screen version of Peter Nichols's National Theatre success, *The National Health*.

Terry's experience in films was long and varied: he started as an accountant and worked thereafter in many different jobs, including

Lolita with Stanley Kubrick where, judging by rosy reminiscences, a lot of time was spent playing table tennis with the director. He had moved on to Michael Klinger, a buccaneering English independent producer, and kept a tight rein on the purse-strings of films like *Penthouse*, a small budget shocker which made a lot of money for Klinger in the 1960s.

I met him while he was working for my agent, John Heyman, a multi-faceted entrepreneur who combined managing Burton and Taylor, Trevor Howard and Hughie Green with raging ulcers and one deaf ear (used devastatingly in negotiation to hear only what he wants to hear). An early scheme had been to book Elvis Presley into Wembley Stadium in a vast magnifying goldfish bowl which would enlarge every pelvic twitch. It foundered with the suggestion that the lights might burn him up like a boy scout's second lesson in fire-making. John was also ambitious to produce movies. He had started by making *Privilege*, directed by Peter Watkins, and he was to continue to indulge his aspirations, notably with *Boom*, with Burton and Taylor, and *The Go-Between*, with Julie Christie and Alan Bates – both directed by Joseph Losey. Terry had been brought into *Privilege* to keep an eye on purse-strings and practicality, and had been successful in both areas. He was keen to co-produce and he combined a practical grasp of most aspects of production with an imaginative approach to problems which I found refreshing and congenial. His attitude was never 'It can't be done', but always 'If it's important how can it best be done?'

He saw us through the intricacies of *Every Home* and together we enjoyed planning our low-budget assault on *Up Pompeii* so that it could still look as handsome as possible. Our luckiest break was to discover most of Rome on the abandoned MGM lot up the road from Elstree Studios where we were due to film – endless vistas of marbled flats and Roman columns and statues of John Gielgud from Charlton Heston's *Julius Caesar*, which we bought for a song and subsequently sold to roughly the same tune.

The interesting challenge was to try to capture Frankie Howerd's unique comic quality on the screen. It was not that he was new to the big screen, but somehow in his earlier films he had never looked like the great stage comedian he is. One of his secrets in the theatre is the extraordinary communion he achieves with the audience. He establishes a conspiracy of two with each ticket-holder and together they undermine the show, the setting, the material, other members of the cast and even other members of the audience. He thrives on the tightrope of live performance, coaxes, cozens or berates his listeners and with unlimited cunning, self-rehearsal and self-absorption squeezes a fresh sense of occasion into each show.

The beauty of *Up Pompeii* on television was that it allowed the conspiratorial affair with the studio audience to be shared by the viewing public, thanks to large close-ups of generous asides to camera and to studio reaction which reassured and inspired the actor. In film studios the cathedral-like silence which is created out of chaos when a director says 'Action' presents an immediate problem to a player who is at his happiest and most masterly controlling an unruly crowd. In the three films which we made with Frankie we failed to find an alternative to the inspiration of the audience. He was often very funny, particularly in the first two films of the series, but the bubble of fun which he could blow at a first reading, delivering a line with rich eccentricity to set off the laughter of the crew, was punctured when the director called 'Action' and they became quiet and the air of solemnity descended. There is still time to transform that cunning, leering, furrowed, leather face into a perfect vehicle for screen comedy, but we failed to help its owner live up to his and our own hopes.

The television shows were written by the late Talbot Rothwell, who was responsible for a substantial number of the *Carry Ons* and who lived outside Brighton, looking like a prosperous, retired squadron leader. He was diffident about committing himself to a series of *Up* films in case he should lose favour with the *Carry On* producers. However, with Sid Colin he wrote the first film and it was a joy to turn the pages of the first draft, so rich in robust music-hall routines, so replete with red-nosed *double entendres*, so redolent of meaty seaside postcards:

My poor child, so lovely and so chaste. And so easily caught!

Let us celebrate the festival of the prolific goose. Laying all night . . .

A: In the great court of Samarkand she once held a unique position.
B: On top of the wardrobe, I should think . . .!

Orgies, stolen parchments, ancient Christians fed to lions, Nero, public baths, the entire destruction of Pompeii – all ancient Roman life was there seen through Talbot Rothwell's vaudeville eyes. Michael Hordern, Lance Percival, Bill Fraser, Bernard Bresslaw, Barbara Murray and Patrick Cargill supported Frankie.

Up Pompeii was a big enough hit to ensure that a sequel could be planned and put into production straight away. By now the problem of 'properties' and 'development' and paying for scripts had ceased to be a headache. We were working with Beryl Vertue, who ran the film side of Robert Stigwood's growing organization and who had long represented Frankie Howerd as an agent. We agreed to deal with Nat Cohen and Beryl, who also represented Alan Galton and Ray Simpson (who had written material for Frankie for years) and smoothed the way to a collaboration between them and Sid Colin, who provided the initial treatment. The picture was to be medieval instead of Roman – for 'slave' read 'serf' – and instead of 'Lurcio' Frankie became 'Lurkalot', his master 'Ludicrous Sextus' became 'Sir Coward de Custard', and his son 'Nausius', 'Knotweed'. The equivalent of a gladiator, 'Prodigious', in *Up Pompeii* would be 'Chopper', a woodsman in this epic – the *double entendres* were doubled ('Oh, me chopper!'). Once again the sense of history was more spirited than scholarly.

> A: Serfs ought to be where you want them when you want them. He'll have to go.
> B: I agree, my dear, let's swap him for one of those nice Swedish girls . . .

Sid Colin's plot revolved around the thesis – not supported by any historical evidence – that King Richard the Lionheart had been born with an identical twin brother. Mr Howerd essayed both roles: the first-born spirited away by evil barons and raised by a sow whom he regards as his mother, and the younger twin, born after the villains thought they had settled the succession, who grows up to be King Richard, not keen on the boring routine of ruling – 'Sod that for a lark. I think I'll go on a crusade.'

This time the medieval panorama included jousting, jesters, crusades, stocks and a ducking-stool, as well as the invention of gunpowder – originally called 'gone' powder because, 'no sooner did you light the fuse than you had gone!' – Robin Hood and his Gay, as opposed to Merry, Men, changing their Lincoln green for black leather cut tight across the hips in the winter; and a grotesque Maid Marian:

> He: How do you do?
> She: Not very often, thank you.

Marginally they failed to corrupt young Knotweed:

> She: Knotweed, you're not one of them!
> He: If he's not, he soon will be.

The plot turned on Lurkalot's new invention, a chastity belt – the Knickerbocker Glory, mark three, and it all ended happily.

One of the best fringe benefits of this sort of exercise is to be able to cast admired comedians in cameo roles. As well as Bill Fraser, Lance Percival and Anna Quayle, we had Roy Hudd, Derek Griffiths, Dave King, Fred Emney and Hugh Paddick, together with Godfrey Winn, who turned out to be a fully paid-up member of Equity and who appeared as the Archbishop – pink and plump and scrubbed. This sort of farcical comedy requires a *femme fatale*, and we invited Eartha Kitt, who had two field-days pretending confusion in a crusader's tent as she seduced the two Frankies simultaneously in the ultimate twist of mistaken identity or mingled limbs. She managed it with a low throbbing purr and a mischievous intensity which never quite allowed her co-star to relax.

Up The Chastity Belt opened even more successfully than *Up Pompeii* and looked like beating it at the box office when, during its first week on general release, there was a nationwide power strike. Cinemas were dark, or looked like being dark, and patrons stayed at home. It was replayed piecemeal after the strike had finished and, although it did well, it never achieved the financial success we had hoped.

Our last film in the *Up* series was *Up The Front*, a First World War saga in which Francis the slave or serf now became Francis, a batman. This was by far the least successful of the series, enlivened in retrospect only by the *farouche* experience of adding Zsa Zsa Gabor to the mixture in a Mata Hari role.

Miss Gabor has a zest for new experiences. We negotiated quickly and pleasantly for her week's work on the film. Most of the questions to be solved concerned travel, transport, accommodation and especially costume, make-up and hair. We had agreed on the telephone that Zandra Rhodes, who was just emerging as a leading designer, should create a wardrobe for Zsa Zsa, who purred delight down the line. She was cast in a tightly contained sequence of scenes which we were planning to shoot at the end of the schedule almost entirely in ballrooms and boudoirs. She was to arrive from Los Angeles on a Friday, be fitted and fêted and fussed over during the weekend, and photographed on Monday.

She has a history of trouble with customs officials, so we worked hard to get her smoothly through at London Airport. The problem of which we had been warned was the agony she felt when saying goodbye to her pet dogs, sometimes so unbearable that she tried to smuggle them in with her. A little caravan proceeded to the airport. We had two colourful members of the production team at the time. My assistant, Nicholas

Page, was young, cheerful, indefatigable, affable and wore his hair very long; my driver was an ex-guardsman who insisted on having a uniform for ceremonial occasions – the colour he had chosen for his suit was a delicate powder-blue. The plane was on time. Nicholas, who is also wily, managed somehow to ingratiate himself behind the customs barrier so that he could make sure that there was no trouble. Accordingly he emerged with Zsa Zsa (who was travelling alone) as her escort or, as some newspapers preferred, her 'hippy lover'. Zsa Zsa came out with the usual hail of 'Darlinks' and was very friendly. The 'hippy lover' had started the good atmosphere, the powder-blue chauffeur completed it. The convoy set off for her rooms in Piccadilly.

The procedure on arrival was fascinating. The hotel's obsequious welcome was followed by her imperious examination of the accommodation offered. Having looked at the rooms she rejected them. The main objection was hanging space. This was, apparently, quite inadequate. It was difficult to decide if the rejection was real or ritual. It was followed by immediate acceptance of the next suite, which to me seemed similar. She swung round for confirmation of how undemanding she was being: 'You see, darlink, this is perfect. Why don't they offer me this first time?'

The next evening I gave a small dinner party for her. The guests included Mervyn Stockwood, Bishop of Southwark, who always loves life, friends and rubbing shoulders with showbiz. Some years before, at Hywel Bennett's wedding to Cathy MacGowan, I had sat him next to Roger Moore, producing a Sunday newspaper photograph captioned, 'What the Bishop said to the Saint.' This time the legend was equally predictable – 'What the Bishop said to the Actress.' I sometimes wondered if Mervyn minded these gross exploitations, but I was reassured later on going through his press cuttings book to find that both photographs were duly pasted in.

Mild tremors started on the Saturday afternoon. I made the mistake of engaging a female hairdresser; a half-wit should have assessed that Zsa Zsa felt more secure with men. Richard Mills, the make-up artist, became her immediate friend and valued confidant. Zsa Zsa had a fixed idea that a stylist of Ricci Burns's – the fashionable 1960s King's Road crimper – should attack her hair. It did not take her long to explain to our appointee that she would not do, and I got a cooing call to explain that she had left 'very happy, darlink! I tell her she is a sweet girl; but not for me. But you do not have to worry, I have found this marvellous man. He is divine! He understand! He work for my great friend ...' (aside) '... what is his name?' (to me) '... Ricci Burns!'

I was about to explain that there could be complications. For example, unions jealously guard the admission of hairdressers to studios and if Mr Burns's man was not a member of the union we could not let him in. I did not get the chance. Zsa Zsa embarked on a perfectly shaped monologue which stays vividly in my memory:

He is so good to me, Ricci. He has sent me this beautiful man. He is the best. The girl was nice, but she did not understand me. This man is wonderful. . . . You are wonderful, darlink . . . he has done all the best people. . . . I have complete confidence in him. . . . Tell me who have you done, darlink! I am talking to my producer, he would like to know . . . (to me) He cannot remember. (to him) You must have done someone. . . . Are you good? . . . I only have the best. . . . Are you very good? Me . . .! Of course I am good! . . . You do not ask me this! How dare you say that! . . . What? . . . What is this? Clapped out! . . . Go away! Get out! (door bangs) Darlink, I do not think he will do. Do not worry, we will find me someone better. Au revoir!

Richard Mills, having gained her confidence, found an excellent hairdresser and no more was heard of that problem. Now the clothes became an issue. 'Zandra is the best dressmaker in the world, BUT! . . . And darlink, she is so amusing, the green and pink hair and the funny accent. . . . BUT! . . . And I am sure the clothes would be wonderful for somebody else. . . . BUT! . . .'

It transpired that Zsa Zsa had brought with her a couple of her own 'old rags' and she thought that even these would be better than Zandra's creations. I suspect that she had never had any intention of wearing anything else. The whole experience was riveting for Zandra. Conspiratorially we conceded the clothes. Miss Gabor was to wear whatever she was happiest to wear. Zandra asked only one favour. Zsa Zsa having given strict instructions that Miss Rhodes was not to come to the studio, Zandra was determined to have a look at this curious creature, strange in her experience, actually at work. We arranged a vantage point on the set from which she watched fascinated and eventually retreated still shaking her head in amazement. Now they have become friends.

Taking Zsa Zsa to a first night was another revelation. She had revelled the night before at her usual stamping-ground, Les Ambassadeurs, and then she had worked through the day. She changed at the studio and we drove in from Elstree just in time. She was very hungry. All the way we hunted for a salt-beef sandwich – her heart's desire – to no avail. We arrived at the Globe Theatre just in time for me to buy a box of chocolates and get to our seats as the curtain rose. The play, written by Frank Marcus, directed by Robin Phillips, earnestly acted by Irene Worth and Nigel Davenport, very quickly put her into a deep gloom. Indeed as the night went on her head began to sag. It is a large, pinkish-whitish head and her shoulders were swathed in white fur. She was not inconspicuous. We invented a routine like Chaplin's in *Modern Times*. As the great blonde head sagged I nudged her side and her right hand stretched out automatically, clutched a chocolate and stuffed it in her mouth. The effort and the munching and the sugar in the sweet gave her a temporary lift and the head snapped up into position. Five minutes later, down went the head, out dug the arm, in went the hand and up went the chocolate. There were just enough chocolates to see the evening and the ritual through.

Terry Glinwood and I found ourselves producing three or four films at once. There was a period when we were starting one on location, finishing one at Elstree, and preparing yet another one at Pinewood. Ironically this was the moment when I decided that it would be wise to have a telephone in my car. I was beginning to resent jumping out to press pennies into coin boxes *en route* or trying to make and take important calls during the few moments of spare time on arrival at a destination. I worked out that I was spending some four or five hours in the car each day. In those days car phones were not easy to come by but I lobbied a lot and eventually, a year later, a telephone was installed. From the moment I had the phone I never completed another film deal.

Rentadick, which we did make, came via David Frost, who had trouble getting a John Cleese/Graham Chapman project to the screen. David's flirtation with the cinema has always been a come-and-go affair and the week we talked about the subject it was very much on the blink. He had paid richly for the development of the script and was anxious to off-load because there seemed little chance that he could get the money together to film it. The prospect of a screenplay by Cleese and Chapman tailored for the *Monty Python* team was exciting and we arranged to buy it. Having become proud purchasers, we discovered that the *Monty Python* team were now disillusioned with their vehicle – a lesson other producers have learned since – and no longer wanted to be any part of it. We had no alternative but to recruit other actors or write off the money. Robbed of the enthusiasm of the writers and the participation of the cast, we were puzzled about how to find the finance. One of the problems of taking over a script from another producer is that he has usually shopped it from backer to backer. We soon found that placing this particular package was not going to be easy.

By a lucky chance I was asked to speak at a City luncheon. I left Elstree Studios reluctantly: we were in the middle of filming, there were problems, and I wanted to stay around the set. However, having got to the lunch, I found that I was sitting next to Graham Dowson, who was John Davis's right-hand man and heir apparent at the Rank Organization. We had had no contact with Rank up to that time, and indeed their film production side was contracting rapidly. 'How extraordinary,' said Dowson, 'you've never done anything for us.' 'How extraordinary that you should say that!' I said. 'I have the perfect script.' I elaborated on the farcical premise and the financial promise of such a venture and he thought about it while I made my speech.

By the end of lunch we had made appointments to discuss the project with Frank Poole who ran the film side of Rank. I got the impression from Graham that he indulged occasionally in a film project and this might be his annual treat. He also confessed ruefully that his other pet projects had rarely been winners. He also told my favourite dieting story. John Davis, in a serious attempt to lose weight, had heard of Limmits, the dieting biscuit. Having admonished Dowson for not suggesting them sooner, he adopted them like a new religion. Some weeks later he was complaining that he had lost no weight. Dowson discovered that Davis had been consuming his usual large meals throughout the day and taking the Limmits as well, with milk as prescribed, instead of morning coffee and afternoon tea, assuming, apparently, that they had some magic dietary effect on a normal intake of food.

There seemed to be a lot of dieting at Rank. Apart from slimming down their film production, Frank Poole, whose appearance I only knew from cinema trade journals as a vast figure behind whom Orson Welles could conceal himself with ease, turned out to have lost several stones and to have that stark, ill-coordinated appearance of people who have lost weight fast. However, he adopted Graham's new baby with wary indulgence and we were given the go-ahead without delay.

Jim Clark directed a clever collection of actor comedians including Donald Sinden, Richard Briers, James Booth, Ronald Fraser, Richard Beckinsale, John Wells (who with John Fortune had done some tailoring revisions to the script), Kenneth Cope, Spike Milligan, Michael Bentine, Penelope Keith, Tsai Chin and Julie Ege; but the mixture which the *Python* writers had concocted for themselves failed to rise in other hands, however skilled. The film was not a success and lost virtually its entire investment. Cleese and Chapman were unhappy and declined to have their names on the script. It was an anticlimactic end to a venture into which we had fallen by accident, sustained by a lucky meeting, and on which we had expended a lot of enthusiasm. The comic spirit is highly individual and we did not manage to keep it alive on this occasion.

While we were still trying to generate as much activity in England as possible, Terry Glinwood and I were beginning to sense that finance for English films was getting harder and harder. We had made a deal with Robert Stigwood for him to buy Virgin Films and this looked like giving us some security; but it also meant that we had to keep active. We bought a West End play, *The Girl Friend*, which had flopped, and Caryl Brahms and I adapted it for the screen under the title *Girl Stroke Boy*. Its premise was a weekend visit home by a boy whose parents (Michael Hordern and Joan Greenwood) have begun to worry if he will ever marry. He announces that he is bringing home a fiancée. They are overjoyed. When the pair arrive, the fiancée is black; and there is also room for doubt if she is a boy or girl. The plot sounds sleazy but the play handled it tactfully and amusingly and the parents and the lovers (played by Clive Francis and Peter Straker) gave elegant high comedy performances under Bob Kellett's direction. It has remained one of my favourite films and I could not understand the very severe press criticism it received. Unlike *Rentadick*, about which I had felt a sense of unease during screening and previews, *Girl Stroke Boy* seemed to delight audiences until the press show, when dismay set in. However, we made it extremely cheaply (for Hemdale) and it recovered its costs.

For Columbia we made the sequel to the original Alf Garnett film which was memorable for the close-up chance to observe the detail which Warren Mitchell and Dandy Nichols poured into their characterizations and for the gallery of cameos.

Finally we made a film of *The National Health* – Peter Nichols's stage play which I had wanted to film since the first night at the National Theatre some years before. On that occasion I tried to persuade Columbia to buy it, but had no luck. Later I heard that they had bought it for Carl Foreman. Once again it had not moved beyond Peter Nichols's preparation of his own screenplay. Then, by one of those lucky ironies, I was called to see John Van Eyssen, who asked diffidently if I knew Peter Nichols's play *The National Health*. Fighting back my desire to say, 'Yes, I tried to sell it to you three years ago,' I professed admiration. He asked if I would like to produce it, and we were away.

The movie had to be done on a small budget and we agreed that Jack

Gold was the right director. Peter Nichols made some tinkering changes
to his screenplay and our only serious problem was to find a hospital in
which to make the film. The Ministry of Health declined to help with a
building - shades of the War Office and *Virgin Soldiers*; but we found a
condemned barracks in Woolwich which was beautifully transformed
into an antiquated hospital. The cast - Jim Dale, Lynn Redgrave, Donald
Sinden, Eleanor Bron, Clive Swift and the group of veterans - were
admirable both in the severely realistic scenes and in Nichols's stylish
parodies of hospital soap-opera clichés. The film won the *Evening News*
award as comedy of the year.

However, although the off-Broadway production of the play had had
a success, Columbia were reluctant to screen it in New York. A change
of régime at the top converted modest reluctance into downright opposition, and although we tried innumerable ploys to have it screened on
television, including the Public Broadcasting Network, we had no help
from the distributor. We prepared a television version changing certain
words and scenes for censorship reasons and some for American tastes
- shades again of *Virgin Soldiers* ('We've got a case of syphilis.' 'Makes
a change from the Lucozade,' becoming 'Makes a change from Coca
Cola.') Nearly ten years later it was finally screened at a small art house
and highly praised by Tom Buckley in the *New York Times* - too late,
too late.

By now Terry Glinwood and I were convinced that we must widen
our horizons and look out for properties that were more difficult, and
more ambitious, than those we had attempted so far. *The National
Health* is a fine and a funny film, but it is also a responsible interpretation
of a major modern play. Now we sought to break away from the pattern
of films which depended on recouping their costs in England.

We started to buy properties, not a cheap hobby. I have a vivid
memory of Jack Gold arriving one morning and saying, 'I bought this
book yesterday,' with great nonchalance; being at that time obsessed
with a negotiation for the film rights of a novel, I automatically assumed
that he was talking about a large sum and marvelled that he could find
it. All he had bought was a paperback to read for personal pleasure.
Along with Beryl Vertue at the Robert Stigwood Organization we developed a screenplay beautifully constructed by E.A. Whitehead, based
on Hunter Davies's novel *The Rise and Fall of Jake Sullivan*, but we
failed to move it.

Again with Stigwood we spent a deal of time working on a screenplay
of *Peter Pan* intended for a Tim Rice/Andrew Lloyd-Webber score with

Liza Minnelli in the lead. This bounded forward with all the enthusiasm a large musical project can generate. Universal Pictures, who had put up the money for the movie of *Jesus Christ Superstar*, were to finance and distribute it. Their television arm had had a success with Patrick Garland's film of Paul Gallico's *Snow Goose* and they were happy for us to commission Patrick to prepare the 'book' of the screenplay, which he did with great finesse.

There was a memorable meeting in Stigwood's office when Ned Tanen, the Universal executive responsible, flew in from Los Angeles – leisure clothes on display, gold chains, bare chest, expansive manner. Patrick is very good at these meetings: 'May I describe how I see it?' he said. 'Please do,' said Mr Tanen. 'That is just what I would like.' Very quietly, very persuasively, Patrick lectured us for thirty minutes on the essence of *Peter Pan*. He told us the story. He told us the story of how the story came to be written. He pointed out its similarities with *The Great Gatsby* and *Le Grand Meaulnes*. His audience hung on every word. Eventually he stopped. There was a long pause. 'Gee, Patrick,' said Mr Tanen, 'you sure do have concept!'

Filled with enthusiasm, Mrs Vertue and I set off for Paris and the Georges V. Liza Minnelli was playing the Olympia. We went to see her. We went round. She could hardly believe her luck. This was the role she had always dreamed of playing. She nearly *had* played it on innumerable occasions. Always the prize had been withdrawn before she could grasp it. Did we really mean that we were offering it? How fantastic! We left in a rosy glow feeling we had made a talented girl very happy. There was an air strike and we took the car, returning to England by the wrong hovercraft and finishing up at Ramsgate instead of Dover and having a clinching celebration lunch.

Then we hit the problem of Tim and Andrew. Andrew had (and has) hundreds of tunes racing around in his head and could not wait to liberate them. He saw no problems – a rich vein of melody was, he was sure, waiting to be tapped. Tim, on the other hand, although he looked forward to meeting Liza Minnelli, could see no way of solving the problem of writing lyrics to fit the fanciful fabric of Barrie's play. His libretti for *Joseph and the Technicolor Dreamcoat*, *Jesus Christ Superstar* and *Evita* have taken famous grandiose stories and then applied an iconoclastic, colloquial idiom which produces a conversational, casual set of lyrics, amusing, sometimes shocking, always popular and easily identifiable. To maintain Barrie's fragile make-believe would, hindsight tells me, have been impossible for him. To have treated it in his house style would have destroyed it. Wisely he decided not to write it at all and another grand scheme faded away.

Meanwhile we bought the film rights to a book called *The Bodyguard Man*, a thriller by Philip Evans, a journalist who specialized in reporting soccer. It was set in Italy and told an exciting but complicated story about an attempt to assassinate an Italian football idol. It was a perfect story with which to explore the possibilities of getting out of parochial subjects and into international film production. To this end we also acquired *Cage of Water*, an ingenious thriller by Alan Scott and Chris Bryant set on a luxury Mediterranean yacht and with a Clouzot-style dénouement in which the entire complement of guests and crew, enjoying themselves in the water, miles from shore, suddenly realize that they have no chance of getting back on the boat and no hope of rescue. Months of negotiation brought both projects near to fruition.

MGM were still producing films from London and, more particularly, in the rest of Europe. The London office liked the script of *Cage of Water*, and Terry and I came away from a couple of meetings with a brief to go to Paris and make a deal with one of a short list of approved French directors. We were keen to interest Yves Boisset, a young director of great promise, who had worked on a lot of American and English films. At that time Terry Glinwood's French was non-existent and mine was rusty schoolboy-standard. We moved in to the Hotel Lancaster, long my favourite Paris hotel, and set up shop. Boisset was immediately interested. He had had a success with a picture which had just opened and he talked perceptively and enthusiastically about the project. He was also involved in setting up another movie and it took us some time to work out that his interest in our property was as much a manoeuvre to concentrate the minds of his rival backers as a desire to bring *Cage of Water* to the big screen.

As the chance of signing Boisset began to slip away we went back to our little list of MGM-approved directors. One after another proved unavailable or uninterested and our chances of going smoothly into production began to fade. Edouard Molinaro, who has since had a huge success with *La Cage aux Folles*, got as far as coming round for an aperitif, but it was plain that although he liked this earlier *Cage* his dates would not suit ours. Only one name was left on our list. It had stayed obstinately unconsidered at the top since we arrived in Paris because of the three initials which stood beside it – 'N.S.E.', for 'No Speak English'.

Jean-Gabriel Albicocco had directed one of my favourite French films, *Le Grand Meaulnes*, shown in an English version as *The Wanderer*, a beautiful lyrical-primitive impression of that elusive novel which when it was first screened chimed with the current mood for psychedelia and was a harbinger of many special effects which later became voguish. It had a success in America because of its beautiful, free-wheeling imagery, and in Paris it is still revived annually. I had left Albicocco alone with some reluctance: at least it would have been pleasant to talk to him about his masterpiece.

One morning we sat at the Lancaster in a deep depression. We had been in Paris some days. We had a lot of MGM enthusiasm but so far no director and no return on our investment. Paris, while pleasant, was also expensive and our chance of involving an important director was slipping away. Terry urged me to call Albicocco – there was nothing to lose. He answered the phone himself and it was clear that 'no speak English' was no exaggeration. In his own language Jean-Gabriel can wax eloquent and expansive. He can also speak in a quiet, puzzled monotone which is what I first heard. I hate speaking French in front of anyone who is bilingual, but I am less self-conscious if no one can monitor my mistakes. I ploughed on and began to enjoy myself. MGM was obviously a magic word for Jean-Gabriel and I sensed that to be offered a film as opposed to having to arrange everything himself from scratch was a welcome change. After half an hour of struggle we decided that it would be easier to talk face to face and he came to the Lancaster – a round, dark, rumpled, friendly man with a passion for filming. We managed to piece together the plot of the film for him and gave him the literal translation of the Scott and Bryant script which we had had prepared.

My memories of Albicocco are among my happiest film recollections, even though we never made the film. With his collaborator, Pierre Kast, we worked for months on a screenplay that he could believe in and we could approve. We worked in Paris and London. We talked to actors, we examined yachts, MGM picked up our development costs – at last – and paid for a reconnaisance in Egypt where they had some currency locked away. We believed that we were within some three months of shooting when suddenly Metro decided that films had lost their charm and hotels were what would keep the lion roaring in future – and just when Jean-Gabriel had learned a little English.

We had sat for three days in my office in Wellington Square and slogged to resolve our script problems. Nobly we had denied ourselves a drink until the end of the day, by which time I must have used the same idiomatic phrase 'Oh, I think it's over the yard-arm,' on each occasion – in inverted commas, I hope. On the third day the going had been especially rough and at about six o'clock I became aware of Jean-Gabriel's dark eyes following me as I paced up and down the room searching for a solution. As I paused a very small, tentative, hopeful voice squeezed out, 'Eees eet over thee yard-arm?'

Jean-Gabriel and *Cage of Water* got away, and I regret them.

We wanted to make *The Bodyguard Man* as an Anglo-Italian co-production, a decision that led us into the strange and exotic world of Italian film finance. There are financial advantages in co-production deals and in the case of this particular movie the subject matter was plainly going to have a greater appeal in the European and Latin American territories than in the USA, where professional football had yet to establish itself.

Italian television also provided a powerful boost to the Italian cinema. To stay at home all evening is anathema to the average Italian. On our first night in Rome we waited for nearly an hour for a guest to turn up and I switched on the television. A full-scale discussion on the drainage in Calabria was in progress. Ranged around a relief model were a gaggle of local worthies. An hour had passed and they got no further than explaining and, more important, admiring the model. When the guests arrived we left for dinner and returned some three hours later. I switched on the set and sure enough the discussion on drains – a little more heated now – was still going on. It was not hard to see why going out to the movies in Italy was still popular.

Most of our plans for *The Bodyguard Man* involved Warner Brothers, but we spent a lot of our own money acquiring the rights to the book, commissioning a screenplay and finding a director who was acceptable to Warners. Our guide through the tortuous byways and back alleys of Roman film-making was Christopher Mankiewicz, the son of Joseph L., the director of *All About Eve*, and – more recently – of the *Cleopatra* epic with Elizabeth Taylor, Richard Burton and Rex Harrison. Chris had been an assistant director on *Cleopatra* and had worked on and off in Rome ever since. When we met he was supervising production for Alberto Grimaldi and liaising on his behalf with the major American distribution companies. Grimaldi, married to Silvana Mangano, had just produced *Last Tango in Paris*, and with Di Laurentiis and Carlo Ponti was a highly successful and fashionable entrepreneur.

Chris cherished an ambition to direct and was pushing a script by James Salter called *Raincoat*, a charming, off-beat, bitter-sweet comedy about an amusing, very fat hero with whom the would-be director – himself a Falstaffian figure – could easily identify. Terry and I both liked the screenplay and our loose arrangement was that we would try to finance *Raincoat* in England if Christopher held our hands in Rome. He was an impeccable guide and an enthusiast for Italian food and wine which, it quickly became clear, were an integral part of Italian movie-making.

Rome was still a busy, bustling film city and every evening hundreds of film deals were discussed with growing excitement and complete conviction. Mountains of pasta moved mouthwards, arms waved, lips slobbered, garlic was breathed, names were swapped, dates decided on, stars suggested and future global profits gleefully added up. Directors and producers juggled their diaries, congratulated one another on their perspicacity, slapped backs and shook hands. Everyone knew that this was how the game was played and no one expected the result to have any effect the morning after.

Our first target was an Italian 'action' director called Sergio Corbucci. Warners suggested him and we screened some of his movies in London – full of bangs and laughs. Sergio showed some reluctance to meet us. He later explained that he had had a quick look at my photograph in a 1960s book called *Goodbye Baby and Amen*, to which his wife took an instant aversion. On meeting him I was able to explain that I had a similar opinion of David Bailey's criminal exposure and they could see that I looked nothing like the photograph.

Sergio is a vivid, buccaneering character. First we became aware of that curious Italian custom which demands that everyone should be invested with a title. When you ring the Corbucci apartment the maid answers all questions with reverent reference to 'il Dottore'. No one less like a doctor – medical, of philosophy or even of animal diseases – could exist. However, on meeting 'il Dottore' all becomes bonhomie and anecdotage. There is much name dropping, waving of arms, and an infectious chuckle. Stories of disciplining recalcitrant actors by raising large bricks and threatening to smash the offenders' faces dissolve amid gales of laughter. Sergio also has some eye trouble, and there is an apocryphal story that on the first day of every film he gets an assistant to disarrange a small item of an actor's clothing. Then, from hundreds of yards away, Sergio 'notices' it and calls to the assistant to correct it – so reassuring any nervous actor or producer who may have started to wonder if he is working with a sightless director, considered a disadvantage in movies. Having worked in the Italian cinema for some thirty years in one capacity or another, Sergio has rubbed shoulders with many Americans and occasional ingratiating American mannerisms have rubbed off.

The Bodyguard Man excited him, football excited him, the faint hint that 'Georgio Best' might play the footballer – lots of action, few lines – excited him; but as our meetings became more serious he began to have great doubts about the story. The characters were perfect, the plot was perfect, the action sequences were perfect. The trouble was that they were Italian. No Italian would believe that Italians would behave like our characters. Now, if we were to set the piece in Spain, everybody would believe that Spaniards would behave like that – except possibly some Spaniards: but this was not important. Spaniards would not matter; besides, there were many advantages. Not only would it be an Anglo-Italian co-production. It would be an Anglo-Italian-Spanish co-production. Maybe if we dealt in a couple of French actors – then we could have a Franco-Anglo, etc., etc. I do not think that working in Madrid would have hurt Sergio's income tax arrangements either.

More meetings, more food, and we got near to signing the contract. This in itself was a highly theatrical occasion. It took place in the offices of Roger Beaumont, the head of CMA, an international theatrical agency, now merged with other initials. Our meetings with Roger had always been jovial. Before, when we had argued hotly about the terms of the deal, it seemed to be a part of the Roman charade. Now, suddenly, a religious solemnity descended on the office. As I brought out my cheque book I felt that Roger might be about to kneel. One of those restaurant romances was actually going to be consummated. Money was going to change hands. The reverential whispers sank into silence as pen scratched paper. It probably happened more often in CMA offices than those of most Roman agencies; but still there was that air of comfortable make-believe metamorphosing into uncomfortable reality.

There was no happy ending. I spent a deal of time in Los Angeles trying to interest stars, and failed. We went often to Madrid and looked at locations and had long unproductive co-production conversations. Sergio worked hard on the script and in between he reminisced. My favourite story beautifully illustrated that hard ruthless Roman attitude. Sergio, an observer not a principal, was sitting in the lobby of the Grand Hotel with a bunch of important Italian producers and financiers and a celebrated English actor. They were joined by a notoriously pushy, self-invited American producer who was married to an English actress who had had some success on the screen – none on the stage. The producer launched into a paeon of praise for his wife's art. Even if these men wanted her for their next pictures they could not have her, no matter how much money. Her English public would not let her go. The

National Theatre would not let her go. Laurence Olivier himself would not think of letting her go. She had just completed three successful plays with Olivier – she had played Hedda Gabler, Juliet and Lady Macbeth. Olivier had told him personally that his wife was the greatest classical actress in England. At this point the senior Italian rose to introduce the celebrated English actor. 'I don't think you have met', he said, '... Sir Laurence Olivier!' 'I think I'd better go,' said the producer.

My other quite vivid memory of trying to produce an Italian action movie is standing at Rome Airport and becoming aware of bullets spattering the walls. I was on the way home and a hijack had started. This was as anticlimactic for me as the attempt to produce *The Body-guard Man*. We were herded on to the outside tarmac of the airport and stood for hours singing 'Why are we waiting?' until we were finally allowed to fly away. The film fizzled out in much the same way.

At the same time as our work on *The Bodyguard Man* we had been trying to promote Chris Mankiewicz's project, *Raincoat*. Chris was determined to make it with Alan Bates, but the longer we worked on it the less enthusiasm Alan showed. There is, of course, a reluctance on the part of leading actors to have their name attached to a script which is being peddled from studio to studio, and this reaction played its part; but he also saw himself less and less in the role as we pursued finance. All these projects (and others) led us into a curious no-man's-land of independent finance. Persuasive Arabs materialized in hotel lobbies. Voluble Italians flew in and lived in a penurious manner which accorded neither with their pretensions nor with the well-reported meanness of the really rich. There was a wildy farcical episode when we camped out daily at the Inn on the Park, having been side-tracked for the moment from the necessity of financing films into a greedy exercise to acquire for ourselves millions of dollars which were supposed to flow from oil rich potentates to hungry Scandinavian finance ministers – leaving us swimming in a hugely lucrative commission for having effected the introduction.

In a lifetime of naivety this was the nearest I got to becoming an unborn babe once more. There is no more dangerous combination than ignorance and greed, and when it came to that crock of gold I could summon up both. Although it was perfectly easy to call a finance minister in Stockholm and have an apparently serious conversation with him, it was hard to believe that the rag-bag of 'international financiers' with whom we were dealing could deliver their part of the bargain. Their trump card was usually called Prince Faisal, and at one moment there appeared to be some seven Prince Faisals alive and well and peddling millions in London. Confirmation of these prodigious transfers of money depended on a telex. The telex was always due to arrive on the very first day of the transaction. The small hitch that day was another regular feature of the negotiation. It stretched interminably. Dapper men with brief-cases flew themselves to Geneva or to Rome or to Paris and tied themselves to telephones in expensive hotels. No one trusted anyone else – sensibly. No one knew more than the next man. I never heard of one of these deals going through. More naivety?

We grasped at other straws in order to keep active. Some were attractive projects which we badly wanted to do, others were exercises in opportunism which failed to provide an opportunity. Tom Stoppard made a funny, elegant adaptation of his novel *Lord Malquist and Mr Moon*. Alan Bennett wrote an ambitious original screenplay called *The Vicar's Wife*, a comedy in the Ealing manner which we offered to Peter Sellers with Harvey Orkin's enthusiastic encouragement. The plot turned on a busty young woman's attempts to exhaust to death her elderly parson husband. Neither of us connected this twist with Sellers's heart attack soon after his marriage to Britt Ekland. When the script came smartly back we ruefully realized that it had not been the most tactful text to offer. At one time it looked as though Cary Grant was going to do it playing opposite Rachel Roberts, and we went some way to negotiating for a part for his estranged wife, Dyan Cannon (who was not well known at the time), in a B picture to be made in England at the same time so that Grant would be able to see his daughter while shooting. When he changed his mind we were nearly left with a commitment to Miss Cannon and no movie to underwrite it. Nearly but not quite. In this nearly, nearly history we nearly did it with Rex Harrison, but once again we were foiled.

We developed a romantic English western, *Gentleman Abe*, another of my favourites: a 'last of the gunslingers' rides out of Buffalo Bill's Wild West Show at Windsor and into the English countryside where, with an impoverished squire's beautiful daughter, he starts a series of bank raids. Once again no one shared my expensive enthusiasm.

Caryl and I adapted a Henry James novel, *The Spoils of Poynton*, which we had done as a play. I sent it first to Katharine Hepburn, achieving my one telephone conversation with her in farcical circumstances. I was having lunch at home when an agent, also called Hepburn, rang and we had a row. It is not my habit to shout at agents and especially such a conscientious one as this victim, but it was an infuriating call. Putting down the phone, I went back to my congealing chop as the bell rang again. As I picked up the receiver and acknowledged the call, a secretarial voice said, 'Miss Hepburn for you,' and I wondered that she should be coming back so soon for another bout of recrimination. I had hardly paused to select a few adjectives, even more choice, when the unmistakable other tones began to question me about *The Spoils*. We did not make it with Katharine Hepburn, nor with Bette Davis and Glenda Jackson, who were both intrigued by the idea of doing it together. It was another Waterloo.

We toyed with a comedy thriller written for Morecambe and Wise, but their properly cautious attitude to embarking on another film put an end to that. We even found ourselves trying to sell a werewolf story which we reckoned could be filmed very largely in my house. Even that economy failed to bring the budget into acceptable figures.

My last excursion into film finance was the least successful. It was a dying throw in our efforts to finance *Raincoat*. Optimism preceded disaster. At last it was all agreed. I was to fly to New York on a Sunday and check into the Algonquin. On Monday all that was required was my signature on a piece of paper. The Monday meeting failed to materialize. Thursday was Thanksgiving Day in New York and from Wednesday it was holiday. Holiday lasted through the weekend, a weekend of gloom, relieved only by kind friends in Bucks County who blotted it out for me. On Monday the saga started again.

I was looking for the last third of the budget. The rest was secured in England but it could not be released until this final contribution had been raised. The moment of truth came at the Plaza Hotel in New York. The broker – let us call him Horace – was the same man who had set up the infallible deal which had brought me into New York. Even though that had fallen through, Horace was still on the job. His invitation was to meet a southern millionaire – he was in coal; but he wanted to invest half a million dollars in a movie. It seemed improbable; but greed and necessity won again.

We are at the Plaza. The millionaire, short, in a blue suit and an open-necked shirt, is behind the door. Horace is bobbing nervously up and down a long corridor, welcoming. In the sitting-room are four men, five women and the remains of an all-day buffet. Introductions. The oldest woman is maybe Czechoslovakian, perhaps the madam. One of the others is French, one English, two are American. They look like the sum total of a last-minute, indiscriminate casting call. The English one was a model in England. No, no particular agency, but she worked with some really nice people and had a really nice time until it became really draggy and then she decided to come to New York. She arrived three months ago and really liked it because, although when she got here all her friends were out of town, she made some really nice men friends and all in all she's got to like New York a lot. Really.

I can't work out the cast yet. I'm not sure if the millionaire is the millionaire though the chances are that he is because he seems to be the worst dressed person in the room. I know that his lawyer is here. He must be the 'distinguished-looking' grey-haired man in another open shirt. He smiles a lot. More champagne arrives. I am joined by the snappiest dresser. I do not recall his name. Maybe he is the millionaire? No, he is too friendly and he lives a few blocks away. He talks about movies. He is a close partner of Horace's; they've got a regular little group going. They get together a lot and have a fun time. Like tonight.

Finally, the millionaire coal-miner is declared. It is the Badly Dressed Man. His name is Joe, or Bob, or Bill. He is wheeled over. I am to tell him the story – strictly for laughs. He is not really interested in the story but if the deal is right he says he will go along. I recite and he laughs a great deal and occasionally slaps a fat thigh. The ladies laugh a little bit but only when they see he is laughing first and slapping. Half-way through my tale he gets diverted into a story about a launch he owned on a lake near the coal-mines and girls and liquor and a storm. . . . The investment recedes.

Sandwiches arrive. An enormous tray of club, beef and chicken – no turkey. Instead there are a lot of turkey jokes at Horace's expense because Horace has raised turkeys since he left Princeton. Horace's big thing now is Celebrity Turkeys and Show Business Turkeys. Horace, a visionary, conceptual thinker, sees a great deal of life this way because some executives also send turkeys to girl-friends. Horace can tell how important the girl-friend is by whether she gets a 14lb turkey or a 20lb turkey.

By now the girls are beginning to look a little bored.

The coal-miner's lawyer descends on me. Are we getting down to business? No. He produces a carbon copy of a poem he suddenly felt inspired to write one dark and stormy night down south. The poem had come to him quite spontaneously, as such things do, and he called it 'Togetherness'. He has made several copies and is in the habit of giving them to friends. 'How can man with mortal words. . .?' it starts.

Business appears to be over for the night. The girls are despondent and start getting their coats. 'We thought there was going to be an orgy,' one says sadly. I suggest that there is still a fair chance and, like a reporter from the *People*, make my excuses and leave.

Horace diverts me to the lobby and says that professionalism is very important and he has arranged many more meetings for the next day and that the coal-miner, who is very professional, has personally said that he may come through. . . .

Walking away I could hear the girlish giggles begin. At least they were getting their orgy. The ladies prostituted themselves to some purpose; I danced to none. That much was confirmed in the morning. There were more outings of the same sort to be suffered before the money failed to turn up.

I had to leave New York just before Christmas. I was contracted to appear on, of all things, *Any Questions?* It put a fitting full-stop to my career as a film producer.

Brahms and Sherrin

While I was at Oxford I had two vague, pipe-dream ambitions. In fact they were the same. I wanted to write or direct, preferably both, two musicals. Today theatrically-minded undergraduates use Oxford as a convenient place from which to select the show business career which most attracts them – star writer, star mogul, star composer, star-star. Had I gone up thirty years later I would have acquired the rights to my two favoured subjects, *Zuleika Dobson* by Max Beerbohm and *No Bed for Bacon* by Caryl Brahms and S.J. Simon, and sat back to wait for them to become enormous West End and Broadway hits. At school I had already attempted a musical version of *Pygmalion*, with an opening chorus set outside St Paul's, Covent Garden, 'Come Out of the Rain', and a stirring song about women's rights for Eliza called 'Emancipation . . . it's a big sensation. . . . All across the nation!' The music-hall pastiche with which I kitted out Doolittle was 'One of the Undeserving Poor'. None of them would have threatened Alan Lerner, and I came, like more experienced writers, to the sage conclusion that *Pygmalion* would never make a musical.

Zuleika was a perfect subject for Oxford. However, although Max Beerbohm was still alive and reasonably well and living in Rapallo, it never occurred to me that he would let anyone set his novel to music. I was reckoning without Cambridge. The announcement in *The Times* that *Zuleika* was to hit the stage at the Arts Theatre was accompanied by a pithy sentence stating that Sir Max was overjoyed that Cambridge was giving his heroine 'theatrical life' and that he had always been disappointed that Oxford had never asked.

I watched the subsequent history of the show. It was pleasant as an undergraduate musical, dominated by Peter Woodthorpe who played Noakes. Later Donald Albery staged it for London, and I went from Birmingham to Wolverhampton to see an early try-out performance at the pretty little green and white Wedgwood Theatre. Woodthorpe was still in it, still funny, but more subdued. Diane Cilento was acting, but barely singing, Zuleika. She left the show at Oxford among traumas. Eventually it came to the old Saville Theatre, starring Mildred Mayne, who had been promoted from inside the company. Until then she was mainly known for a bra advertisement on the underground. *Zuleika* languished and died.

However, back at Oxford Sir Max's rap on the knuckles emboldened me. 'So,' I thought, 'Caryl Brahms is still alive. I'll write to her.' As soon as I came down and was installed in semi-permanent lodgings (semi-permanent lasted eight years) on Chelsea Embankment, I checked the London telephone book and there she was, no ex-directory nonsense, 3 Cambridge Gate, London NW1. S. J. Simon, her great collaborator, had died some years before and since then she had finished a novel which they started together and written another by herself, *Away Went Polly*, which I admired. I had already started to toy with songs for *No Bed* and I wrote to her to suggest that I might perhaps send some lyrics to see if she would agree to an adaptation of the novel, for the stage.

I posted it late in the afternoon, and next morning Kenneth Fortescue, one of my landlords, called me down to answer the telephone. I found it blearily and awoke quickly at the sound of a sharp businesslike voice at the other end of the line. 'Caryl Brahms,' she announced. 'Is that Mr Sherrin?' I admitted it. 'Of course we have met,' she said firmly. I doubted it. 'Oh yes,' she said, 'I'm trying to remember where; I'm sure I know your work.' I doubted this as well and said I was just down from Oxford. 'That must be where we met,' she persisted and continued until I weakly agreed that we probably had. 'There, you see, I knew it,' she triumphed, and went on to explain that she would much rather I did not send her lyrics because people were always doing that and then she lost them or failed to find brown paper and string with which to return them, provoking accusations of theft from the would-be adaptors. I suggested that I should come and talk to her about the idea. She could see nothing wrong with that and suggested that I should come for a glass of sherry the next Tuesday evening.

So I did. As we talked we moved round to the idea of doing it together. I have since realized that Caryl is one of those writers who hates other hands to adapt her work for a new medium. Her humour is too delicately balanced and too personal to her and Simon. Apart from one exercise in adapting *Away Went Polly* as a stage play, with Christoper Hassall, she had not wanted to embark on another collaboration after Simon's death. However, I was very different from him and did not challenge memories of what had been a highly successful, close and idiosyncratic partnership. They both had their alternative professional interests. Caryl had her ballet criticism until she tired of swans, Simon his bridge; but their work together was the principal concern. They were both funny and together they were formidable. (My own taste in the humorous British writers of this century is Waugh, Firbank, and Brahms and Simon. I understand the passion for Wodehouse; but I cannot summon up the same enthusiasm for him that I feel for the others.)

Caryl does not have the most logical mind, but her descriptions of Simon suggest a rare Russian anarchy. Together their strange imaginations took off on excursions into laughter using routes no one else had explored. They were unique, and they influenced a lot of writers who came after them.

My own collaboration with Caryl is of a very different order. If she most nearly approximated to an organizer in her work with Simon, in our partnership she had to be the free spirit. My instinct is more literal and earthbound. I am inclined not to allow her the chance to explore untravelled areas, being too sure too soon that there is nothing there to discover.

We started working on *No Bed for Bacon* over a ritual luncheon at the Ivy. I was determined to start 'professionally'. The Ivy meant West End Theatre and it was my first visit. I was unaware that it was no longer the last word, but Caryl had used it a lot during the war and was delighted. We met on a Saturday and I began with an artichoke, another first.

As *No Bed* was to be a musical we had to find a composer. Caryl had done some work with Leslie Julian Jones, one of the composers for the Gingold revues during and after the war. He lived in West Horsley with his wife, Hazel Gee, a choreographer, and we began with him. However, rather like a Ziegfeld or a Cochran collecting tunes from a number of sources, Caryl was not happy with one composer. She was a close friend of the Australian composer Arthur Benjamin and admired his popular 'Jamaican Rumba'. So it was assumed that he would contribute one or two songs. Caryl kept talking airily about a drinking song which she insisted on calling a 'Brindisi'. Then there was Larry Adler, from whom we solicited a couple more. When we went to see him I carried the tape-recorder and he still thinks of me as Miss Brahms's electrician. A few years later an actor mistook her for my secretary, which made honours even. In the end most of the score was Leslie's.

The novel is a warm and witty, anarchic, anachronistic examination of the court of Elizabeth I and the playhouse of Shakespeare and Burbage. The starting point is Brahms and Simon's reluctance to believe that Shakespeare could have written Cleopatra for a boy actor. Viola, a lady-in-waiting, falls for Shakespeare and the theatre, disguises herself as a boy and is taken on at the Globe. When Shakespeare finds out her secret he declares that at last he is ready to write the great woman's role now that he has found an actress worthy of playing it. It was always a problem for us to tell the story in sufficient depth and to balance it with the running gags which pepper the book and the revue numbers with which we dramatized other comic setpieces like the 'Tasting of the First Potato'. We played it to innumerable managers, never with much luck.

I remember the series of auditions principally because it was my first experience of a managerial excuse which I soon realized was a universal cliché for rejection: 'Of course,' they said, 'we think it's very funny, but it's too sophisticated for the public.' There were also private backers around to lead us up other garden paths. At one house we were to be dined lavishly and then, in an after-dinner glow, to play our demonstration tape. Before dinner I started to set up the tape-recorder and by pushing two plugless ends of flex into a metal wall fixture I fused every light in the house, putting an end to dinner, audition and that source of money. When we performed live Leslie played and sang the love songs, I chimed in with the comedy numbers and told the story while Caryl enthused – though a manager told me years later that his clear memory of one such occasion was 'of this tall, fair young man singing away to the accompaniment of a wild gypsy lady at the piano'.

Auditioning a musical is always a depressing process, but we were extraordinarily ill-prepared. Some listeners would preserve a stony silence throughout and beat a retreat the moment it was over. Others would laugh along, tapping merry feet and smiling appreciatively. They would linger to discuss casting and theatres, unable to come out with a rejection face to face. Two days later that would arrive through the post – or they would find it easier to forget and let it fade away. Private backers often looked on these occasions as a free concert at home and asked friends who were supposed to make the evening go with a swing – invariably they grew bored and talkative five minutes in. Ours was a hopeful, naive approach, especially as the private backer was usually good for no more than an investment of a few hundred pounds. They never told us that until they had had their free cabaret.

It was Leslie Julian Jones who first got the play to a stage – the village hall at West Horsley. He and his wife were leading lights at the WHIPS, the local amateur dramatic society. We went to the last night, and very spirited the WHIPS were. One of them, a commuter to the City, was so impressed that he recorded the performance and, encouraged by Bernard Miles to treat the Mermaid as the City's private theatre (not unreasonably as the City had provided most of the money), he submitted the tape with an enthusiastic letter.

Bernard reacted well. He liked the idea and the frequent references to Elizabethan London. He summoned us to Puddledock and said that he was delighted by the plot, 'Bloody girl, dressed up as a boy – going to bloody Shakespeare!' The Mermaid was still an ex-warehouse and he showed us proudly over the rubble with Josephine Wilson, his wife, and Gerald Frow, his son-in-law and PR assistant. Josephine wore a permanent worried look, as though in constant anticipation of the next brick which Bernard would surely drop. She kept her distance, rather like the English lady five yards behind her husband in *Monsieur Hulot's Holiday*.

Inside the bare walls of the warehouse a theatre was taking shape among the mud and concrete, and the thrust stage was being installed. Bernard delivered a tirade against theatre in the round which was plainly a setpiece. He had been to see it. He had not liked it. His neighbours in the theatre had not liked it. 'Couldn't bloody concentrate. No play's half as interesting as how far the bloke on the other side's got his hand up his girl-friend's skirt' – end of theatre in the round. Administration was being carried on in a small hut on the building site and we finished up there with the Miles family, sausages, and some very sharp white wine which played hell with Caryl's digestion on our next few visits.

These stretched into a saga. On that first meeting Bernard was expansive. What a wonderful idea! What a perfect play to open the Mermaid! A play about Shakespeare and a play about the City of London. He retold the plot of her novel to Caryl with delight – a conversational gambit which he repeated on each of our subsequent meetings. He had heard the tape and vetoed our choice of composer. This was not a battle which we minded losing. We were beginning to feel the need for a coherent score and were aware of the weaknesses in ours. Bernard suggested John Addison, whose work we all admired. However, first he said he wanted some changes to the script. He was glad we had written as we did because, he said, it enabled him to see clearly where we had gone wrong. He sent us off to rewrite while he went to America to appear in a remake of *Wuthering Heights*. 'A great man of the theatre,' we said to each other on the way home. 'We can learn from him. . . .'

At the end of four weeks we sent in the rewrites and a couple of days later went down to hear the great man's verdict.

'I'm glad you did those rewrites,' he said. 'It's all wrong, but I can now see exactly what to do about it.'

He gave us more sausages and white wine and sent us away to do more work.

'A great man of the theatre,' we said to each other once again. 'We can learn from him.'

Two weeks later we were back again.

'I'm glad you did those rewrites; it's all wrong but now I can see exactly how to bloody do it.'

He told us the plot again and with rich enthusiasm centred his attention on one particular scene. 'Nothing bloody like it has ever been seen on the stage. Just bloody think. She's rehearsing with bloody Shakespeare and he gives her this speech. Remember he thinks she's a boy and she knows she's a bloody girl. So she gets to this line, "Bare thy bloody breast", and she can't: but he doesn't know that so he keeps after her. "Bare thy bloody breast", and she doesn't so he rips her bloody shirt off and he sees both of 'em and he knows. Never been seen on the stage. Bloody marvellous!'

Accepting that he may well have been ahead of his time, we were beginning to have doubts about the direction in which our man of the theatre was leading us; however, we had one more go.

Returning, we found Bernard in an exultant mood.

'Bloody marvellous!' he enthused. 'It's all wrong, but I'm glad you did it. Now I know what to do. Throw out all your dialogue. Every bloody word! Go through Shakespeare. Shakespeare has a word for everything. Find 'em all. I don't want a word of yours. All bloody Shakespeare's. I want an under-water-over-air-tapestry of Shakespeare's language.' (And if anyone doubts that this flight of Milesian fancy ever dropped from his lips, I have been repeating it without embroidery regularly since the memorable day on which I first heard it.) Bernard had not yet finished. He was having a vision.

'I can see the opening night,' he said. 'We'll have the Queen and we'll have bloody Philip! Both at the Mermaid. London's theatre! She'll come down by barge, sailing down London river; and she'll get out of the bloody barge and she'll sit herself down and when the play starts every

bloody word'll be Shakespeare's – not one of yours – just bloody Shakespeare's for bloody everything; and after about five minutes Philip'll get
the idea and he'll dig her in the ribs and say, "That's where the bugger
got it from!" '

We parted at that, and found out that Bernard, like any sensible
manager, was talking to several teams about providing the opening show
for the Mermaid – Lionel Bart and Laurie Johnson were chosen, and
Bernard earned his hit with *Lock Up Your Daughters*.

His devotion to his theatre is legendary. I relish one irreverent legend
which is told of Robert Atkins and other actor-managers, but somehow
sits more authentically on Bernard's lips. Bernard raised money tirelessly
over years to realize his dream. He was particularly good at cozening
City money into the City's theatre. On one occasion he was showing a
group of City businessmen around the growing building. Picking their
way past the mud and cement, the party fetched up on a platform
overlooking the Thames. Pausing, Bernard drew a breath and surveyed
the picture of misty, urban beauty. Everyone was duly impressed by the
site when Bernard decided to gild the lily. Spotting a large barge making
its slow course down the river, he waited until it drew level with the
already softened-up City fathers.

'Ahoy there, skipper!' he yelled to the barge master. 'Where are you
going with your cargo of ivory, and apes and peacocks, sandalwood,
cedar wood and sweet white wine?'

There was a pause as the barge master picked up his loud hailer and
the City fathers hung on his warm response to Bernard's poetic outburst.
They did not have to wait long for over the loud hailer came: 'Fuck off,
you silly old bugger!'

Before we finally got *No Bed for Bacon* to a stage at the end of the
1950s we wrote our first produced work – directed on radio and then for
television by Charles Lefeaux, a senior BBC producer. We called it *The
Little Beggars* because it was a loose retelling of *The Beggar's Opera* for
very young kids living rough on a bomb site. Alec McCowen played the
Macheath figure in both productions, David Hemmings was the child
lead in the radio play but had outgrown the role by the time we got it to
television.

No Bed for Bacon finally found a home at the Bristol Old Vic. A new
composer had arrived on the scene. Caryl inquired of the music publishers, Boosey & Hawkes, if they knew a young writer, classically
based, with a melodic gift. They suggested Malcolm Williamson, an im-
mature Australian whose orchestral music was full of big tunes and who

turned out to be keen to try a musical play. Heavily under the influence of Richard Rodgers, he produced some broad romantic settings for the songs for hero and heroine, and bouncily effective tunes for the comedy numbers. A problem was to get him to play the score to managers if he was not in the mood. Frank Dunlop directed, the cast was full of first-class character actors – Lally Bowers, Michael Bates, Peter Jeffrey, Robert Lang, John Woodvine and Donald Pickering – and the principals were Marion Grimaldi and Derek Godfrey.

The balance between plot and incidental diversion had still not been found and our collaboration with Williamson ended on the last week of the run. After a substantial disagreement about rewrites we all went to the pub next door for a lunchtime drink. Malcolm surprised me by buying the first round. For himself he ordered a pint of bitter which he soberly proceeded to empty over Caryl's head. The story has gathered variations whenever I have had it told back to me; but those are the bare facts. I still regret not having punched Williamson very hard. As an excuse I can only say that it is not every day that someone pours a pint of bitter over a lady and my reflexes were below par. The victim insisted that she would rather leave quickly than stay around to argue with the future Master of the Queen's Musick – so we went.

It was three or four years before we had another go at *No Bed for Bacon*. This time it was in the Ashcroft Theatre, Croydon. By now we had a new score composed by Dave Lee and John Scott. Again the cast was good, led by John Wood as Shakespeare, with Vivienne Martin, Angela Baddeley, Stephen Moore and William Rushton. Again incidental performances and comedy setpieces came off; but we had not solved the conundrum of reconciling the drive of the romantic plot with the jokes that pepper the book. A pattern of disasters dogs our theatrical experiences and here it focussed its attentions on our opening night.

At the dress-rehearsal the leading lady was in tears about her costume, and with good reason. Robin Phillips, now a distinguished director but then a fledgling actor not involved in the production, volunteered to make another overnight. He is the most prepared theatre director in the world – his versatility covers wig-making, and wig-dressing, dress-designing and making, the practicalities of lighting, scene construction and rudimentary choreography; box office and theatre cleaning are second nature, and his comprehensive supervision of press and public relations, though more controversial, is spirited. None of this was known to the young woman in question, who simply saw a pale young actor promising

to make a suitably grand gown in twenty-four hours. If she was Cinderella she was not going to recognize Robin as a Fairy Godmother. She
burst into tears and went missing.

She was still missing the next day, and as the time for curtain up
approached general nervousness spread. Not only was the girl nowhere
to be found: but the dress was on the other side of London with Robin
and a girl-friend still stitching. Realizing that time was running out, they
transferred their workroom to a taxi and as they hit a traffic jam from
Streatham to Croydon commuters were treated to the puzzling spectacle
of a young man and a young woman bent over a mass of apricot silk,
sewing pearls into it. In Croydon we had no idea where they were and
no way of finding out. We hoped for the best. The leading lady returned
to the fold just in time, having spent the day stalking Croydon in a
successful attempt to control her emotions. She arrived rather too soon
for us, as her first request was to see her new dress which had still not
turned up. Before a massive relapse could set in, the dress came through
the gates of the car park and with a pin here and a tuck there brought
about her complete recovery.

It was not enough to save the play. It languished in Croydon and
stumbled as far as the cavernous wastes of the Golder's Green Hippodrome. There was enough going for it to make a transfer to the West
End a possibility, but no more.

One of the great problems of doing musicals in this country is the
prodigious effort it takes to get them produced. So often it is necessary
to agree to a try-out on an undernourished repertory company budget.
Some musical shows thrive on an air of improvization; but the very
nature of most of them requires that they should have more people,
more scenery, more costumes, more rehearsal, more musicians, more of
everything than the average straight play, and all that adds up to more
money and more risk.

Caryl Brahms and I developed one sideline which helped nudge our
work towards the stage. With *The Little Beggars* on radio (which became
a BBC nomination for the Italia Prize) we started a vein of ballad
musicals. For a 'sort of sequel' – *Bigger Beggars* – we used English and
American folk songs in a story of teenage gang warfare in South London,
which we pushed as far as a student production at RADA with would-be
actors like Tom Courtenay, Nicholas Pennell, David Burke and Derek
Fowlds. We called it *Shut Up and Sing* (echoing one of the projected titles
for *West Side Story*, which was *Shut Up and Dance*). We did not succeed
in setting it up in the West End, though some managers came to see it

and Tom Courtenay's fighting performance focussed early interest in his career.

One visitor was Jack Minster, a producer and director of long experience who, in spite of the number of comedies he had directed, never allowed his features to relax into a smile. 'Jolly Jack' sat grim-visaged through the first half when he was spotted by Basil Dean – an even more senior director. Dean turned to me in some surprise – 'What's Jack Minster doing here?' he asked. There was only one answer. 'Leading the laughs!'

Another play in the same tradition was *Benbow Was His Name*. Our musical starting point in this case was *Sea Shanties*. After its radio production it graduated to television and a brave attempt to stage it at the Worthing Rep.

Of our shows which started in this way the one with the longest life is *Cindy-Ella* or *I Gotta Shoe* – the Cinderella story played out in the Storyville area of New Orleans. A mother narrating the traditional story of Cinderella to her child holds the show together, and the dialogue is an anthology of received white attitudes to black people. Mostly traditional Negro songs are used, which fit the moods of despair and elation that characterize Cinderella's progress to the ball and back. 'Sometimes I feel like a motherless child' spells out her loss of her own mother. 'Nobody knows the trouble I've seen' heralds the arrival of stepmother and sisters. She goes to the ball to 'Swing low sweet chariot', and comes rushing out at the stroke of midnight to catch the Midnight Special – 'Git on board!' The resources of radio drama enabled us to engage a large cast and an orchestra conducted by Peter Knight, who also composed the music for some new songs.

The large and ebullient company, which included Elisabeth Welch, Bertice Reading and Cy Grant, carried the carnival mood of the studio into the lifts at Broadcasting House, and I retain a vivid picture of Charles Lefeaux, a man excellent at his job but with a rolled umbrella in his soul, being serenaded by 'Swing low sweet chariot' as a lift took us up to the canteen. Bertice Reading narrated the piece during the day and then carried out a demanding night club routine. At the final recording the sound mixer turned up her microphone and all that emerged was silence followed by a deeply contented snore and then a wheeze. I sympathized years later when I was waiting to be interviewed on a particularly dull talk show and was surprised to find the studio manager whispering into my ear that I was on next and would I wake up as I was only about two feet away from the interviewer and about to be asked a question.

Now we had a recording of *Cindy-Ella* to give us something we could play to managers. To make a demonstration record is always expensive and often frustrating. Here we had in our hands a first-class cast and beautifully orchestrated songs, and we began to prepare a stage version to go with it. We took it to Michael Codron, who was to become one of the most enterprising and innovative of West End managers and at that time was still producing musical plays. His reaction was good and prospects began to look rosy. Then Sandy Wilson finished his version of *Valmouth*, Michael produced it and we lost Bertice to the venture, in which she played Mrs Yaj.

Cindy-Ella was shelved for the theatre for the meantime, but we were still in love with the subject so we attacked it again as a novel. In 1962 W.H. Allen published the slim volume with beautiful illustrations by Tony Walton. At that time I was waiting to go on the air with *TW3* and still directing *Tonight*. I persuaded the editors that we could make an attractive item by singing the story of a black Cinderella in three and a half minutes, and produced it by stringing together snatches of the show's key folk songs and spirituals, sung by Elisabeth Welch and Cleo Laine, using a split screen technique to decorate the musical summary with Tony Walton's black and white illustrations.

By a happy chance Michael Codron was watching and became excited all over again about the show he had passed up a few years before. There was a catch. He thought it would be best performed entirely by Elisabeth Welch and Cleo Laine. The era of the two-character play was approaching. We persuaded him to accept two men as well – Cy Grant and George Browne who had also been in the radio version. The four were to play all the parts and share the narration. We redressed the script once again.

Christmas and the start of rehearsals were perilously close, and to add to the risk Cleo was some six months pregnant and had to be dressed in an apricot tent – the most pregnant Cinderella ever to meet her Prince Charming. We played matinées at the Garrick Theatre and opened in a record snowbound winter. For the revival the next year at the Arts there was no snow; but audiences were still not big enough. Since then we have done *Cindy-Ella* on record, on television, and revived it at the Criterion in 1976–77. Disney decided not to make a movie; but there is still ice.

Other disasters come back like old friends. There was a revue which Caryl and I were paid to translate from the French. We did the job to the best of our ability and advised the manager who had commissioned us not to proceed. It was essentially a small-theatre, absurdist show which he was determined to tour around the larger Moss Empire provincial houses. He supplied the title *Oom Pah Pah!* and engaged a director just down from Oxford and a perfectly respectable cast who suffered enough on tour not to be reminded of the nightmare experience. The manager thought a reasonable economy would be to leave the engagement of a musical director for this musical piece until the second week of rehearsals and a stage manager until a week later. Somehow they rehearsed and got themselves to Bristol.

I was just about to start *Not So Much a Programme* and arrived in Bristol late on a Monday. They had had Sunday to get the modest set in and were due to do a dress-rehearsal on Monday evening. I waited until it was time for the milk train to take me back to London. Next day I got back to Bristol to do a promotional interview on the local television news, and checking at the theatre found that only the opening number had been roughly run through on stage. I went to the BBC to breach the Trades Descriptions Act, lavishly assuring viewers that they were in for a feast of fun. Returning to the theatre, things were running true to early form. The audience, which no more than half-filled the enormous barn, were welcomed by the director, who stepped through the curtains to inform them that the show was not really ready and if they would prefer to go home they would get their money back. Their appetites whetted by the promise of impending disaster, not a soul moved. Or at least not until we were ten minutes into the show. Throughout the first half there was a steady trickle of leavers. At the interval I eavesdropped the bars and would have been surprised to hear an encouraging word. I was not surprised. On our return the half an audience had shrunk to an eighth. The eighth were even more restless and kept up a movement towards the exits livelier than anything that was going on on stage.

A heavy pall of gloom hung over the two translators, especially as Caryl had a large clutch of cousins living around Bristol. They all turned up to cheer her on and we were to meet for dinner. The wake (good food and reproachful looks) ended for me when I got back on the milk train: but the humiliation was not over. The press cutting agency sent weekly reports as the show moved from town to town and bitterly reproachful criticism from local papers trickled in.

The tipping up of theatre seats is never an appealing sound. We heard it again in our one venture into opera. Colin Graham, who had directed *Cindy-Ella* beautifully for us, asked us to translate some dialogue in a Carl Orff opera, *Die Klüge*, which he was to produce at Sadler's Wells in a double bill with Dallapiccola's *The Prisoner*. *Die Klüge* has a buoyant, tuneful score, but the dialogue scenes were as earnestly German as the revue we had translated was feyly French. There was one other stumbling block – the plot, which Caryl could not understand. It hinged on the biological fact that mules – the result of a union between horse and donkey – cannot reproduce. This was a new piece of information for Caryl, and she was reluctant to believe it or to believe that anyone in the audience would know or believe it. We reached an amused compromise. Colin Graham suggested a programme note, 'N.B. Mules cannot have babies.' Caryl accepted that and we set to work from a literal translation to cut and sharpen the scenes. It was not a labour of love, except in the sense that it was unpaid, but we did it, sent it off and forgot about it.

Some twelve months later Caryl got a call from a friend who said he was looking forward to seeing her at her first night at Sadler's Wells. We checked in the newspapers and there it was, a double bill: *The Prisoner* and *Die Klüge*. Getting into appropriate clothes, we shot off for our première. The Dallapiccola was a tremendous success. The foyer buzzed with approbation at the interval. We went back in to see what would happen to *Die Klüge*. For the first time we paid attention to the programme. There was an asterisk after the title. I looked at the bottom of the cast list. There it stood in all its inexplicable clarity: '*N.B. Mules cannot have babies.' Colin is a man of his word.

The curtain rose on one of Orff's lively melodies, but as it finished every word of the appalling spoken passages rang out with that uninflected, sing-song flatness that only Welsh opera singers can render to perfection. Whatever percussion Orff included in his score was overshadowed by the relentless seat-tipping exits of the paying public. Almost alone, but for a sympathetic Arthur Benjamin who was too polite to leave, we sat it out. We have not been asked to improve another opera.

A subject for which there was no easy route to the stage was our attempt to make a stage musical out of the life of Marie Lloyd. We had already dabbled in late-Victorian, early-Edwardian music-hall atmosphere in a radio play called *Mr Tooley Tried*, in which we were embroidering around a Crippen-like marriage between a meek little man and his overbearing singer wife. The music-hall songs ran through the play and once again we felt that we had the basis of a stage show – with music by Anthony Bowles and a tape of the original songs which we wrote with him, generously recorded by friends who included Barry Humphries. Just as we were trying to set up a production, Wolf Mankowitz announced a musical, *Belle*, based directly on the Crippen theme, and once again we had to retreat and use our material as a novel which we called *Rappel 1910*. However, while we researched the period music-hall material, we became interested in Marie Lloyd and started to chase up the surviving contemporaries who remembered her.

Ada Reeve, who was over ninety when we met her, grew up in the next street to Marie Lloyd and was some three years younger. She admitted frankly that although Marie was universally loved she herself had never really liked her and had indeed been rather afraid of her. The older girl was too brash and too noisy in spite of her open heart. On one occasion when Ada was playing at the Tivoli she bumped into Marie in Leicester Square. It was her first West End engagement and Miss Lloyd decided that it was an occasion for celebration. She hustled Ada into the Queen's Bar on the north side of the square and called for champagne, which Ada had never tasted before. She took a sip, was disconcerted by the bubbles and did not like the taste.

'Drink up!' her hostess commanded. 'Have another!'

'Oh, no!' said the debutante.

'Go on – bloody virgin!'

'I'm not, Marie! I promise I'm not.'

Ada was always looking to better herself and felt that she had made it when she married the stage manager of a legitimate theatre company run by Johnston Forbes Robertson. Recollecting him bitterly she said, 'He had all the appearances of a gentleman.' Thrilled by keeping company with her gentleman, she married him and they went to Brighton for their honeymoon. Showing him off on the front she was dismayed to see an effulgent Marie Lloyd approaching. In her new-found gentility she was sure that Marie would say something shocking in front of her 'gentleman' husband. She tried to head him off down a side street, but it was too late. Marie bore down on them and looked Ada's catch up and down approvingly: 'Nice bit of cock you got there, dear,' she said and sailed on.

Ada had another grievance, which was really against Marie's first husband Percy Courtenay, a racing hanger-on. She was taken to Brighton races on this occasion and given a hot tip by the lord who was escorting her. Courtenay offered to place the bet and the lord handed over the money. The horse came home at thumping odds, only for Ada to discover that her bet had not been placed. 'Didn't think it could win, old girl; just trying to save your money.'

As we talked to her in the upstairs dining-room of a pub at Notting Hill Gate, her strong voice rose to a pitch in moments of excitement and swooped to a conspiratorial whisper at others. Her stage training meant that even the conspiratorial whisper carried throbbingly around the room, and at one point an old Cockney woman some tables away bustled across, drew herself up beside Ada and said sharply, 'You're a wicked old thing. Don't you say a word against our Marie, she's twice as good as you'll ever be.' She stomped out leaving Ada no room for reply, and for a moment the old lady's eyes looked puzzled. Then she shook her head in disbelief and applied herself again to her lunch, which she was attacking vigorously, carrying on with her story between and during mouthfuls.

All the old ladies we met had the same tendency to whisper their confidences: plainly the thirty-odd years since Marie Lloyd's death had done nothing to diminish the aura of scandal that surrounded her. One of the most interesting was Clarice Mayne, who used to feature an imitation of Marie Lloyd in her act. Her first marriage was to James Tate, who accompanied her and wrote songs for her including 'Oh, You Beautiful Doll', and who was billed with her on the halls as 'Clarice Mayne and That'; after his death she married Teddy Knox of the Crazy Gang. Her imitation of Marie was generally held to be the best and she was happy to slip into it. She clucked with disapproval when I told her that we had been to see Marie Kendall, whose great song was 'Just Like the Ivy' and who went out of her way to say what a lovely girl Clarice had been. 'I dare say she did,' snapped Clarice, 'old cat. Always trying to pass me off on some follower or other,' hinting darkly that Miss Kendall's motives in urging these introductions were not always of the purest.

She also harboured a grudge against Vesta Tilly who, unlike Marie Lloyd, had not relished her impersonations and who, as Lady de Frece (when she married into music-hall management), was in a position to make her displeasure known. 'I saw her years later in the south of France,' said Clarice with uncommon relish. 'She was very old, and I cut her dead.'

On one visit to New York I tried to track down another contemporary, 'Happy Fanny Fields', an American who had a success in England before the First World War. She had retired in New York and married a Dr A. J. Ronjy. I looked her up in the phone book and found that she was living on Central Park South. I had little time to spare but I did not want to alarm her with a call out of the blue. I checked with the editor of *Variety*, Abel Greene, who told me that as far as he knew she was well and that anyway if I rang the number in question I could get a switchboard operator who would be able to give me the up-to-date information. I rang and got no switchboard but a very suspicious maid. I asked if I could speak to Mrs Ronjy. 'What about?' I explained that I was researching the background to one of Mrs Ronjy's contemporaries on the stage in England. No luck. 'Ah'm sure Mrs Ronjy don't want to be bothered by a little thing like that,' she said, slamming down the phone. When I left two days later I could see her point. I opened my *New York Times* and read Mrs Ronjy's obituary.

Marie Lloyd's life runs too true to the traditional show business story. A love life littered with unsuitable husbands, and a professional career which goes up and up as personal happiness goes down and down. In the end she was too sick to earn the huge sums she had commanded all her life; but she continued to perform and to scatter money with extravagant generosity, until her death – on stage.

Once again as we thought we were near a production a rival version reared its head. This time it was Dan Farson who provided the competition. It was staged at Joan Littlewood's Theatre Royal, Stratford E15. Joan Littlewood directed herself – it had long been her ambition to do a show about Marie Lloyd: 'Silly old Joan,' Barbara Windsor used to say, 'she's in love with cockneys' – but it was not one of the productions she touched with her special magic. It languished and did not move. However, we reckoned that we had to put our version away for a few years. In the meantime we kept working at it and rewriting, helped at one stage by Peter Wood who cooperated closely and imaginatively with us and with Ron Grainer on script and music, cutting a swathe through the clutter of detail which we loved because of its accuracy but which we began to see was killing the play's theatrical life. At another stage we persuaded Alan Bennett to write a couple of important comedy scenes with which we were having difficulty.

The years of research, writing, rewriting, cutting and re-examining paid off when the Greenwich Theatre opened. Ewan Hooper, whose brainchild it was, was looking for a musical which could fill the new theatre with familiar songs as well as for a London subject. We talked to him about Marie Lloyd and he was enthusiastic – the only problem was a shortfall of a few thousand pounds on the sum required to budget it adequately. It was time to do the rounds of the London managers again, but this time at least we had a theatre which was staking some of the money, so for a limited investment a punter had a chance to see if his gamble would pay off and could then complete the flutter, should he wish, by financing a West End transfer.

In fact we found Robert Stigwood, who was busily expanding his empire into theatre and films. We lost Millicent Martin, whom we had hoped would play Marie, to an engagement at the Talk of the Town (not one of her best career decisions, I felt), but Barbara Windsor came in instead, with Denis Quilley and Maurice Gibb of the Bee Gees as two of her husbands. The Bee Gees were separated at the time by bitter differences and casting Maurice as Bernard Dillon, Marie's disastrous young husband, was as much an act of therapy on Stigwood's part to keep him happy as it was a piece of commercial casting. A few eyebrows went up among the cast on the first day of rehearsal when Maurice's road manager solicitously helped him into his rehearsal sneakers and took away his street shoes; but pop stars do get used to the attentions of their road managers, and the word when Maurice's marriage to Lulu broke up was that he was given custody of the 'roadie'.

Robin Phillips directed *Sing a Rude Song* in a set by Roger Butlin and it had plainly benefited from the long history of rewriting. Barbara Windsor's keenness was a major problem. She saw herself as some sort of reincarnation of Marie Lloyd, which was not hard considering her cockney background, her volatile character and her turbulent private life. As the opening drew nearer she rehearsed more and more strenuously, taking a tape of her songs home and singing them through the night. Her voice, though pleasant and practised, was not elaborately trained and during the dress-rehearsals and previews signs of strain were beginning to show.

We opened on a Thursday and she was fine. Friday morning brought a crop of good notices. Bookings, which were already good, shot up, so Greenwich could be fairly certain that the theatre would be full for the run. On Friday night Harold Hobson was in for the *Sunday Times* and Barbara did her best, but the voice was going and by the end of the evening it had gone. Because of the short-handedness of suburban companies her understudy, Pat Ashton, was not adequately rehearsed, and after curtain-fall Robin Phillips and I tried to prepare her for two performances on Saturday. Both were fully booked and Greenwich, which had only been open a few months, could ill afford to give the money back. At three in the morning we gave up: Pat was too tired and nothing was going in. We decided to sleep on it and prayed that Barbara's doctor would work a miracle.

We had called the company for eleven the next morning and they straggled in, cold, damp and apprehensive. The verdict from Barbara's doctor was depressing – in no circumstances could she sing until next week. We were not sure on which day. Pat Ashton was not nearly ready to go on alone so we worked out a compromise. I had told the story to so many managements over the years that I was to stand at a lectern at the side of the stage and ad lib my potted history of Marie Lloyd, leading into scenes and numbers which did not include Marie and could be played as staged. The snag was that she was in virtually everything. Robin, the director, wearing black sweater and black trousers, would read her scenes; the choreographer would dance her dances; and Pat Ashton would sing the songs. And so this extraordinary hybrid with a narrator and three Marie Lloyds was launched. I shall never forget the look of puzzled horror in Denis Quilley's eyes as I explained the plan; but there was no alternative and everyone agreed to give it a try.

It worked like magic. Indeed one critic suggested that it was the most perfect Brechtian approach to a musical that he had ever seen. No one asked for their money back and our only anxiety was that this was a trick that could only work once. Luck and nerves had got us through the matinée. Would we get our come-uppance in the evening?

There is a famous theatrical story of a music-hall tenor who, just after the war, at the height of his fame was engaged for two Sunday concerts at Blackpool. He arrived and sought the manager in a sepulchral whisper and said, 'My throat. I cannot sing tonight.'

'Well, I'm not going to tell 'em,' said the manager. 'They'll tear t'seats aht.'

So after the first act and the interval the tenor parted the curtains and whispered to the shocked house, 'My throat.... I cannot sing to-night....'

Into the shocked but sympathetic silence came a voice from the gallery saying, 'All right, show us your cock then.'

The house dissolved in good-humoured laughter and the audience went their ways peacefully. Unfortunately the manager decided to repeat the device for the second house, this time carefully planting a stooge in the balcony to say the magic words. Timing, insincerity, something, robbed them of their healing effect and everything the manager had feared came home to roost a thousandfold. They tore the house apart.

Were we, we wondered, due for a similar come-uppance? But no, it worked even better now that the actors were emboldened by seeing that their scenes played just as well. An extended season at Greenwich was followed by an anticlimax. We had to wait weeks to get a suitable theatre, and when we did move into the Garrick the excitement that

surrounded the run at Greenwich had disappeared. The opening coincided with an election, a world cup, a test match, a heat-wave and
Wimbledon. We were not short of alibis: but the trouble with alibis is
that some shows do not need them.

Some years later we wrote another musical for Greenwich, with a
book by Dick Vosbrugh and music by John Cameron; Gillian Lynne
directed and choreographed. Once again we were trying for a recogniz-
able style of popular music, in this case country and western. We used
Goldsmith's *She Stoops to Conquer* as a basis and it proved a perfect
vehicle for Vosbrugh's twin skills – scholarly analysis of the virtues of
the original and an impeccable ear for pastiching the clichés of western
literature. Instead of riding out from London to the countryside around
Bath, Marlowe and Hastings set off from Boston for the Wild West of
the 1890s. Tony Lumpkin became an irresponsible Indian speaking only
in Hiawatha-ese. Kate, when she stooped to conquer, became a saloon
bar queen instead of a serving girl. Derek Griffiths's half-caste was his
first theatrical breakthrough; but the show has still to find a West End
home.

For a saga to match the length of time it took to get *Sing a Rude Song*
to a stage we have *Nickleby and Me*. This dramatization of *Nicholas
Nickleby* we first undertook for Giles Havergal for his opening season at
the Glasgow Citizens' Theatre. Again we were working against time and
had no clear idea how we could condense 800-odd pages into two and a
half hours of stage time. The solution came in our first conversation with
Giles. We were most attracted to the Crummles family – the touring
theatrical troupe with whom Nicholas and Smike find shelter and work
in Portsmouth. Among Nicholas's duties is the translation of French
plays, but instead of translating we had him write an original play and
like all beginning playwrights his first attempt was autobiographical. In
this way we were able to have the Crummles company play the *Life and
Adventures of Nicholas Nickleby* – in grand barn-storming style, with
Mr and Mrs Crummles claiming the plum roles. As an additional device
we invented a miser for whom the company is giving a dress-rehearsal of
the play in the hope that he will see the promise of a hit and leave his
£50 investment with Mr Crummles.

The play went well in Glasgow and had other provincial productions
at Nottingham and Crewe, but we began to see possibilities of making it
into a musical. At one point, when the craze for inflated movie musical
spectaculars was at its height, I talked to Columbia Pictures about it.
Columbia suggested that with a score by Richard Rodgers they might be

interested, so we set off to talk to Richard Rodgers. By that time he had had a stroke and spoke with some difficulty; but he was still due to write a couple more shows for Broadway. He was polite but unenthusiastic, and we retreated without the necessary trump card in our hand.

Back in England we started to think of the theatre again and talked to Arthur Schwartz, the redoubtable composer of 'Dancing in the Dark', 'By Myself', 'I Guess I'll Have to Change My Plan' and a string of other standard tunes. Arthur, though senior in years, has bursts of tremendous activity and always keeps several projects on the boil. With most of our other composer collaborators we have worked separately – delivering a lyric or setting words to a tune and then improving and polishing the finished result together. With Arthur we worked far more closely, meeting at his house in Walton Street, where he proved a witty and receptive collaborator, delighting in a felicitous phrase, lavish in his encouragement and boyish in his enthusiasm.

As the score progressed and the book was pruned down we started looking for a star and a management. We went to America on a forty-eight-hour trip and played to Alfred Drake one evening and to one of the producers of *Man of La Mancha*, Al Selden, the next morning. Caryl's usual vivacity at the second audition was replaced by jet-lagged sleep. The response was polite but lukewarm. Back in England we played to Harry Secombe, and in spite of my urgent setting up of the songs and Arthur's pounding at the piano and his vivacious attack on the lyrics, this time it was the turn of the music publisher who brought Secombe along to snore and whistle in contented fashion throughout. Harry did not see himself in the role so we attacked Harold Fielding, one of the few managers who mounts large-scale musicals. He was enthusiastic and suggested Ken Dodd as a possible star. The idea appealed to us and we drove Arthur and his wife, Mary, to Nottingham to see a Dodd pantomime. His command of the audience and his effervescent humour appealed to them and we arranged to go to Liverpool to play to the man himself. Ken Dodd was a lively audience, especially for one of the novelty songs in the play. All seemed to be going well.

At this time Harold Fielding went off to America to oversee the production of Harold Rome's musical version of *Gone With the Wind* which had already played in Tokyo and London. (The London production spawned one of those glorious first-night disasters when a horse comprehensively fouled the stage. It was also the first time Bonnie Langford burst on the British public as the unacceptable face of moppetism. The two phenomena prompted Noël Coward's famous cracks: 'If they'd stuffed the child's head up the horse's ass, they would have solved two problems at once,' and 'Two things should be cut: the second act and the child's throat.' We have heard no more of the horse, but Bonnie Langford has developed into an ambitious, talented, regular actress.)

Fielding set off for California (and another first-night mishap when his Rhett Butler wandered off stage muttering oaths, not realizing that his radio microphone was still switched on). Arthur Schwartz was travelling to and fro across the Atlantic and it was our understanding that we should start work together when Fielding was back in England at the end of the summer. I wrote to him to ask if he was ready to start discussions and received a puzzling letter to say that surely there was the question of which book we were going to use to be settled. It was the first that we had heard of a second version.

It appeared that Arthur had submitted his own text under the impression that chances of production were being prejudiced by ours. We have never been able to work out if this was on information from Fielding or simply born of frustration caused by waiting around for the manager's return. Arthur is impetuous and given to third-person pronouncements like 'Arthur Schwartz cannot be treated like this.' It also transpired, in a long letter that he wrote in response to mine asking what he was up to, that he had been keeping a diary of any disagreements we had had while working, including one memorable phrase documenting my bad behaviour. I had been reluctant to accept one suggestion and, heinous crime, '... Ned looked at the ceiling.'

Arthur kept custody of his tunes and Caryl and I hung on to our book and lyrics and reworked the whole play with Ron Grainer. Backed by his manager, Deke Arlon, who later became mine, we put our new version on at the Theatre Royal, Stratford E15, for Christmas 1975. In rehearsal some fine character performances began to emerge but disaster struck again when we moved to the theatre. Arriving to light the show on the weekend before we opened, I found that very little of the scenery we were expecting had actually been built, let alone painted. 'I'm sorry,' said the man responsible, 'I have let you down; there is no scenery.' He had not liked to disappoint us by relaying the news before. Nor were there many costumes, and for three days cloths and clothes were chased and found from stores all over London, and moonlighting crews from West End theatres worked through the night to get the sets up and working. For the first preview, a free performance for old-age pensioners, very little had arrived and I had to do my Marie Lloyd act filling in the details from the side of the stage. By the press night two days later most of it was in place, and we got a remarkably good press in the circumstances; but once again the show was in no shape to justify a transfer.

We finally got it right in 1981–82 in a Christmas season at Chichester.

Side by Side

Compared to our other interminable sagas *Side by Side by Sondheim* and *The Mitford Girls*, two more recent adventures in the legitimate theatre, had charmed lives. The genesis of *Side by Side* was a series of fund-raising shows I did with the Dankworths for their tiny stables theatre at Wavendon. (The Wavendon All Music Plan grew out of a dream shared by John Dankworth and Cleo Laine. They wanted to bring an education in the best of all types of music to children interested in any kind of music.) The first show that we did together was a Gershwin concert which established a pattern for others including *Side by Side*. The setting was simple – four stools (Elisabeth Welch's idea: she thought she would like to sit down now and again), three singers and one narrator. On that first show Denis Quilley joined Cleo Laine and Elisabeth Welch as the singers and Larry Adler was a guest. Later David Kernan replaced Quilley.

When, some years later, Kernan was playing in a long run of *A Little Night Music*, he thought it would be pleasant to sing something else on Sundays. In neighbouring theatres Millicent Martin and Julia McKenzie were also in long runs – in plays by Alan Ayckbourn. (Kernan had spotted McKenzie's special versatility long before, when she seemed condemned to life as an understudy and a take-over artist.) The girls welcomed his suggestion that they might care to keep their voices in trim, and when David asked if I would like to organize and link a Sondheim night on the lines of my Wavendon formula, I jumped at the chance. We had vague hopes that a short late-night theatre engagement might develop out of it.

Kernan enlisted the musical director of *Night Music*, Ray Cook, and with Sondheim's puzzled agreement and the Dankworths' enthusiastic offer of a couple of Sundays at Wavendon we set about devising the programme. Julia McKenzie knew exactly what she wanted to sing and suggested tearfully that she would probably kill herself if she did not do 'Broadway Baby' and 'Losing My Mind'. Millicent Martin, on the other hand, was less well briefed and had to be shoe-horned into 'I'm Still Here' and told that Sondheim wrote the lyric for 'The Boy From' which had been in her cabaret programme for several years. Finally we agreed on a two-hour programme and they set to, rehearsing it and working with exemplary discipline. They had a fortnight to get that formidable body of material under their belts. For once in building a revue there was no room for the usual arguments about the running order. All three performers were of course in every trio, and duets just gave the third time to get breath back from a solo. The general shape of the programme hardly changed from the first performance.

It was an extraordinary evening. It was billed as a dress-rehearsal and tickets were sold at half the usual prices which, at Wavendon, were low anyway. Even so, many of the seats were unsold and a bus load of pensioners were brought in to fill them. The girls had been out to Oxford Street and bought little green dresses. Kernan and I had our dinner-jackets. The entire set consisted of a platform, the four bar stools and two pianos played by Ray Cook and his assistant on *Night Music*, Stuart Pedlar, who also arranged the final, show-stopping medley of Sondheim songs with Caryl Brahms.

Ray Cook's great contribution was to insist on the accompaniment of two pianos. The rest of us tacitly assumed that at least the bass and drums of a rhythm section would be added if the show was ever staged on a more ambitious scale. Cook alone realized that Sondheim's music was best served by two pianos – especially as all his scores were very fully written for piano as a guide for his orchestrators.

We wandered into the small, oddly-shaped stables theatre that morning fussed over by Cleo, but not John, who was pole-axed by a violent migraine. Millicent Martin looked puzzled by the presence of a fourth stool – she had not realized that I was going to narrate the show, but conceded graciously that it would help them to remember the running order. We went slowly through the songs and finished with time for make-up and a short break before the audience arrived. It was a quiet, methodical day with three professionals tucking their notes and effects into place in a businesslike fashion.

I watched the audience arrive – very few show business people, mainly the hard core of Wavendon's local supporters and that bus load of OAPs. Suddenly it seemed impossible that we could hold them with a body of material that was likely to be so unfamiliar. Only 'Send in the Clowns' was universally known, and many of the numbers from *Company*, *Follies* and *Night Music* were quite strange, let alone some of the obscure songs which I had turned up from odd sources.

I had reckoned without Sondheim's craftsmanship. In presenting evenings like the Gershwin compilation we had been capitalizing on the *frisson* of recognition, the glow of nostalgia which the famous melodies inspired. In *Side by Side by Sondheim* – which was still at that time called *A Sondheim Songbook* – we found as the evening went on that the effect was of sharply observed sketches set to artfully appropriate music: monologues, dialogues, conversations, usually planned so that each item told its separate story. The simple presentation allowed the audience to go straight to the nub of the situation, to follow the skeletal plot without the sugaring assistance of a familiar tune. Of course they could relax when they got one, as in 'Send in the Clowns'; but they could be held equally firmly by Julia McKenzie's interpretation of 'Broadway Baby', which she had explored entirely by herself.

I had seen the artist who originally sang this in *Follies*, Ethel Shutta, a fine, feisty old lady, well into her seventies, and she brought the house down by her energy and the convention that this was an old star recreating one of her long-ago triumphs. Julia chose to interpret it as a piece of realistic acting for a young hopeful pounding the streets and climbing the stairs to the dusty offices, cold rehearsal rooms and echoing stages around Broadway.

Half-way through the second act there was a disturbance on one side of the audience. The room is long and narrow and the stage was in the middle of one side. I realized that the OAPs were going home as a body. Had we lost them so completely? They had seemed to be enjoying it. Later it transpired that their exit was determined by the arrival of the bus to take them away. The rest of the house was happy and we reached the climax with no further deserters.

I soon learned to look forward to the three great songs which complete the main part of the entertainment. Julia McKenzie found another powerful acting piece in 'Losing My Mind', a Gershwinesque tune for a lament by a bored housewife regretting a marriage which might have been. She was followed by David Kernan, who chose to sing a song, 'Leave You', written for another embittered wife, but to deliver it as a contemptuous kept man might have done. It was a daring idea, again entirely his own, and especially risky because Sondheim's approach to his songs is so specific in the delineation of character that to tamper with them to the extent of a sex change is playing with fire. We learned that it could inflame the audience rather than destroy the material.

'I'm Still Here', Millicent Martin's last number, is a great cry of a survivor. The references are all to the Thirties and Forties in America, but the defiant message is universal; and Millie, who has had her ups and downs, had no trouble in identifying proudly and passionately with the sentiment. I had first played her Yvonne de Carlo's original cast recording and she thought it too slight for her big spot. However, after a week I let her hear Nancy Walker's superb recording made at a benefit in Sondheim's honour in New York, and this time she realized its potential. 'Oh yes, I think I can do something with that,' she murmured, absently.

I realized that there was something splendid and cathartic about these three songs. The tight team of three singers had juggled the numbers brilliantly from one to another all through the evening, staying on stage for virtually the whole night, relishing one another's skills and loyally laughing when they judged that I had hoped to make a joke. Although, as the performances got into the several hundred count, I used to change the jokes quite a lot, there were still a load of asides which they had heard to distraction; but they still managed to crack a smile, which helps the audience share the illusion that the remark is new-minted.

For the last three songs they came up on stage separately, rather like weight-lifters taking the spotlight for a tremendous throw. The three exhibition bouts over, the final medley was a perfect chance for them to resume their former partnership and appear to relax and let their hair down with the audience. The complexity of the medley ensured that this had to be an illusion; but it was always convincing as they mined the text to cap one another's laughs. The evening finished with 'Side by Side by Side', that charming pastiche from *Company* which was eventually to provide us with our title.

One impresario came to Wavendon and was full of enthusiasm; another, Cameron Mackintosh, drove up the wrong motorway and did not arrive at all. As the weeks went by we found enormous reluctance on the part of managers to consider presenting the show, but from that first dress-rehearsal none of us had any doubts that it could work.

The generally expressed doubt was whether this tiny gem, perfectly set in a mini-theatre, could grow to fill a West End house. We tried the Gardner Theatre at Brighton: it was a couple of hundred seats bigger and we thought we could lay the 'too small' rumour once and for all. No chance. Again we were considered too small, except by one fledgling impresario who thought it was a wonderful body of material but could I not replace the performers with sixteen- or seventeen-year-olds because the critics loved welcoming young talent. I relayed this to the rest with some relish because we were in fact a self-administering group under the title 'In Comes Company' (a pun on the money we hoped to make from it and also Stephen's title song for *Company*). A return visit to Wavendon brought us no sponsors and we were beginning to find Sunday dates hard to come by. Chichester turned us down but we found a home at Bury St Edmunds to which we could invite Michael Codron, one of the shrewdest managers, and at that time the employer of Julia and Millie. On this visit we were also being looked over by Burt Shevelove, one of Stephen's closest friends, and one of mine. He wrote the book for *A Funny Thing Happened on the Way to the Forum* with Larry Gelbart, and on the way up to Bury found us our title – improving on a suggestion that, as we had three singers, *Side by Side by Side* would be a good idea.

The theatre at Bury St Edmunds is a beautiful early nineteenth-century hall in warm terra cotta shades and we admired its exquisite proportions until we became aware of a keen, cold, fenland breeze sweeping across the stage and through the house. The hall was not full, but the drive of the programme worked its magic by the end, and perhaps the biggest laugh came during the sentimental encore when the frozen audience saw the shivering singers link arms and sing 'Isn't it warm, isn't it cosy, side by side by side?'

We were all sharing a dressing-room and we waited anxiously for Michael Codron to come round. I am always fascinated by watching tact exercised in dressing-rooms after performances. No one did it better than Noël Coward, but Michael's performance was masterly. However, it left me in no doubt that he was not going to present us in London. He came a couple of steps into the dressing-room and opened his arms expansively. 'Show me,' he enthused, 'show me three more talented performers in the whole country!' This was high praise, sincerely offered, and it was exactly judged to hearten the performers. Through the glow of approbation I heard the sinister words, 'Let's talk on Monday morning,' to the business manager and I wrote off Michael there and then as a potential impresario. It seemed heartless to pass on this instinct to the others as they all had high hopes and Burt Shevelove said he would give the thumbs-up to Sondheim.

He had heard a tape already – not sent by us (we wanted to be sure that as many rough edges as possible were rubbed off before recording), but by two musical 'buffs' who had sat in the audience with a tape-recorder and got it all down. This was perhaps lucky because their seats were in the centre of all the applause, giving a very favourable perspective of cheering in relation to performance.

Monday produced the expected rejection and we were running out of possibilities. We found one further date at the Greenwood Theatre, a versatile but rarely busy auditorium in Guy's Hospital which doubles as a theatre and a conference hall. The charming rumour is that a benefactor left money to the hospital for 'a theatre' and a theatrical theatre was built instead of the operating theatre he had hoped to supply. Again we were a sell-out, and again a gaggle of managers made their excuses like Sunday newspaper reporters and left. However, one backer, George Borwick, a modest investor in many West End productions, was loud in his praises. We went to dinner with him and he insisted that he would call Cameron Mackintosh – the man who mixed up his motorways – in New York next morning. 'He must do it.'

And he did. He joined forces with Helen Montagu, an energetic and enthusiastic Australian who was working with H.M. Tennent, one of the senior West End managements. They were by now about the only two impresarios who had not seen the show and they had only the evidence of some tapes recorded at the Greenwood. The problem of a theatre arose, but Julia McKenzie heard that the Mermaid was suddenly desperate for an attraction, and a deal was struck with Bernard Miles for a limited engagement.

It was an odd nostalgic trip to talk to Bernard again about a musical. He listened to a few minutes of the tape, appallingly garbled on a machine which was malfunctioning, but appeared keen to take us on board sight unseen ('Ahoy there, skipper!'). We agonized a little about the set and it became simpler. We did some rehearsals and then broke for a short holiday preparatory to a concentrated bout with Sondheim before previews.

The first day of rehearsals with Stephen was critical to the final polish of the piece. We ran through the whole programme with him song by song, and his mixture of enthusiasm and instruction – the first generous, the second precise – was compulsively interesting. He is an instinctive teacher, certain, lucid and concentrated. He had doubts about David Kernan's choice of 'Leave You', but realized that there was not an equally powerful alternative and accepted it. He worked on Julia McKenzie's 'Broadway Baby' and then retreated, sensing quickly that she had found her own way of singing it – an interpretation which was faithful to every line he had written. He was a lesson in how to intensify an actor's performance by illuminating any moments of uncertainty with a reasoned explanation of the effects he had written for and which they were hoping to achieve. Most of this he achieved on one day and very soon we were at dress-rehearsal time.

The dress-rehearsal will remain a treasured moment. Not being a professional comedian, I hate to risk jokes before a few colleagues. Millie, Julia and David were used to not hearing my commentary before the audience came in. Stephen had heard the tape and knew roughly what was coming – he also turned out to be a bad barometer, rarely laughing at a joke which was tried out on him, but seeing the humour when he heard a positive audience response. When we ran through before a gaggle of colleagues at the Mermaid I did my usual trick of saying a few words loudly for sound balance and then gabbling through the rest no louder than a mutter and getting back to full strength at the final cue for song. As the evening wore on I became aware of a shadowy figure flitting in some agitation through the stalls. It was Bernard, now Sir but not yet Lord, Miles conveying his anxiety to Caryl and Stephen. I was inaudible. They failed to reassure him and as the rehearsal ended he came bustling up on the stage expressing his heart-felt thanks and deep admiration to the singers. He then bore down on me with a lump in the throat and moist eyes. 'How can you do it?' he said. 'Those bloody kids are working their guts out and every time you open your mouth you put the show on the bloody floor.' I tried to explain, but to no avail. 'Disaster,' he prophesied. 'Sorry,' I said, 'that's what happens if you hire amateurs.'

The picture of the first night is evoked for me more vividly by the diary I was asked to concoct for the *Sunday Times* than by memory. (I was also finishing off a disastrous television series called *Terra Firma* for BBC-2 at the time and had, on the previous Sunday, arranged for a profile of Millicent Martin and presided over Stephen Sondheim's first meeting with Christopher Bond, the writer of the version of *Sweeney Todd* on which Sondheim based his Broadway musical. It was a prickly encounter with the Marxist Bond treating Stephen as a Broadway light-weight, a role which he found some difficulty in accepting.)

Monday
Final rehearsals for *Side by Side by Sondheim*. We are supposed to have fixed the running order on Saturday night, but Sondheim still has

a reservation about cutting one of the Japanese numbers from *Pacific Overtures*.

I am fascinated by the way my three colleagues warm themselves up and create diversions in face of nerves. Millicent Martin bangs around a great deal. Her dressing-room is next door and her adrenalin can be heard being built up as she usually finds some minor irritation about which to be shrilly vocal. Julia McKenzie arranges a lot of flowers and swishes about purposefully in a green housecoat. David Kernan is exercised over his suits.

Sondheim is an expert at word games. Tonight I try a new pun on the first preview audience. 'A cunning linguist.' No response from the audience. It's out for tomorrow. We call the cast at five o'clock the next day for notes. Stephen has decided to put the Japanese number back for the first night and we opt to tell the company just before the first night.

Tuesday

Present buying. Find Sondheim, who is a puzzles fanatic, a Victorian musical game at John Hall's shop in South Kensington. Have lunch alone at Alexander's in the King's Road and see an old friend, Paul Dehn, looking very ill, for the last time.

Slowly to the theatre, which is very quiet and dark and cool in the auditorium. Sit there with Stephen and David discussing nervousness. David admits to an uncontrollable desire to weep on first nights, Stephen on last nights. The girls come down. There is a suggestion of sleep-walking. We drop the bombshell about restoring the Japanese number. It fails to explode. Very quietly and very professionally they rehearse it twice and get back to unpacking presents, sticking up telegrams. The time gets nearer. Millie begins to bang about. To a novice the call 'Beginners please' still sounds self-conscious, but here it comes.

The best fun of the show is to be sitting so near three splendid artists performing such demanding material.

Fascinating to watch the Critical Brethren from the stage – to wonder why heads bow and pens begin to scribble at particular moments.

Emotion takes over as Stephen bounds down the aisle emerging from a dark cavern of clapping forms, loping slowly like an action-replay. His speech is choked and simple. The evening ends at the Double Dutch in York Street with a lot of food, a lot of drink and the first papers, fetched by Alan Ayres of the Mermaid. *Telegraph*, Barber, favourable.... Caryl drives me home. For some reason I am convinced the time is 1.30. Checking on arrival that it's 4.30 I wisely have two alka seltzers....

Wednesday
0900: Woken by Miss Godfrey who used to be my housekeeper. I take none of it in and go back to bed convinced that I have a first night tonight and must conserve my energy.

  0905: Come to and go down to the papers which leave very little to be desired. Struck by the way in which Stephen's writing seems to have challenged all the critics to write more considered, more elegant, more important prose.

Thursday
Trying to pick up other threads. Going to the theatre each night plays hell with the balance of a daily routine. Off to the theatre.... How long, O Lord, how long?

'How long?' turned out to be an extended season at the Mermaid followed by the rest of the year at Wyndham's and then a trip to America.

Our original idea of a series of one-night stands went out of the window with the success of the Mermaid and West End runs. The morning after the Mermaid opening at least four pairs of eyes were firmly set on Broadway. An encouraging number of American producers made enthusiastic approaches, but we were well aware that Stephen controlled the property and that his first loyalty would be to Hal Prince who had produced most of his shows. Hal was at the first night and made canny but hopeful noises. As negotiations for New York started, the main obstacle was the perennial problem of the exchange of actors between England and America. Usually the factors which encourage the unions on both sides of the Atlantic to allow such an exchange are the stellar status of the performer in question and the indigenous quality of the material. Our singers were expert but not international names and the material was not essentially British. I was luckier because the convention that I was giving a largely improvised critique of Sondheim's work was soon accepted as an individual contribution.

Prince lobbied American Actors' Equity cleverly and persistently, and eventually they agreed that if Julia McKenzie stayed three months, David Kernan four, Millie Martin five, and I six, they would let us all in. There were some demonstrations from rank-and-file members of Equity, but it was a compromise that suited us. There was one snag: Millie had agreed to extend her West End contract while we were awaiting the good news from America. The theatre owner refused to release her and our Broadway opening was postponed by a month. As a result, although we had gratifying notices and an exciting first night, we opened in the same week as two other musicals – *Annie* and *I Love My Wife* – which were also hits. Had we opened on the earlier date we would have had a clear month of capacity houses – Broadway had been starved of a single musical success that season. As it was, we slogged it out with the other two shows and were not the blockbuster we might have been.

There were no changes in the Sondheim material for New York but I had to revise my contribution comprehensively. Although the spine of biographical information about Sondheim and my evaluation of his work survived, the narrator of the show has to fulfil other functions. Sondheim's is a highly idiosyncratic point of view. In many songs he deals with a specialized set of Manhattan characters, and the narrator has to help the audience to understand and sympathize with that rarefied world. He also has to supply light relief and remind the audience that Sondheim's people exist in the centre of contemporary society.

In London topical local references were a reassurance for British audiences picking their way gingerly through Stephen's thickly stacked American allusions. The size of the Liberal Party, the Slater-Walker débâcle, Marcia Falkender's notorious Honours List, followed by Lew Grade's *Life of Our Lord*, '... which turned out to be autobiographical', and the ever-present Mary Whitehouse were constantly recurring themes. Arriving in America, it was clear that new references would have to be found. I would have to 'translate' a lot of my material.

Hal and Stephen were anxious that I should find a romantic paragraph suggesting the genesis of the show – on the lines of a group of kids getting together in a barn and doing the show right there. This sort of American sentimentality was foreign to our instincts, so I had to find a way of accommodating the idea inside my own vocabulary. Eventually I produced a mocking paragraph in which I explained that the show was born out of two ideas held by three English entertainers. One was to provide themselves with gainful employment, the other was to do missionary work in England on behalf of Sondheim's songs. Accusations of tunelessness are often (unfairly) levelled at his music and *Pacific Overtures*, then his most recent work, is perhaps his hardest score to assimilate. I got a ready response from sophisticated early audiences by saying that I knew it might be difficult to believe that Sondheim needed any introduction in London when, in New York, '. . . on every street corner you can hear the newsboys whistling the love theme from *Pacific Overtures.*'

The first lines of the narration were the most important because if they could be seen to have a specific reference to that day's news the audience assumed that the rest of the narrator's contribution was ad lib and new-minted. In England the opening line was an apology for the size of the company, usually '. . . Roughly half the number of Liberal MPs in the House of Commons . . .' – in America I had to find alternatives and there was no reference which was similarly perennial. I tried a wide variety: 'Half the size of the Saudi Arabian Olympic ski-team . . .'; 'Half the size of the Idi Amin Fan Club . . .'; after the Koreagate scandal in Washington, '. . . half the number of people in Washington who admit to knowing Tongsun Park . . .', and most effective of all for a few weeks after Polanski's arrest on a morals charge, '. . . half the American Mothers' Committee for the defence of Roman Polanski'.

There followed another convenient device for a topical joke – an apology in advance for any verbal slip on account of being an Englishman in a foreign country: '. . . so please remember, if I do say something wrong, so, from time to time, does X.' 'X' could be switched to suit whoever had made the most recent gaffe. Andrew Young worked for months; but when he was switched from his job at the UN others had to be found. Hermione Gingold, who understudied me in New York and then took over for the end of the run and the national tour, came regularly to see the first six months of the show and record the lines which got the biggest laughs. Once she had heard a solid response it was hard to persuade her that the joke was losing its topicality and potency. She clung to Andrew Young for months after I had let him go and indeed until the show arrived in Los Angeles, by which time he failed to raise a smile. Mercifully Vanessa Redgrave made her notorious Oscar speech the night before our opening in LA, and by various subterfuges I was able to inveigle Hermione into introducing the new reference, which brought a monster laugh that she then flogged with professional persistence long after its topicality had gone.

With a view to Americanizing the text, I tracked down an American writer, Tony Geis, a man of wide interests, great sensibility and a bubbling wit who has a facility for spotting the pertinent topical target and encapsulating his trenchant comment in a 'one-liner'. Nothing dates more quickly than humour from the headlines, but it was a vintage time in America with Carter as President, Andrew Young at the UN, Bert

Lance in trouble, John Mitchell, Dean, Ehrlichman and Haldeman in custody, 'the first person to be sentenced to three to seven years in jail and a 100,000 dollar advance'. Kissinger was on the sidelines, 'admitting that his German accent was a plea for sympathy...' and that '...the bombing of Cambodia was an error of the heart'.

Nixon and Frost were doing their interviews, Nixon supposedly replying to Frost's overworked question, 'What is your definition of love?' with 'Love is never having to say you're sorry', and describing living the simple life in California as 'leaving his house only once a week in order to take his money to the laundry'. Barbara Walters, Pierre and Margaret Trudeau, Truman Capote, Studio 54 and Farrah Fawcett Majors were suitably frivolous names which could always be relied on to trigger an instant reaction. There was a convenient week when the election for Mayor of New York coincided with the election for Miss World. As Tony pointed out, the two elections were similar except that the questions asked of Miss World candidates were harder. We all know where we stand on capital punishment, but how would we answer, 'Would you kiss on your first date?'

He also found a perfect comparison to illuminate the mystery of the monarchy at the time of the Queen's Jubilee. 'The Queen of England reigns but she does not rule – like the Mayor of New York.' By great good luck America produced its own equivalent of Mary Whitehouse in time for our opening. Anita Bryant, a singer who appeared in orange-juice commercials, mounted a ferocious anti-gay campaign and inspired the slogan 'Squeeze a fruit for Anita'. After Anita I was particularly fond of Tony's disclaimer about *Pacific Overtures* – 'This is not a story about foreplay in a Californian beachhouse.'

Our first night climaxed at Sardi's. Hal had avoided that restaurant for first-night parties for some years because of the legendary risk of disapproval, disappointment and dispersal which attends a flop. However, he argued generously that for an English cast a Sardi's reception would be something to which to look forward. He also felt that for once the risk was minimal.

The Sardi experience is splendidly routine. There is no English equivalent. On ordinary nights a third of the room is held for regulars and celebrities – the rest of the restaurant is packed with rubber-necking out-of-towners. When a first night takes over, most of the room, depending on the generosity of the producer or the amount of optimism which attends the production, is occupied by cast, creators and hangers-on. The writers, directors and performers usually manage to linger until their supporters are seated. Then they enter as their loved ones or agents keep an eye on the door and start the required ovation. It would be idle to pretend that, however obvious the artifice, the moment is not a powerful, emotional, theatrical up after the tensions of the evening.

There is a famous story of the near identical Shaffer twins. Peter, having had a success (and a Sardi's ovation) a couple of times, turned up to support his brother Tony on the first night of *Sleuth*. Appearing accidentally before Tony at Sardi's he garnered the applause which was rightfully Tony's from a roomful who had wrongly identified him. The proud author of the evening's hit arrived later to total silence from a group who thought that they had already applauded him quite enough.

We had no such mishap. We enjoyed our cheers, and the notices – telephoned before the papers were on the streets – were good enough to make everyone happy. The party was spiced by an unlooked-for note of romance in that one of my guests, Marc Alexander, cornered Millicent Martin and, in no time at all, married her; and there was one of those dramatic, shallow 'incidents' which sprout so readily from the fertile soil of Broadway hysteria.

For over a year on stage I had quoted an old Broadway joke about one of Sondheim's less successful musicals, *Do I Hear a Waltz*. Owing to a reluctance to buy seats, this joint work of Sondheim, Richard Rodgers and Arthur Laurents, based on Laurents's charming play *The Time of the Cuckoo*, was frivolously nicknamed *Dearth in Venice*, the town in which the story was set. My reference to the joke title had been on the tape which Stephen had heard before giving final permission to stage the show – and Arthur had listened to that tape before urging Stephen to give us the go-ahead. However, on that first night it struck a wrong chord for him and he assailed Stephen bitterly for this betrayal of their long collaboration and friendship. Oblivious of all this, I sailed into the storm just as the evening was coming to a mellow conclusion and collected my share of passionate moans.

Nothing happens bigger in the theatre than it happens in New York. Success, failure, envy, bitterness, triumph, betrayal, congratulation, re-crimination – the hothouse of theatrical Manhattan is a powerful forcing ground for every emotion, and in retrospect I realized that I was privi-leged to be an extra in a wonderful row which had no business being a row at all.

Setting off for New York, I had arranged to stay for the first few nights at the Algonquin, sharing a suite with David Kernan, but once we began our performance routine we had to find somewhere to live on a more reasonable basis. Eventually, through the columns of the *New York Times*, we happened upon a delightful house in Washington Mews in Greenwich Village, roughly the place whence Henry James's heroine in *Washington Square* expected her lover to spirit her away. The house divided itself conveniently. The living-room was a high studio giving on to a small garden at the back where the grey squirrels from Washington Square played and marauded and sometimes scampered across the roof. Of all the happy memories of that house and of other premises in New York, my abiding joy is the lady whom we inherited with Washington Mews and who looked after us – a joyous eccentric, Amy Allenby was handsome, statuesque and eminently quotable. After David left the cast, I moved to a smaller apartment and Amy followed me to its roach-infested, scraped pine and open-brick walls on the Upper West Side. You get quite fond of roaches in New York. Then we moved together to two other premises in the more fashionable Sutton Place area. The first looked like an off-Broadway set for a revival of Noël Coward's *Fumed Oak* and was owned by an elderly scoundrel who migrated to Miami each winter where he had a handbag-shop concession in a large hotel.

To all these desirable residences Amy would journey from the Bronx once or twice a week. She arrived at about eight o'clock after two changes of train and a bus which brought her to within a couple of blocks of her destination. She cleaned and washed and laundered from eight until three with a very short break for lunch. She wanted little: a pickle, a couple of slices of garlic-laden processed meat and a thimbleful of juice. She is (she still remains on call if I go to New York for a longish visit) very thorough and very talkative. Twenty minutes at least, prefer-ably at the beginning of the day, must be devoted to news of her family and her other employers. Ten minutes at the end must be spent in admiring the miracle of transformation she has wrought around the premises.

Amy had two other regular places of work until recently when one of her ladies 'passed on'. After the tragedy we spent many mornings trying to decide whether Amy should enter the old apartment at the behest of one surviving daughter in the face of the opposition of the other. A *Dallas* family power struggle was building up and Amy wanted to be sure of her rights to take away 'what I bin left'.

She had dire forebodings about another employer who refused to buy her an upstairs vacuum cleaner, insisting that she carry the heavy down-stairs one up a flight of some twenty steps to the bedroom. This, coupled with the fact that she was only allowed either paper towels or dishcloths, but not both, plainly presaged immediate financial ruin.

Amy's husband is a Jehovah's Witness, which takes him out most evenings. Her daughter has married a ne'er-do-well who leads his wife a terrible life and habitually leaves his shirts to dry over a naked flame, invariably setting light to them and to the apartment.

In the *Fumed Oak* flat Amy took a dim view of an indelicately disrobed lady, artwork vintage 1940, whose sharp, naked breasts pointed out aggressively from their gilt frame. Amy dismissed her as 'unnecessary'. She was much happier when I covered her over with green tinsel at Christmas. After Twelfth Night the complaints started again.

She has an individual way with the English language. One of her blind spots is the plural of the word 'actor'. She has no idea that actors multiply by the addition of the letter 's'. When Kernan and I were in Washington Mews she could never quite understand why we went out on Wednesday afternoons. 'Where you going?' she would say. 'To the theatre, Amy.' She heaved a heavy sigh, 'Always enjoying yourself, you actresses!'

David's friend Basil Poole stayed with us for a time. He is a professional chef, a black mark in Amy's book. 'Mr Dazzle', as she used to mispronounce him, 'does leave a lot of dirty plates – but that's that chef-type cooking he do.' Dazzle also gave her an exaggerated idea of my importance. 'Mr Sherrin,' she asked one day after they had gone, 'do you control *all* the television?' And on another occasion, 'Does Diana Ross work for you?'

Amy has her own view of England, which she has never visited. It is based on the certainty that everyone lives in a 'spacious mansion'. 'I expect you'll be looking forward to getting back to your spacious mansion,' is a phrase often on her lips. On one occasion there was a variation.

'What is Miss Caryl Brahms's spacious mansion like?'

'It's more of an apartment, Amy.'

'Oh, that can be nice.'

'Yes, it's a very nice apartment. She has a lot of antiques.'

Amy frowned. 'I don't like antiques. Sometimes they just junk!'

After leaving the cast of *Side by Side* in New York, I stayed on to direct the replacement casts and the National and Chicago companies. An extraordinary range of performers have done my narrator's chore. Gingold, Cyril Ritchard, Arlene Francis, the puppeteer Burr Tillstrom and, I am reliably informed, Dorothy Lamour are among the Americans.

In England they include Michael Parkinson, Robin Ray, Russell Harty, Michael Aspel and Sheridan Morley, a rather more conventional list.

When I rehearsed the Chicago company Cyril Ritchard's understudy was English actress Brenda Forbes, long resident in America, where she originally arrived to understudy Edith Evans as the Nurse to Katherine Cornell's Juliet. Cyril had asked for some songs to be added when he played my role and the lady was anxious to get hold of all her material on the first day of rehearsal. I went off to get scripts duplicated and brought the pages back to her – she was thrilled.

'Oh, how wonderful,' she said. 'Everything is here, the script, the jokes – even the songs. . . .' She leant forward conspiratorially. 'I'm told', she confided, 'that the poor boy who did it in New York wasn't allowed to sing them.'

Cyril Ritchard performed with apparent relish and was a charming survivor of an older tradition. He hated much of the material and could not bear any skittish religious reference. He relished a long ago row with Noël Coward with whom he had queried a line in Coward's song 'I Wonder What Happened to Him':

> Whatever became of old Keeling?
> I hear that he got back from France
> And frightened three nuns in a train in Darjeeling
> By stripping and waving his lance!

Cyril wanted the three nuns out. Coward wanted to know why. Cyril explained that it was offensive to him because he had a cousin who was a nun. 'Oh, very well,' said Coward. 'Make it four nuns.'

After scoring a success when we opened in Chicago, Cyril had a heart attack on stage and never regained consciousness.

The Chicago cast contained two of our New York understudies, Carol Swarbrick and Bonnie Schonn. With Jack Blackton, who understudied Kernan, they had done a special Equity matinée performance of *Side by Side by Sondheim* a few weeks after our opening. The show was free and an enormous line of Equity members stretched around the block. I had to narrate the piece as Gingold was not anxious to go on so soon, and it was an eerie experience which I enjoyed enormously. The audience were hanging from the rafters, determined to cheer the local performers home and prove that it had been unnecessary to let in an English cast in the first place. When the English stars took round collecting boxes for Equity charities during the interval they faced a deal of hostility. It gave me great pleasure to watch the understudy cast have individual successes; but also to have a chance to point out bluntly to the partisan audience that the show would not exist but for the imagination, skill, sacrifice, faith and talent of the three English performers who had made it. There is no feeling quite as exhilarating as saying something you know to be true and relevant to a very large audience who do not want to hear it. 'You do like to let them have it straight, don't you?' said Sondheim, looking puzzled.

Beecham to Mitford

One Sunday in Manchester, when I was recording *Terra Firma*, a magazine programme for BBC-2, I ran into Arthur Lowe at the Midland Hotel – much put out because his boiled egg kept arriving at the breakfast table too hard. Eventually the egg arrived in a satisfactory condition and we talked of his recent success as Louis Pasteur in a drama documentary on television. He mentioned that it had drawn a letter from an accountant who had managed many of Sir Thomas Beecham's affairs towards the end of his life. In his eye Arthur was the epitome of Sir Thomas and Arthur was interested in playing the old boy. I talked to Caryl about it and we became enthusiastic about devising what would be virtually a one-man show, although Beecham was so inclined to score off people that we reckoned there must be a second actor to set up some of his memorable cracks.

I have always found one-man shows rather decorous, quiet affairs, though some exert a special magic, like Roy Dotrice's *Brief Lives*, Max Adrian's *Shaw*, Gielgud's *Ages of Man* and Micheal MacLiammoir's *Wilde*. The attraction of the Beecham idea was the extra dimension the music would bring. We started to work on the material while I was in the Sondheim show in London, and went in the first place to Beecham's own autobiography and to Neville Cardus's warm and witty account of his conversations with Beecham. Helen Montagu, who was co-presenting *Side by Side* with Cameron Mackintosh, encouraged the enterprise and we produced a very long script.

Discussions carried on for the best part of two years. Arthur thought there was too much musical material and not enough about Beecham – man and especially lover. Eventually he passed on it, and with his defection we lost Helen Montagu too. However, by now we had per-suaded Patrick Garland to interest himself in directing the play and with him we cut and reshaped the material and began to choose the music passages which were to give us a special bonus.

Patrick suggested Roy Dotrice as Beecham and we took Roy to see Shirley, Lady Beecham, the conductor's widow. We seemed set to go ahead in time for Beecham's centenary when Roy was offered a lucrative West End job in *Oliver!* and we were again without a star. By a great stroke of luck Patrick was talking to Toby Robertson, who was then running the Old Vic Theatre. Toby mentioned that his wife had been pondering a play on the same subject and had discovered that Timothy West, whom we had always known to be a fine actor, was also a frustrated conductor. By now the form of the plan was a Beecham rehearsal, and a great deal of credible conducting, even to the playback of Beecham recordings, was required. Tim West leapt at the chance and Patrick Garland found a stage on which we could try the play out at Salisbury. It was a great success and we found ourselves in the unfamiliar position of being courted by half a dozen managers. Finally three of them united to bring the play to the West End and the impresarios outnumbered the cast by one. (There is a charming story of an American impresario, Arthur Cantor, who had two one-man shows following each other into the same theatre – Alec McCowen followed by Emlyn Williams – and is said to have given a 'joint cast party'.)

Our three brave managers presented *Beecham* at the Apollo Theatre, where Beecham *aficionados* and old colleagues gave it enthusiastic re-ceptions, but we were never able to persuade a large public to attend – possibly because an unusually long excerpt, filmed at Salisbury, was shown on television just before we opened. However, whenever Timothy West and Terry Wale take the show out for a Sunday night performance in the provinces the houses are packed and enthusiastic.

A more melancholy episode was an adaptation of a thriller which we called *Hush and Hide*. We admired the novel on which we based it. We liked our adaptation – so did the managers, the director and the cast. We liked the rehearsals and had high hopes for the play. We opened at the Forum Theatre, Billingham, planning a twelve-week tour and a triumphant London opening. It was a sober experience to see the curtain rise for the first time on the play and to watch each cast-iron scene, each exciting twist of the plot, each great dramatic moment dwindle into decorous boredom. The cast were committed to tour the 'turkey' around England and we could find no way of enlivening it. It was dull and worthy and when it finally died in Richmond there was nothing to do but try to learn a lesson. Unfortunately I still have not decided what the lesson is so I cannot even take that satisfaction from the enterprise.

While I was in America for *Side by Side* I was approached to find a way of anthologizing Lieber and Stoller's songs. These two doyens of rock and roll gave me access to all the songs they had written: 'Hound Dog', 'Charlie Brown', 'Stand By Me' – the list is endless. A formidable body of work, it did not seem to fall easily into the same format as the Sondheim show. However, the acute observation of street life in urban East Coast America lent itself to a 'day in the life of' picture of inner-city behaviour which I found irresistible and called *Only in America*.

I developed it with David Yakir and Susan Crawford, who had grown up in the sort of streets in which we were setting the musical. After the usual chapters of hope mixed with disaster, we opened at the Round House, financially undernourished but with the catalogue of irresistible songs working their magic on the audiences. Best of all, the show provided an excuse to bring back Bertice Reading, after some fifteen years out of the country. Her personal triumph was enormous, and though it did not keep the show alive it has served to keep her in Great Britain since then. *Only in America* is a major regret, one of those shows I would dearly like to find an excuse to stage again with adequate resources and, of course, Miss Reading.

Another musical, *The Mitford Girls*, was an altogether happier experience. Choosing a subject for a musical is a lottery, especially a British musical, that much maligned art form. Gilbert and Sullivan are the best starting point. No one in this country has been as good or as radical. America inherited their mantle. Early American practitioners, informed by a European tradition and inspired particularly by Gilbert's verbal dexterity, especially as they were working in a language which many of them were still struggling to master, crossed Gilbert and Sullivan with continental operetta, nurtured and developed the form and triumphed in it. Subsequent Americans have continued to infuse the musical with that competitive frontier energy which colours American life, and they continue to do more musicals better than the British do.

It is possible to pluck English names at random and come up with a formidable roster of talent – P.G. Wodehouse, Basil Hood, Lionel Monckton, Noël Coward, Ivor Novello, Christopher Hassall, Desmond Carter, Vivian Ellis, Eric Maschwitz, A.P. Herbert, Sandy Wilson, Lionel Bart, Leslie Bricusse, Anthony Newley, Peter Greenwell, Rice and Lloyd-Webber – but the American list is automatically longer and more impressive. Quote titles of shows which have worked overseas – *Oliver, The Boy Friend, Stop the World, Jesus Christ Superstar, Evita* and now *Joseph and His Technicolor Dreamcoat* – and in spite of their success the English musical remains a joke. In America, one way out of the ghetto has always been to box or play games or run fast or jump high; another is to act or sing or dance or write hit shows. Do the English lack a similar incentive? The argument is harder to sustain now that nice middle-class lads like Alan Jay Lerner and Stephen Sondheim are beginning to write their way to success from security.

It cannot be the climate that we lack and certainly not the performers. Perhaps it is an English reluctance to take the music hall seriously. We chose the Mitfords as a subject because they were quintessentially English, and we enjoyed the exercise of attacking a story in which any spurious, second-hand, American energy would be out of place: and the Mitford daughters have their own vitality, which is urgent and all-embracing.

Part of the excitement for us lay in the apparent problems – a mass of material but hardly a plot – although we were also aware that stories that seem to cry out to be set to music must be viewed with grave mistrust. The classic example is the irresistible temptation which *The Importance of Being Earnest* offers to every generation of songwriters; once they tamper with its delicate, impeccable clockwork, they sabotage their songs in the process. And surely Hal Prince and Stephen Sondheim were being watched over by a particularly discerning Good Fairy when they failed to persuade Anouilh to allow them to make a musical around the obvious charms of *Ring Round the Moon* until it was too late? They had to make do with the challenge offered by Bergman's *Smiles of a Summer Night* for their *A Little Night Music*, and how lucky (as well as clever) they were.

The starting point for the Mitfords was an American house-guest with a highly developed sense of snobbery who asked me to tape Julian Jebb's television memoir of Nancy Mitford, remembered by her four surviving sisters. He could not see the programme when it was transmitted and could not bear to miss a duchess, a real lady and two hon. missuses. As we watched the programme, the idea of six leading ladies telling the story of their public and private lives and slipping in and out of character and in and out of song began to form.

We talked to Julian Jebb who produced the television show and he explained that the Duchess of Devonshire (Deborah Mitford) was the key to securing the rights, the whipper-in. It was our intention to make a collage of the memoirs of Diana and Jessica, the novels, essays and letters of Nancy, and some of the reminiscences added on television by Pamela and Deborah. The Duchess (Debo) is Nancy Mitford's literary executor and controls the copyright in all her material. She also maintains easy contact with her right- and left-wing sisters, Diana and Jessica. I wrote to her at Chatsworth and got an immediate reply, which I soon learned was characteristic, suggesting 'lunch at Chatsworth on the 6th, 7th, 8th, 9th October or 13th, 14th, 15th October', enclosing detailed train arrangements from St Pancras to Chesterfield, where I could be collected, and a postscript: 'You don't think the poor old British public have had enough of our ugly mugs?' By the time I made the journey we had done most of the initial reading and had a fair idea of the shape we wanted the show to take. We arranged with Peter Greenwell to compose the new music and arrange the evocative standard songs which we felt would add to the nostalgic period flavour.

I arrived at Chatsworth in time for lunch and was butlered into a small sitting-room which I recognized from the television documentary. I turned to find the Duchess and Mrs Jackson (Pamela) prowling in, both with blue eyes wide open, rather like very well-mannered, welcoming big cats. The beam of Mitford charm is bright and direct, but the aspect remains formidable and the suggestion of a claw, however deeply sheathed, is ever present. They laugh a lot and the laughter is infectious, not empty. The importance of 'jokes' is paramount, and the passion for nicknames, well-documented, has not been dissipated. Mrs Jackson, as I knew from Jessica's *Hons and Rebels*, was immediately 'Woman', the two other guests at lunch had their labels, and within a few weeks Peter Greenwell, our composer, became 'Perfect'. In the course of two letters Debo called his piano playing 'marvellous' and 'wonderful'. He was a little dimmed by 'wonderful', thinking the praise was not quite as extravagant as 'marvellous'. I told Debo that she must be consistent or it would breed insecurity, so she plumped for 'Perfect' and adopted it as a nickname – 'Perf'. When her husband went on record as finding the show 'plotless', I had a letter starting 'Dear Plotless', which has not stuck.

After lunch we settled down to discuss the project. The question of over-exposure was aired, and Debo produced a fat file labelled 'The Industry' (the Mitford Industry). My own theory was that people enjoy the ingenious retelling of a well-known tale. In *Cinderella* everyone knows the heroine is going to get to the ball, the interest lies in the attractive and inventive manner with which her progress is plotted. Familiarity with Mitford myths – which have reached folk status – would be an asset if we could be sufficiently beguiling in our presentation. The two sisters thought about that and labelled it the 'Cinderella Theory'. Debo wrote later detailing the amount of Mitford lore due to hit the screens, including an eight-episode family history, inspired by Diana's book, with three actresses playing each sister, '... older and older. I suppose I end up as a furious old woman permanently wearing a tiara! Oh well ... I can hear the groans of our friends and the switching off nightly of many a telly....'

However, the Cinderella Theory carried the day and I went on to explain our idea of mixing new and old songs, and found an immediate response from both sisters. Pamela Jackson in particular launched into a repertoire of Twenties and Thirties numbers, some of which the family had sung in their original form, others elaborately parodied. 'You must have "Ukulele Lady",' she pleaded. 'Nancy always sang that. She learned the ukulele specially.' 'Write to Decca [Jessica] straight away,' Debo advised; and indeed we had already approached her English agent. 'Dear Mr Sherrin, ... Sounds like a marvellously comic caper....'

Back in London we talked to Patrick Garland, who had taken over the Chichester Festival and was looking for some Sunday night programmes. We thought our Mitford anthology could perhaps be tried out at one of those and, if successful, it might be specially mounted the following summer.

We finished a first draft in November and arranged to play it to Debo, who was by now referring to it as 'the high-kicking musical', and was coming to London for the 'Dairy Show'. It took about three hours. I read all the parts and Peter Greenwell sang all the songs, with which she was much taken. She had very few complaints apart from correcting a few inaccuracies and pointing out a few sore points which might upset one sister or another. She was rather caustic about Decca's suggestion in *Hons and Rebels* that 'Debo always wanted to marry a duke', pointing out that Andrew Devonshire had been a second son when she married him.

She followed up with a letter the next day:

... Thank you very much indeed for yesterday's memorable afternoon.... I've no idea what Decca will make of it, I never have. ... I've had another thought, my mother never said 'Do admit', it was us who started that – silly fools. Oh dear, I did love the music.

I'm in an urching mood ...
An anti-churching mood
That's the mood I'm in!
I'm urching, not churching,
I'm in a researching mood....

[At that time we were including 'I'm in a Dancing Mood', which we later cut; it had been a Mitford house parody.]

Get marvellous Mr Greenwell to sing that. THANKS again,

Debo.

I sent copies of the text-so-far to all the sisters. ('Woman won't open it. Too busy feeding those chickens.') By this time we had agreement in principle from Jessica, subject to a television option on her book, which looked like lapsing at any moment. We took a chance on that.

At about this time we played to Patrick, who had lost one play and decided to put ours on as a full production at the Chichester Festival for the main season. Things were moving almost too fast for us. Together Caryl and I had worked on various television shows for a couple of decades and separately we had spent years trying to get musicals written and staged. We had started on this one in October and by Christmas it seemed we had a production scheduled for that summer.

We arranged another play-through for the European sisters just before Christmas. Diana Mosley was coming to London and letters arrived from her and Debo on the same day. 'I think Diana might be able to snatch the time to see and hear *The Girls* on December 10th, latish afternoon if you could put it on again? [I love 'put it on'.] And Pam says if Diana comes she will ... if wonderful Mr Greenwell and you have got the time?'

Lady Mosley was due in London because she had promised to do a TV interview on Henry Williamson; I pointed out that we had used a phrase of hers from the television documentary as a song title, '... I laughed at the idea of a sequence of songs ... "Why *do* people fall in love?" Did I really say that? It must have been in connection with Nancy, who did fall in love with rather strange people; at least so I thought.'

Two or three days before the day appointed Oswald Mosley died. I was interviewing Pamela Jackson about the television version of *Love in a Cold Climate* on a radio programme that morning and we heard the news after the broadcast. She was an enchanting guest, treating the BBC studio like a dinner table, oblivious of the microphone and engaging guests on her right and left in polite succession, showing equal interest in the odd range, from A.L. Rowse to Clive Powell, a young footballer, and his manager. She told an unexpected story of trying to introduce her obscure Swiss breed of hens, Alpenzellers, to this country. The Ministry of Agriculture refused an import permit so, she explained with a wicked smile, 'In the end I just brought in a dozen eggs and hatched them!'

Mosley's death meant a postponement of our audition until well after Christmas. I went to America for a few days to set up a revue I was directing in Connecticut – Christmas dinner at Sardi's, half-empty, and no special menu until Anthony Hopkins at the next table insisted on plum pudding and we shared it. When I came back we prepared for the final test.

It was an uncanny feeling reading all six Mitford sisters aloud to three of the survivors and braying like six demented impersonations of Edith Evans in a hopeful approximation of 'the Mitford Voice'. They followed their scripts carefully and only really relaxed when 'Perfect' Peter Greenwell launched into their favourite songs. It was not made easier by the fact that Lady Mosley and Mrs Jackson are, in one case very and in the other quite, deaf; but they laughed at the familiar jokes and it became clear as we ploughed on that we were winning. Lady Mosley wanted a stronger case made for her parents. Mrs Jackson wanted a reference to John Betjeman corrected. Basically they were happy with it. Debo marshalled them out with, 'Come on, Mrs Nozel Wurzle,' another nickname, 'they're bored with us, let's bugger off.' She insisted that we got pretty girls to play them. 'We may have been dull, but we certainly weren't dowdy!' We taped the entire afternoon for Jessica and sent it off for her approval, which came back smartly. By the time I left for rehearsals in America we had everything but a cast.

I heard from Lady Mosley just before leaving:

> It is so kind of you to think of ways round, so that Muv gets anyway part of her due. . . . Last night my son Alexander, who has seen *Love in a C.C.* which I have not, made a rather good point. He says that in Nancy's novels Uncle M. is eccentric and funny but he is not a buffoon. He says the whole tension in the novels, which makes them something a bit more than simply 'funny', is a result of the fact that the children were in fact quite afraid of him, as well as being amused by him. Decca of course makes him a buffoon and rather a nasty one at that. . . . I remember Alexander was asked to stay with him up at Redesdale and I asked him, 'How did you know which was Farve on

Newcastle Station?' And Alexander, aged about twelve, replied, 'Well, I looked and then I saw a noble old gentlemen and I knew it must be Farve.' I told Andrew Devonshire this ... and he said, 'A perfect description of your father.'

I felt such a fraud the other day, poor old black crow [she was in deep mourning], at the idea of being 'beautiful' [the text made constant reference] ... It made me laugh and cry. The song 'Some enchanted evening, you will see a stranger across a crowded room' [the song is not in *The Mitford Girls*] ... always reminds me of Oswald Mosley. It was at a ball at Philip Sassoon's house.

With so many thanks for Muv.

I collected the fourth surviving Mitford sister, Jessica, in New York. Like all Mitfords she was exactly on time. Indeed she had arrived at 1 Fifth Avenue before the one o'clock date on which we had agreed, and I was further delayed as I got out of my taxi by seeing an elderly man knocked down by a car. He was dazed rather than hurt and had only walked a few steps from his doctor's office, so I pushed him back inside and hurried to the restaurant. Once again the Mitford obsession with the popular songs of their adolescence surfaced over lunch. I was treated to a spirited 'Brother, can you spare a dime?'; and Decca's greatest enthusiasm was reserved for my suggestion that her voice was marginally better than Debo's (not difficult). 'Compared with Debo you are Callas,' I said rashly. The news winged its way to Chatsworth by the next post as though a childhood argument was being carried to victory fifty years on. Decca now often signs herself 'Your loving Callas' in letters to Debo.

The clockwork of *The Mitford Girls* was a delicate piece of machinery involving long musical rehearsals because of the number of songs which were treated to intricate harmonies for the six girls' voices. We were lucky to find six actresses all of whom were potential or actual leading ladies. Patricia Hodge was Nancy; Julia Sutton, Pamela; Patricia Michael, Diana; Colette Gleeson, Unity; Liz Robertson, Decca; and Gay Soper, Deborah. Oz Clarke, actor and wine expert, played most of the men, sprinkling the season with wine tastings and inspiring the girls to order house wine on arrival at any restaurant table lest their constant search for expensive vintages should ruin their bank balances. ester's summer festival season breeds a more leisurely, expansive mood than most theatres. Two plays are rehearsed simultaneously in rural surroundings. Cut off from London, except perhaps at weekends, the players become a close knit unit more quickly than they do when they rehearse in town and go home to families at the end of the day's work.

The play opened at the beginning of June, and was a perfect Chichester choice. West Sussex enjoys its summer theatre: black ties and long gowns parade in the parklands surrounding the theatre. Mitfords came in stages. Jessica planned to bring a large party of 'country relatives' in the second week. Debo was on parade for the first preview. The Duke of Devonshire had announced his intention of staying away: he preferred *Anyone for Denis*, in which he was mentioned, to an evening of Mitfordolatry. Interviewing him on *Midweek*, I managed to get through a whole hour without mentioning the Mitfords, a record which pleased him enormously. Later he dismissed the play, which he had been allowed to read, as 'plotless' and rechristened it *La Triviata*. However, in one interview he confessed to a great liking for Decca and her books – which surprised her: 'I could scarcely believe it – always thought he loathed me.... I have long yearned to review his book *Parktop: A Romance of the Turf*. It is up amongst my favourite books such as *Modern Pigsticking*, published in 1913, which begins, "It is now some twenty years since Baden-Powell published his charming brochure on pigsticking ..." and goes on from there. Dedication: "To my Mother."'

I had had special badges made for the cast: 'I am a Mitford Girl' they proclaimed, and we distributed them without regard to sex. Four special ones were created for the surviving sisters saying 'I Really am a Mitford Girl.' They wore them loyally, to my surprise, on their visits to the theatre (Diana: 'I wore my "badge" which made my companions shun me (shyness) but nobody noticed it because my clothes were black and white so my bold gesture was wasted.'). For Devonshire and Bob Treuhaft, Decca's husband, two more badges announced, 'I'm Married to a *real* Mitford Girl.' I don't think the Duke wore his, even in the intimacy of Chatsworth.

Debo categorized the first preview audience – almost entirely local – as 'her people': largely Women's Institute. She was more suspicious of the first night crowd two nights later, which included a generous sprinkling of Londoners and critics. On this occasion she came with Pamela, who was still happily reliving the old songs.

With Decca's visit the element of controversy which surrounded the show came into focus. What we had attempted was an essay in style. The essay was designed to chart in their own words the development of a rich, eccentric English country family in the Twenties and Thirties –

six girls who had wilfully and often wittily gone their very different ways. It had seemed to us unnecessary to editorialize or to judge the girls and the events in which their lives became entangled. Our main focus was on the characters of Nancy and Jessica. Patricia Hodge lent exquisite elegance and wit to her Nancy: beautiful, sharp, poised and precise, switching effortlessly to suggest the heavier step of her mother.

The real Decca shared the doubts felt by those who wanted us to make a more political statement of values which we assumed were obvious. To the *Sunday Times* readers she confided her doubts. She characterized the Chichester audience in her mother's words as 'a youngish crowd in their early seventies', and went on to say that she found the lack of dimension in our sketch of her first husband, Esmond Romilly, troubling; she objected to what she saw as a romanticization of Hitler in his brief moment on the stage, and she was critical of our bare statement of her sister Diana's marriage to Oswald Mosley.

I had a three-hour session with her at our hotel in Chichester, during which it was interesting to watch the technique of a self-proclaimed 'muck-raker'. I had noticed that in all her best pieces she found a dramatic structure, a hook on which to hang her investigations, a per-suasive way of presenting her argument. In this interview she deputed the job of questioning me to Polly Toynbee, a pretty young reporter and long-time family friend, rather more critical of the play than Decca herself. Decca took no notes and, I think, recorded nothing. She listened with great concentration and hardly intervened except testily on occa-sions when she sensed that little Polly was overplaying her hand. The technique lent an objectivity to the article which was very effective. Caryl and I happily conceded the point about Esmond Romilly, and we in-cluded a paragraph from the peroration at the end of *Boadilla* – his account of his experiences in the Spanish Civil War – at the climax of our play which added greatly to its poignancy.

I am still surprised by the need to underline the revulsion against fascism which most critics who disliked the play have expressed. It strikes me as naive and superfluous. However (in a triumphant mixed metaphor) we had started a hare which became a red herring up which we were unable to bottle! The play filled Chichester and moved to London. At the Globe it had a rapturous first night, a divided press and an uncomfortable rumour that it was 'that play about Hitler'. Two sentences spoken by a supporting character who was on the stage for less than a minute evoked that label. However, I suppose that if you embark on an exercise in style and your pyrotechnics allow the audience time to look elsewhere, then you must accept that you have not lavished enough craft on the piece to justify your original hopes.

To close this theatrical chapter on a more amused note, I am an inveterate collector of foyer remarks and I offer these personally monitored examples. I started taking the hobby seriously in the 1950s, when an American matron at Stratford, after a performance of *Julius Caesar*, turned to her companion in awe and intoned, 'That Brutus! Was he noble?'

Then there was Noël Coward in New York with Claudette Colbert after Arthur Miller's autobiographical play, *After the Fall*. She could sense an impending indiscretion and sought to put as many playgoers as possible between them. This only made it worse as Coward had to shout, 'I preferred *This Is Your Life* when it was a television programme!'

Then there was one elderly impresario hissing to another as they left the first matinée of Osborne's *The Entertainer* with Olivier at the Royal Court: 'If that's a play, I'm Mistinguett!'

Burt Shevelove reported a Knightsbridge blue-rinse lady at the interval of Stephen Sondheim's *Company* at Her Majesty's Theatre. She approached the barmaid urgently. 'How long is the second act?' she inquired. 'About an hour, madam.' 'Oh,' she considered the prospect, 'I think I'd rather go home and watch the King of Denmark's funeral.'

More recently I overheard two men at the National Theatre discussing a forthcoming play at the Haymarket. 'It's bound to be good,' said one, an incredible optimist. 'It's by the man who writes Mrs Thatcher's speeches.'

Performing

To start a career as an occasional performer at thirty-five is to self-inflict all sorts of indignities, and award yourself all sorts of bonuses and fringe benefits. One small bonus is that journalists no longer feel obliged to offer their readers a physical description of their subject. They yearn to supply vivid sketches when capturing producers, directors or other back-room boys on the page. While I was involved in *TW3* I was variously described as a 'fat, fair, yoghurt-eating west countryman'; 'tall, with the shoulders of a rugby forward'; 'blond and bulky'; and, most puzzling, 'small, dark and darting'. Putting your face on the screen stops all this, although recently a couple of radio series have reactivated the urge. Two profiles have just landed on my desk. Ms Lynn Barber thus: '. . . Actually he is not *bad* looking – tall and rather gangling with a wicked Cheshire cat grin – though he does wear strangely hideous clothes . . .'; and Ms Maureen Cleave thus: '. . . He is a very tall man of fifty with a barrel-chest that looks good in a waistcoat and watch and chain. Got up in three-piece suits, he looks the last word in suavity. . . .'

The change of life into occasional performer was wrought for me by Tony Smith, a producer at the BBC who had come late to the *Tonight* team, being of that generation who, when schoolboys, had announced their ambition not to be engine drivers, but to be editors of *Tonight*. Tony both cherished the ambition and achieved it. He also devised a series called *Your Witness* in which distinguished legal luminaries debated topics of public concern, calling and cross-examining witnesses in front of a studio jury under the presiding eye of Ludovic Kennedy. Stretching his point a long way, he invited the vestige of barrister that lingered in me to debate censorship with Sir John Hobson, a previous

Tory Attorney-General. The programme lasted ninety minutes and I enjoyed it no end.

My witnesses included Michael Foot, Ben Levy, Mervyn Stockwood (Bishop of Southwark), Anthony Storr the psychiatrist, and Ben Daniel, a ten-year-old whose parents (Dad, a parson) had allowed him to read *Lady Chatterley's Lover*. Ben was happy to give evidence that he had not been corrupted. He knew what he meant and was very cool, collected and lucid. Sir John wisely did not cross-examine him. Sir John's own witnesses included the romantic novelist Denise Robbins and Donald Wolfit, and it was exhilarating to sense the partisanship generated on both sides in the couple of hours of preparation, and to feel the needle which the brief confrontations produced. We won, but the triumph was obliterated when Sir John smiled generously in defeat and I kept what I thought was a becomingly modest straight face. Most viewers who had not attended to the announcement of the score assumed that I was a glum loser and Sir John a gloating victor. Sadly, he suffered a brain haemorrhage and died a few weeks later.

Tony Smith then set about finding another vehicle for his discovery. We embarked on a Saturday night series in the old late-night spot. He called it *Quiz of the Week*. A team of *Private Eye* regulars, groupies or sympathizers were pitted against various generic groups. On the pilot, Margaret Thatcher, in acid lime-green, distinguished herself by getting the most correct answers and by making the smallest number of jokes. After one happy series we returned for a second. The first programme coincided with the declaration of a Conservative victory in the General Election, which put Ted Heath in power. As a result the *Private Eye* team, capitalizing on his musical prowess, paid innumerable compliments to the Prime Minister's organ, and although Norman St John Stevas who was on the other team strove manfully to keep a straight face, and succeeded, both he and I are sure that this ill-fated appearance on a frivolous programme in the very middle of the Cabinet-making process set back his hopes of promotion into Government by several years. In 1981 on *Friday Night, Saturday Morning*, in one of the most enjoyable interviews I have ever done, I reminded Norman of the previous débâcle. He expressed the hope that the return engagement would not have a similar effect. Mrs Thatcher sacked him a week later.

Back on *Quiz of the Week*, on the second show Ted Heath's organ was forgotten in favour of Lord Hill's wife. Lord Hill was currently pretender to the chairmanship of the Governors of the BBC. We lasted very few more weeks.

Acting is something I have not done since Oxford – apart from an enjoyable day, just before going to America, playing the late Noël Coward in a two-minute scene opposite the late Alan Badel, who was playing the late Michael Arlen. The director was exactly right when he rang to ask me to do it 'rather than a proper actor'. I have perhaps listed too many 'enjoyable' experiences in this book; a humiliating one was to be nominated for a Tony on Broadway (mercifully I did not win in it as 'Best Featured Actor' in *Side by Side by Sondheim*. The winner, a bright, particular talent, was the late Lenny Baker.

Side by Side provided my first prolonged exposure to audiences, and a year and a half at the Mermaid, at Wyndham's Theatre in London and at the Music Box on Broadway gave me a new chance to observe them. Sybil Thorndike used to say that there was nothing you could do to predict an audience. They bring their own varied and corporate life into each theatre which they jointly and severally enter. 'Some nights', Dame Sybil confided, 'they're porridge; some nights – electricity!'

It came as a shock to discover just how much I could see from the stage. In the stalls I could pick out a face as far back as Row J. I could spot a sleeping head in Row M or N, especially if it was thrown back in abandon rather than cunningly posed forward. In the circle, or mezzanine as they call it in America, only the front row is clearly discernible, but that was enough to witness one death in New York, completed by the removal of body and return of companions to see the rest of the show. You pay too much to waste a ticket in New York. *Death in the Mezzanine* sounds like a good title for a theatrical thriller.

It is the front rows of the stalls that provide the most consistent entertainment for the alert performer. Some people look up expectantly, seeking a personal communion with the players or, in occasional cases, they treat the evening as an introduction to be followed up after the performance ('I am the youngish, not unattractive fellow who was sitting in the front row last night wearing a brown shirt and white jeans. I live with my mother in New Jersey and would love to meet you for supper and to discuss the show, which I have seen eight times'). Others look resolutely down, too shy to catch an actor's eye, denying themselves more than an up-to-the-knee-level view of the show – not very good value in our case, as both women wore full-length dresses.

Then there were couples with questing hands who convinced me that they believed in a mysterious insulating fourth wall between them and the stage. Hands reassuring, hands massaging, hands exploring, hands off on ambitious voyages of discovery around the body of a partner. I watched with fascination one night as a very old gentleman, I should guess about eighty, sat down in the front row, flanked by two 'girls' of around sixty. He held hands, or rather a hand, restlessly and relentlessly with each of them throughout both acts. Millicent Martin had a theory that one was his mistress and the other his blind wife, an explanation which at least seemed to fit the observable facts. Occasionally front rows talked animatedly, just as they might in their living-rooms in front of Parkinson or Robin Day. At the end of one of David Kernan's more lyrical songs, one which he delivered with considerable quiet charm, I saw an old lady nudge her neighbour as the last lovely note died away. She was pointing at his trouser legs with some animation. 'Look,' she said in a clear, bright voice, 'turn-ups are coming back.'

It is easier to understand the unself-conscious behaviour of the middle rows. One night I spotted Gregory Peck sitting bolt upright in an aisle seat, roughly Row F, concentrating with impeccable courtesy on the entertainment. Beside him sat a young girl, perhaps his daughter, equally engrossed. Next to her I could see a lady I identified as Veronique, Mrs Peck, a dark, attractive Frenchwoman, going through all the agonies of trying to stay awake. Jet lag, I assumed, judging by some of my own theatre-going experiences.

As each evening started, I made a furtive check of the audience while my three colleagues were singing their heads off. Sad faces, experienced faces, bored or disgruntled faces; faces of unwilling husbands dragged there by purposeful wives; faces already composed for sleep and looking forward to it as the lights went down and the seductive music started.

This was the time when my eyes went off on a celebrity hunt. Most celebrities arrange to buy their seats through the management, so they can usually be spotted somewhere between A and J. Robert Redford spoiled the game by lurking in the back row of the stalls. In England the presence of a royal person always makes a theatre audience slightly self-conscious. We had Princess Margaret and Princess Alexandra on separate occasions, and although both enjoyed the show and took pains to show their enthusiasm, half the house inevitably spent the evening craning necks to check on the royal reaction. This divided attention diminishes audience response dramatically. The only Americans whom I have seen have a similar effect are Henry Kissinger and Jackie Onassis.

Great ladies of the theatre – legitimate, like the Hepburns and Colberts, or musical, like the Mermans, Channings and Mary Martins – bring their own brand of extra excitement to the audience of a musical. The ticket buyer feels he has been given a bonus when one of them is in the house. Burt Reynolds, on the other hand, escorting Sally Field looked thoroughly preoccupied and shrouded in a spreading gloom throughout the proceedings. I hope he enjoyed the show more than his face did.

One of the most attractive sensations is to watch a genuinely miserable face relax as the evening goes on. I found it hard not to invent scenarios to explain the sadder spectacles – bad day at the office, incipient ulcers, threats of redundancy. Another melancholy exercise is to wonder which seats may not be occupied after the interval. It has to be admitted that, like most entertainments, *Side by Side* was not to everyone's taste and there were those who occasionally slunk away. A disgruntled television peer boasted to Bernard Levin that he had left at half-time and was promptly told that he would lose Levin's friendship and esteem if he did not go back and sit it out. Loyally Bernard reported that it worked better the second time and the peer stayed. On the other hand, persistent 'returnees' in London included a handful of attractive young women who turned up regularly with a variety of older gentlemen in the 'tired businessman' category. I assumed that they were girls from the escort agencies who had channelled their punters our way, and was duly grateful.

Late arrivals were a problem, but a problem that had to be lived with. My favourite was Douglas Bunn, the Master of Hickstead, the All-England Showjumping course, who is ceaselessly hospitable in Sussex and who came up with a girl-friend, being at the time between marriages. He had asked her if she would like to see 'something with Ned Sherrin'. 'Jolly good,' she said, 'isn't he the Irish showjumper?' 'No,' said Douglas patiently, 'it's some sort of theatrical thing.' They arrived at 7.45 to collect their tickets, assumed it was an 8.30 curtain, and went off for a couple of scotches to put them in a receptive mood. Returning in good time at 8.20, they found us twenty minutes into the revue. 'Ah,' said Douglas to the helpful usherette on the way downstairs, 'can you fill us in on the plot so far?'

In America, more than in England, the decision to come to the theatre seems often to have been made by the woman. I watched couples and knew that, while she had been looking forward to it, he only wanted to get home. The evening acquired a little dramatic subplot. Would we get him to admit that she was right, forget indeed that he ever opposed the visit? Or did his steady frown mean that she was going to be dragged away protesting at the interval?

Sondheim's dense and literate lyrics are something of a trap for foreigners who speak English less than fluently. One night I watched a sad Spanish lady grow sadder and sadder as the evening went on and her English-speaking daughter laughed more and more. Then suddenly, late in the second half, a smile lit up Mama's face as she heard the line, 'I wish I could speak Spanish', winging out in Millicent Martin's precise pronunciation.

In England, three Germans spent half a first half in the front row about five feet away from me loudly discussing their bewilderment – in German. Finally they stomped off up the aisle and I saw Bob West, the company manager, pursuing them to pin down the nature of their displeasure. 'Ve don't understandt it,' they told him, 'and ve don't understandt vy three must sing and not talk and one must talk and not sing?' Had they heard me sing, that part of the mystery would have been solved.

Of course, the business of enjoying a privileged vantage point from the stage opens up other risks. 'Coming round' is an enjoyable nightmare. This theatrical tradition consists of coming round to the stage door and visiting the performer in his dressing-room after the entertainment. When I was appearing I enjoyed seeing people after the show, and I always noted those who came back and those who slunk away. The latter I resented. The feeling is quite irrational. I dislike going round myself when I am in an audience, but that does not stop my interpreting absence as criticism when I am on the other side. But the risks! In the space of two nights at the Music Box, I was compared by one visitor to Orson Welles and by Carol Channing to 'the spirit of Robert Morley', neither description encouraging for a man on a diet.

At the Mermaid I took two American friends-of-a-friend in to congratulate Millicent Martin. They seemed short on charm, but they were very insistent. The wife sailed in first. 'Oh,' she said, her face dropping, 'but you looked beautiful on stage.' Millie is well able to take that in her stride, but I'm not sure she was prepared for the husband's follow-up: 'You can't fool me,' he said, as he waggled a knowing finger under Millicent's nose, 'you've done solo work before, and', encouragingly, 'you'll do solo work again.' I dined one night at a restaurant a couple of tables away from Millie and an American friend, a girl who had been to see the show and at whom I had been talking for some two hours from the stage. I joined them for coffee, and after another half an hour of conversation a dim light began to shine in the lady's eyes. 'Wait a minute,' she said, 'are you the guy who reads out the announcements?' So much for charisma. On another occasion a London ticket agency sent in a number of the staff to see the show. They had a drink with the cast afterwards. I worked hard for twenty minutes with a nice young woman who had a ticket booth somewhere along the Strand. At the end of it she asked what I did.

'I work here at the moment,' I said.

'What as?'

'Sort of on the stage.'

'Oh,' she said, accepting the evidence. 'You look more sophisticated up there.'

One night on leaving the Music Box (quite sober), I slipped on the sidewalk and fell into the gutter on 45th Street. Two rather precious young men who had clearly been in our audience surveyed me with no enthusiasm. 'Well,' one of them said, considering the fallen spectacle, 'it's funnier than anything he did in the show.'

Each evening passes and, watching as the audience warms, you get your own idea of the class of, say, Thursday night; but I noticed that the people out there always wanted to have been part of a good audience when they came round, so a ritual conversation was usually conducted:

'Were we a good audience?'

'Marvellous.' (They were terrible.)

'Do audiences always cheer like that at the end?'

'Well,' the lie creeps in, 'perhaps not quite as much as tonight.'

'No, we thought we were pretty exceptional.'

While I was playing nightly in *Side by Side by Sondheim* in New York, it seemed sensible to drum up some alternative work during the day. *Quiz of the Week* was an obvious vehicle, and Alasdair Milne arranged for me to acquire the North American rights to the programme, which I set up with Channel 13, the New York Public Broadcasting Station. Tony Geis, who had worked with me on 'translating' the Sondheim commentary, invented the new title *We Interrupt This Week*. I was lucky to be produced by John Gilroy, a droll Irish-American who had at various times the responsibility of working on both Johnny Carson's and Dick Cavett's shows and who brought with him a highly professional team.

We started with a live pilot on a Saturday night immediately after I had left the Sondheim show at the Music Box. Although Public Broadcasting is a different kettle of barracudas from American Network Television, there is more of the nervous anxiety which characterizes that vicious, insecure animal than you find in any part of British television.

Tom Slevin, George Page, Bob Kotlewitz and Jay Iselin for the New York station went out on a limb to promote the pilot, largely backed by my English friend, John Heyman. Then they had to sell the series to the rest of the network.

We were anxious to find new faces for the teams. Americans love the familiar, appear to resent the strange and resist it as long as possible. However, if something slips through the net they embrace it with unreserved admiration and start to search for more in that vein. There was no obvious comparable home team to take the place of *Private Eye*, although we occasionally used contributors to *The National Lampoon*. However, in the *New York Times* I came across a profile of Marshall Brickman, a writer and director who has directed his own films and collaborated on many of Woody Allen's most successful movies. He had worked with Gilroy before, and one lunch at Sardi's was enough to convince us that if we could persuade him we had found our first panellist. He has a whimsical, comprehensive grasp of current affairs and a mysterious sense of humour.

I had seen my second target, Jeff Greenfield, cross-examining distinguished adversaries on a PBS programme hosted by William Buckley. A prodigal wit, Jeff slipped most easily into the new convention. Encyclopaedic in knowledge and salting his debating finesse with street-smart wisecracks delivered from the face of an irresponsible schoolboy, he was at home at once. Nora Ephron, having appeared on the pilot, asked not to be considered for the series because, she said, it took away all the pleasure she had hitherto derived from reading the newspapers. Jimmy Breslin, the New York columnist, Pat Buchanan, previously a Republican journalist and speech-writer for Agnew who coined the phrase 'Nattering nabobs of nonconformity', and Richard Reeves, national editor of *Esquire* magazine, completed the teams.

An unlooked-for aspect of playing the game in America was the shock wave created by our 'irresponsible' attitude towards scoring in a game-show. I introduced each programme with the statement, 'I shall award points to those who give correct answers as well as to those who are evasive in an inventive, charming or provocative manner. Those are all the rules, except to say that my decisions will be arbitrary, prejudiced and final.' Nobody noticed, probably nobody heard this in England. In a country where spectacular prizes are the stock-in-trade of game-shows, where the competitive spirit is a religion, where the game-show itself is an indigenous art form as much as the Broadway musical or the western movie, it took time for audiences to get hooked on arbitrary irresponsibility. At first it looked like spitting on the flag. On one occasion a woman erupted in the small studio audience yelling, 'You didn't give her two points! She was right and you didn't give her two points!' One critic took some weeks to surrender and then confessed that the scoring was 'a delicious un-American concept'.

Once Channel 13 had achieved a tape of the live pilot show they set about placing it on the rest of the PBS network. For all the valuable work it does, Public Broadcasting in America has grown up in a haphazard way. Across the land individual stations were created as a result of personal energy and a sense of mission, or on the campuses of various universities, or in areas where groups of citizens found that the service offered by the big networks was wanting. Just as the size of America requires a proliferation of local newspapers, so it demands myriad local television and radio stations.

Funding is provided by membership subscription; by auctions of antiques (referring to commercial re-runs Tony Geis once defined the difference between PBS and the networks by suggesting that one exists on selling genuine antiques, the other by showing antique programmes in re-runs); by on-air subscription marathons and substantial under-writing by major companies – notably the oil giants. (Again Geis once described PBS as the two-car network that pulls into Mobil and Exxon every year and says, 'Fill 'er up,' and comes back three months later and says, 'Top 'er off.') Finally there is a certain amount of government funding which under reactionary administrations makes this source doubly precarious.

Many local stations cling desperately to their autonomy, either to preserve their identity or more frequently to protect the vanity of some big fish in that small pool. The larger stations, particularly Channel 13 in New York, are aware of the need to unite the network. In the first run of *We Interrupt*, Channel 13 shouldered the main burden and offered the programme to those stations which were prepared to take it. We taped the shows in an old CBS studio on 9th Avenue on Friday afternoons between 2 and 2.30 and they were beamed to the other stations at that time. The stations could then choose whether they wanted to transmit at all and at what time they would put out the programme. In New York it had a peak spot on Fridays and was repeated at 11 pm on Sundays. This was a particularly good time for New Yorkers, who caught it on their return from weekends spent out of Manhattan when there was no enjoyable alternative on the other channels.

Outside New York programming was much more hit and miss. When

I went to Tallahassee to do one promotion I found that they were transmitting each show for its first airing on the Sunday lunchtime nine days after it had been recorded. Then they repeated it early the next Tuesday evening. It made fair nonsense of the title *We Interrupt This Week*; but America is so conditioned to repeats *ad nauseam* that they were surprised to find that topicality played a part in the show.

The first series of *We Interrupt* lasted from October to just before Christmas and its impact was immense. With the exception of John O'Connor, the *New York Times* critic, the major national reviewers were enthusiastic. The new wave of panellists were generally welcomed. Only one had a rough ride – Carrie Nye, a fine actress and a formidable wit, who is also Dick Cavett's wife, found the experience difficult to gauge. As an actress she was used to learning her lines and judging her performance, as a renowned dinner-party wit she was accustomed to delivering scathing impromptus in a private situation. Somehow she never managed to strike a comfortable balance between her public and private personas during the early weeks of the show, and then she had to go off to fulfil a theatre commitment. However, her mannered voice, exotic appearance and excitable behaviour provided one of those flash points of controversy – love her, hate her – which can help a programme discover a valuable, early talking point. One critic unkindly wrote Miss Nye 'tried to be Bette Davis playing an actress on a game-show and [she] didn't quite pull it off. . . . "Carrie Nay" is a slogan among *aficionados*. The good good news is that her appearance on the show two Fridays ago may have been her last. The wit of Mississippi and Montauk is appearing in some repertory company play in Princeton or Yale. We may have seen the last of her. Keep your tongues crossed. . . .' She had focused a great deal of interest before she retired, and she is a very funny woman.

At the end of the first series Channel 13 announced that the show would come off. Not enough stations across America were willing to pay for it. The more sophisticated cities were happy – Boston, Washington, Los Angeles, Chicago, San Francisco – but the Middle West was under-whelmed and I became particularly irritated with station managers, who would tell me proudly how they taped the show every week and showed it at private parties to friends and *aficionados* while deciding that it was, of course, far too sophisticated for their viewers.

The season ended with a final *Week* and a special hour-long *We Interrupt This Year*, both recorded on the same marathon day. The result was extraordinary. First the press created an unprecedented fuss about the show's demise. Tom Shales, a prestigious critic on the *Washington Post*, led off, '... 1978 was a no-frills year, but it did have its little luxuries and compensations. One of them was *We Interrupt This Week*, a lovably malicious current events quiz featuring media cut-ups waxing wary, wry and witty about people and events of the day. This made for a lively, funny, and infernally informative show....' Earlier he had welcomed it as 'the merriest and most pleasingly snide weekly brawl in all of television ... the zest of tennis, liquid protein and the inescapable Perrier ... the snappiest and crackliest smug amusement show to hit television since the inception of *Saturday Night Live* on NBC.'

Jack O'Brien in New York wrote, 'This gleeful, witty, informative show ... capsules the week in uproariously amusing fashion ... a minor miracle in itself.' Another, '... Channel 13 should sign it for Ned Sherrin's life. It is one of TV's rare exercises in intellectualism – almost its only spontaneously and dependably witty cavalcade of knowledge, observation in communications in risible depth.' Again, 'This chaotic satire represents the most stimulating television available....' The Tallahassee *Democrat* was another loyal friend, 'Like no quiz show you've ever seen ... [it] lampoons not only the quiz show format but American political life as well ... the panellists can't win, it seems, but you can't lose.'

Terence O'Flaherty in San Francisco found it 'the most amusing and intelligent game-show on the air' and characterized the chairman as '... keeping the thing moving with all the dictatorial authority of an English nanny refereeing a neighborhood croquet match'. The 'Chairman of Cinema Studies' at NYU, Robert Sklar, spent 'several afternoons at the studio observing the show.... [Sherrin] is playing not merely himself, or appearing as a British Television Personality: he is portraying the American fantasy of the urbane British intellectual – quick-witted, sharp-tongued, imperturbable and ineffably superior. He performs not only as host and quizmaster but as our image of the British schoolmaster. Some of the panellists respond by approaching the experience as an oral exam....'

I visited San Francisco and Los Angeles on a promotion tour with David Yakir, one of the show's associate producers. Our visit to San Francisco coincided with the morning assassination of Mayor Mosconi and Harvey Milk, one of the city's leading officials, famous in San Francisco as a leader of the large homosexual community. As we watched a local morning television magazine before our press conference, the young woman who was hosting it was interviewing an overpowering lady novelist when suddenly a studio manager stepped into shot and handed her a note. She read it, looked shocked and read it again. Then she stared up at the camera, somewhere between shock and tears, and said in an incredulous voice, 'The Mayor's been shot – and Harvey Milk!' There was a pause and then she added, fighting back a sob, 'This is terrible!' There followed a triumph of opportunism as the lady novelist leaned forward and slapped a brusque hand on her shoulder. 'Terrible, dear,' she said in a gruff voice. 'Let's get back to my book.'

The volume of press support for *We Interrupt This Week* was underlined by an extraordinary response on the part of viewers. After I had announced the demise of the show on the last transmission I came back to England. The show's staff arrived next week to clear up the office and were much dimmed when there were no letters in the in-trays: we had anticipated a trickle of public support. Some hours later it transpired that there were so many bags of mail for the show that they had been diverted to a special sorting office. An 'enormous response from viewers' usually means a few hundred letters. We got about 15,000, many including cheques, dollar bills and touching messages. Our favourite, from one George Diskant in LA, pointed out that he had been watching the show for five years and could not bear to lose it. As we had not run more than a year we wrote back to ask him what he was smoking.

As a result of this extraordinarily large demonstration, the Corporation for Public Broadcasting came up with a subvention of $100,000 to produce five more shows; and I set off to New Orleans with the Channel 13 executives to lobby the heads of the other PBS stations for the future. There were three hectic days of blandishing in 'smoke-filled rooms'. It was a losing battle which continued to be lost as the year wore on. We were fighting for a return in the autumn season, but as the Middle West failed to come through we started to hunt for sponsors: if you can give PBS a show for free the chances are that they will take it. The programme had two built-in problems. It was recorded virtually as live, it was spontaneous and it could be controversial. The big firms prefer to back decorous, pre-filmed, 'classy' costume drama. Moreover, it was intensely topical, and repeats and residuals, shown again to infinity, which help to balance the budgets of most series, could not apply to us. (A Dick Cavett interview show on the PBS network went out first in the early evening, then late evening and then early next morning. It was then repeated under the title *The Best of Cavett*. Then years later there could be *A Decade of Cavett, Cavett on Humor, Cavett on Politicians, Cavett on Actors* – in the same way that *I Love Lucy* shows are infinitely repeatable.

Tony Geis believes that a distinguishing feature of American television is that by turning a switch around the myriad of channels you can see Lucille Ball at any age.) The title *We Interrupt This Week* had built-in obsolescence.

We failed to get the money and the series did not return; but it remains my favourite way of appearing on television and I look forward to reviving it in one continent or the other. Radio borrowed Tony Smith's formula for its *News Quiz* and BBC-2 has produced two lack-lustre versions under the title *Scoop*, but there is plenty of room for the original and, revived as the centrepiece of *Friday Night, Saturday Morning*, with Willy Rushton and John Wells, it worked well.

In self-indulgent mood I include a few echoes of *We Interrupt This Week* – because they evoke a happy period for me and, as I no longer collect scrapbooks, they will be fixed between covers for me as memory grows dim. We saw the heyday and the busting of the socially impregnable club Studio 54: 'How to get in?' – 'Get a warrant.' Gore Vidal, assured as usual but woefully unbriefed after having flown in from Rome, answered only one question – 'Who said this week, "The possibilities of heterosexuality are soon exhausted"?' The correct answer was a prominent pornographer, but Gore saw his moment. Hopefully he inquired, 'Did I?' He got two points on the grounds that though he had not said it that week he had probably said it most weeks down the preceding two decades.

Barbara Howar was one of the sharpest contestants. I had seen her on a Johnny Carson show decimating Robert Blake, an actor who was boring away on a chauvinist trip. On one of our programmes she was sitting next to Ron Nessen, who had been Gerald Ford's beleaguered press secretary. Helpfully he attempted to rephrase Barbara's answer. Jeff Greenfield leant across with a nostalgic smile, 'It's wonderful, Ron, once again to hear you explaining what someone *meant* to say.'

While the state of California was indulging in a stampede of 'propositions' to vary their Constitution, Marshall Brickman and Richard Reeves competed for eccentric proposals. Tax, sex, and air transport were all under consideration. 'Proposition 5' was the question. 'That homosexuals cannot smoke in airplanes,' suggested one or the other. We had an eclipse to contend with, 'the last this century, unless Lily Tomlin makes *Moment by Moment II*'. A California sculptor threatened to chisel Governor Jerry Brown's features into a rock hanging perilously over a Malibu hillside – 'she has already started work on both faces.' Peter Stone, the playwright, mourned the end of the series: 'I have completely abandoned a very lucrative career to work for $186 a show.... I spend all my time reading newspapers....'

The week before we finished, my work permit ran out. Coming through Kennedy Airport for the penultimate show, I wondered whether I should risk the last trip and not bother to get it renewed, relying on my non-working visitor's visa. As I went through immigration the officer said, 'Who's on the show this week?' The customs man asked, 'Got a good one tomorrow?' And as I gave the taxi driver my address in Manhattan he said, 'You sound like that guy on *We Interrupt This Week*.' I began to believe that it was not quite the elitist excursion the Middle West would have had us believe. And it was fun.

While I was in America my manager, Deke Arlon, made an arrangement with Yorkshire TV to do a series on distinguished lyricists using the same formula as the Wavendon Gershwin programme and *Side by Side by Sondheim*. We had already had a preliminary canter for the BBC examining Ira Gershwin's work. The series provided two seasons of happy television directed by Vernon Lawrence. We worked on lyricists as varied as Alan Lerner, Lorenz Hart, Oscar Hammerstein, Dorothy Fields, Sheldon Harnick, Johnny Mercer, E.Y. Harburg, Irving Berlin, Cole Porter and Noël Coward. There were many old friends and American guests like Lena Horne, Barbara Cook and Howard Keel.

My happiest single memory of the series, called *Song by Song*, is playing 'Yip' Harburg in the programme we devoted to his work. He is one of my favourite lyric writers and he was then, some three years before his death, already into his eighties. His enthusiasm was matched by his eagle-eared attention to see if any of his words had been rearranged. The occasion also had its wry side. There are those terrifying times when you know that certain subjects are taboo with a person. With Yip it was *The Wiz*. Without doubt, Yip's best-known score is the one he wrote with Harold Arlen which provided the springboard for Judy Garland's success in *The Wizard of Oz*. Among the colleagues in the viewing theatre was my friend David Yakir, who had made a vow not to mention the black version of the Frank Baum classic, *The Wiz*, which he had enjoyed, but which we both knew Harburg disliked. After Yip had enjoyed the celebration of his work we chatted happily until David and I took him home in a cab. We were all going up-town and he lived where so many songwriters hang out in style on Central Park West. Suddenly, out of nowhere came the 'brick'. 'Mr Harburg, how did you like *The Wiz*?' The old man was civilly dismissive, David bit his tongue off, and I remembered a similar occasion when I had done much the same to Judy Garland herself.

She threw a birthday party for the American actress Marti Stevens at a large house in the Boltons. It was a reasonable 1960s mix, a lot of actors, half the Ad-Lib, Danny La Rue, one or other of the Kray Brothers. Miss Garland was attended by her newest husband, a tall, handsome, dark young American called Mark. I had seen her on stage some years before at the Dominion Theatre in a programme in which she and her company played the second half – the first was looked after very capably by Alan King. Since then she had had rougher times, and her recent tour of Australia had been a nightmare. She had often been late on stage – her subsequent appearance greeted with cat-calls – nor had her performance always banished the displeasure. In the end she left in a hurry, grabbing the first plane out that she could hop. She came to London via the Far East, and Australia was her number one unfavourite subject. In no circumstances was I going to mention it. I was introduced to her. 'How did you like Australia?' I said.

I need not have worried. She took a breath and launched herself into a vivid monologue. 'It was terrible! That country! They were so awful! I was a little late a couple of times. But they were so bad! In the end I said to Mark, "Let's get out of here"; and we got a plane. I said, "Get any plane," and we got one. . . . We got the last one out! We didn't even know where it was going! We didn't know where it was going until it touched down. It was the Philippines! When we got out, there were all these little yellow men waiting for us and cameras and all! And they started shouting and asking questions and I couldn't hear what they were saying; and then I heard one say, "Miss Glaland" . . .'

She began to relish the oriental accent and to tell the story with that committed, infectious, comic quality which so often informed her acting. ' "Miss Glaland," he said, "is it tlue you tlied to slit your lists thlity-thlee times?" Well, I didn't know what to say, and I looked at Mark there.' He was standing by her and she looked up at him. 'I looked at Mark there, so big and strong, and another one said, "Miss Glaland, is it tlue you slit your lists thlity-thlee times?" and Mark was so good, and big and strong, and he said, "We don't give a press conference here. Let's go to the airline building." And he took me along and there were all these little yellow men and the cameras flashing, and we got to the building and they were all around us, and Mark was so big and good and calm and strong, and he cleared a way and said, "Let's have a press confer-ence," and all these little men said, "Miss Glaland, is it tlue you slit your lists thlity-thlee times?" And I still didn't know what to say and I looked at Mark and he just looked right back and said, "What was the question?" "Miss Glaland, is it tlue you slit your lists thlity-thlee times?" And Mark just said, "Who counts?" '

I saw her offstage once again, trading happy insults the length of a dining table laid for thirty in friendly, fishwife style with another American actress. It was a celebration dinner in a Chinese restaurant, and when Miss Garland was on form no celebration was dull.

Among other things *Song by Song* led to an appearance on a Royal Variety Show. The royal shows are familiarly called Royal Command Performances, though only the first in 1912 was in fact by Royal Command. That was the famous occasion when Marie Lloyd, the outstanding performer of the day, her name synonymous with 'the Halls', was not invited (or commanded) because she was felt to be too blue for King George v and more especially for Queen Mary. Furious, she arranged to perform down the road at the London Pavilion and added to her bill matter, 'Every performance is a command performance: by command of the British public.' She might not have suited Queen Mary, who averted her eyes from the stage even when confronted by the genteel *travestie* of Vesta Tilley.

There were no such shocks from the stage in the one Variety Performance in which I was involved (though I did have a personal brush with authority – more of that later). It is fashionable to decry the honour of appearing on a Royal Command Bill: I found it engrossing. It begins with a great deal of conspiratorial secrecy. Louis Benjamin was arranging the 1979 bill. He is addicted to the telephone and in love with the dramatic whisper as a device. In the first place he finds out if you would say 'yes' if you were asked. That year the show was at the Drury Lane Theatre and he wanted to include a musical comedy section recalling some of the Lane's big hits. The *Song by Song* formula from our Yorkshire Television series was a convenient device, and meant a great deal more secrecy as we went down another list of performers who in turn had to be asked if they would say 'yes' if they were asked.

There was a pleasant irony in asking Millicent Martin, Julie McKenzie and David Kernan. Some years before, when we were all doing *Side by Side*, Bernard Delfont had asked us to perform an excerpt in the 1976 Royal Show. The owner of the theatre decided that it might be bad for business, so the answer 'no' was whispered back up the line. We all fretted a great deal.

In 1979 there was no obstacle for Millie, David and Julia; we added

Elisabeth Welch, Marti Caine, Hinge and Brackett and Carol Channing, who finished the first half with the title song of *Hello Dolly*, and a forthright Welsh chorus never heard in Jon Scoffield's television version because no microphones got near them. Silent, they looked like geriatric chorus boys gone to fat.

The two rehearsal days were attended by heavy security. Passes were demanded. Performers were denied entry. It was all very clandestine. Our dressing-room was a wonderful cross-section. James Galway, accustomed to flying into a town and carrying a whole concert, was rather bemused by having to perform no more than three items and hang around a great deal. Noel Edmonds was not entirely sure whether hosting a pop music section would prove the most popular part of the show, which has a notoriously unpredictable audience. Bernie Clifton, who was to score one of the big successes, came surrounded by a little family of woolly ostriches and camels inhabited by an army of assistants, or was it just one? – I could never quite discover; poor Jim Davidson had the traditional comic's Royal Variety dilemma – which one of his best jokes could he possibly get away with in front of the Queen?

Just before the performance was due to get under way I was standing in the wings with the group of artists who had assembled to watch the Queen's progress from Buckingham Palace on television monitors. Suddenly I was aware of a small Indian man at my side carrying a piece of paper. 'Mr Sherrin?' he inquired.

'How nice,' I thought, 'an autograph hunter.' I smiled in agreement.

'Mr E.G. Sherrin?' he continued.

This sounded less like an autograph hunter. Those are indeed my initials: but few people know them and fewer use them. However, I could not deny it. 'Yes,' I said lamely.

'Will you please accept this?' He put the writ firmly in my hand, thanked me politely and left through the elaborate security precautions which he had breached so easily on behalf, it turned out, of Her Majesty's Inspector of Taxes.

I took the writ up to the dressing-room the better to read it and was immediately struck by the archaic form of address. It purported to be a directive from the Queen herself. Her Britannic Majesty was instructing me in no uncertain terms to pay a sizeable chunk of surtax. It was hard not to see the funny side. After all, I was due to be presented to her in about three hours' time. I began to ponder possible approaches. Rather than answering the writ it would surely be more sensible to have a word with her personally – something like, 'I got your note....'

I stuck it in my briefcase and we did the show. Sitting around through Act Two, waiting for the walk down, discretion banished such fantasies. When the Queen did her rounds I bowed low, listened politely as she said, 'Very enjoyable', and watched her pass on to the late Bill Haley to whom she talked with great animation. Louis Benjamin sent me a picture of my bow. My eyes are closed tight. Under it he added a caption: '... And when you woke up she was still there.'

My accountant sorted out the writ the next morning. They were very apologetic: but they did not shave anything off the total.

Father of the Man

A green field covered in cowslips. A small boy just over two years old. An indulgent aunt. Together they pick the flowers until the boy is bored. The aunt demurs. The boy surveys the carpet of cowslips and says with awful cuteness, 'We must leave some for another little boy to pick for his mother.'

I have been told this story so many times that I now believe that it is my earliest memory. However, it is no longer possible to distinguish between the event and the account ... and my infant instinct to find an excuse for going home which would leave me in a better light rings true – in the light of later developments (as the rest of these pages should have borne out).

The green field lay between the villages of High Ham and Low Ham, on part of my father's farm, Gawler's Farm, in Somerset. We left it in 1934 when I was three.

Two more authentic memories. The first visit to the new farmhouse still occupied by the previous tenant – tears and disgrace. Then, moving into the new home which was much larger, an old coaching inn at Kingweston. I ran lost around the unfamiliar stone passages crying, 'Mummy, where is I? I's lost.' The dialogue is perhaps too fey to be true and the grammar may have deteriorated in the years of indulgent retelling; but that is how I recall it.

My father, Thomas Adam Sherrin, was the son of a small farmer who died when he was twelve. Straightaway he left Langport Grammar School to run the farm for his mother and his two cottage-loaf sisters, Mary Louise who was older, and Emily Grace who was younger. This Sherrin family unit was undisturbed until the late Twenties. Aunt Lou taught several generations at the village school. Aunt Em helped around the house. Then a new teacher, Frances Drewett, arrived to teach at High Ham School. She lodged with the Sherrins and my father married her younger sister, Dorothy Finch, when he was just over forty, she just under. The newly-weds occupied the farm, the three ladies moved to the Lodge, High Ham. My brother Alfred was born on 25 March 1928 and I was born two years and eleven months later on 18 February 1931.

The village of Kingweston as I became aware of it was still feudally organized. The squire, Captain W.E. Dickinson (suddenly OBE during the war – for organizing local knitting for the troops: as they said in the village, '' 'Ee be OBE, 'ee be'), trained as an architect and was, as far as I could see, occupied entirely in watercolour painting, amateur theatricals and fierce readings of the lessons in church on Sundays with scant regard to punctuation. He was thin and later bent. Mrs Dickinson was ample and cloaked, in my memory, in long businesslike but flowing suits of blue or brown. Miss Dickinson was the older of two children – a tall, shy girl. The son and heir was Caleb, handsome, charming, fair and fresh-faced, apparently ill at ease with the restrictions of Kingweston life and keen to be one of the boys. In the background, sinister so it seemed through my father's eyes, loomed the stumpy, sturdy figure of Miss Buckle, the children's governess, who stayed on, he asserted, simply to meddle in village business.

The village itself is strung out along one street. Some eight cottages, the post office (one of the network established by Anthony Trollope), and Lower Farm, in which we lived, border the main road; two more farms, the Dower House and some twenty more cottages straggle beside another road which winds round a sharp corner and up towards the 'Big House' and the church. Two elaborate cedar walks lead away from Kingweston House and up into the woods where I wandered and fantasized and avoided gamekeepers. Home Farm was the home of the Maunders, Middle Farm the Sawtells; both solid farmhouses, full of comfortable furniture, surrounded by big barns and yards. All had lofts and stables ideal for hiding in and were fronted or backed by large lawns on which the unmowed tennis courts were falling into mole-mined undulations while they waited for a new generation who would hardly use them.

Old Mr Maunder was a stalwart Devonian, a bulky bachelor, tolerant and genial and crippled with gout. I was fascinated by his Devon accent and especially the Devonian habit of saying 'us' when he meant 'I'. A natural gent, he appeared to farm with one hand and to ease his way through life troubled only by the pain in his foot. The Sawtells were the 'gentlemen farmers': Mr Sawtell, tall and droll, and Mrs Sawtell, inquisitive, pious, organizing and the village organist. They had two daughters – one dashing, one studious – who are a few years older than my brother and I; and whom we saw as dauntingly worldly and sophisticated.

During the war there were a few winters when the three families indulged in a triangle of dinner parties. The practice started with the Sawtells. My father was loud in his condemnation. My brother and I rather liked the idea of a large three-course hot meal and relished the moment after dinner when the women would retire to the drawing-room and the men and boys stepped out expansively on to the darkened lawns and stood around relieving themselves on the grass with choruses of 'I'm here!', 'I'm here!', 'I'm here!' to avoid damp catastrophes.

My father was a 'country character', a wag who, once he found a joke on someone, worried it mercilessly. Short, paunchy, with a Mr Punch nose and a crafty glint in his eye, he had no taste for the 'gentleman farmer' label. On one rare excursion into national celebrity he was profiled in the *Farmer's Weekly* under the heading, 'He doesn't want to be a "Dog and Stick" Farmer', a proud boast which turned to exasperation when he was baited at Glastonbury Market about how much he had paid for this lurid but, in fact, unsolicited publicity. A relentless jokester, he was slow to see a joke against himself. His passion was a deal and he would happily haggle for hours over a gatepost or through a car window, with enough patience to exhaust an Egyptian bazaar salesman.

Pre-war memories jostle – a kaleidoscope of images – treats and disappointments. Summer fortnights in a boarding house, 'a stone's throw from the front', at Burnham-on-Sea, Knickerbocker Glories and North Poles at the ice-cream parlour round the corner overlooking the model railway which disappeared one year, bought up by a 'rich man' who removed it to the grounds of his stately home so that only 'rich children' could ride in it. Early socialist stirrings were wiped out by a couple of North Poles. Pre-war bananas; pre-war lights on the way home from Sunday mystery tours in the Austin Seven, AYA 422, or later the bigger ELB 359. Mystery tours might dwindle into a visit to the cattle on the nearby moorland or flower into trips as far as Minehead and Dunster, with an exotic polo match thrown in for excitement or a boiling radiator on Porlock Hill for exasperation. Smashing crabs on the muddy beach at Blue Anchor; wool sales at Dorchester followed by sorties deeper into

Hardy country and on to Weymouth; strawberry gathering at Cheddar, or White Horse watching on Salisbury Plain. Sleepily scanning the lights of tiny towns on the low, undulating hillsides on the way home and cherishing the memory through years of blackout and bicycling. Mars Bars and Milky Ways – soon to disappear with the lights and the bananas . . . 'for the duration'.

The village school was Barton St David, C. of E. I was very proud of my first day at school: my brother pushed me into Miss Barrington's infant class. Cyril Bailey, starting the same day, cried all morning and they had to send for his mother – I stayed dry-eyed and pleased with myself. First essays in sexual exploration took place in the boys' lavatory behind the school. 'I'll show you mine if you show me yours' – I showed mine and then he ran away. A car trip to school each morning and, at the end of the day, the mile-and-a-half walk back in all weathers. The fury when the new teacher, Miss Williams, gave my drawing of her fewer marks than the one drawn by the boy at the next desk. What other reason could there have been than that I put (accurately) such a network of lines across her face and he drew none? Tadpoles. Pressed flowers. Another injustice: I collected hundreds more flowers than anyone else, correctly labelled; but I lost because of too many ink blots.

About now my first public performance – a non-speaking role in an Empire Day pageant as a New Zealand sheep farmer. Pre-war cricket, watching Somerset: seeing Arthur Wellard hitting five sixes in one over at Wells – all off Frank Woolley, an elderly gentleman whose reputation was unknown to me. Wellard was my hero, and the grey day and the record number of balls sailing up against the drab houses which fringed the ground stay vivid. Constantine, at Taunton with the West Indies. Measles in 1938 while Howard Marshall was warmly commending 'young Hutton' for his record at the Oval.

After the war my brother and I stepped up our visits to Taunton, and eventually I saved up for a membership subscription and rejected the biscuit tin of sandwiches I brought from home in favour of the sophistication of a ticket for the first or second sitting for a member's salad lunch. We used to look with some amusement at an elderly colonel who sat in the Somerset Stragglers' stand, whom we christened 'the Food Hog' on account of the wicker picnic basket which he set down on arrival and to which he applied himself throughout the rest of the day.

I went by train through the Somerset countryside, through the litany of station names reeled off by the porters. Charlton Mackrell, Somerton, Long Sutton, Langport, Lyng Halt, Durston, Athelney – hardly even a 'halt', surrounded by willows, the place where King Alfred burnt the cakes. Coming off the moors and arriving at Taunton there was a short walk over the bridge and into the ground. A glance on the way at the river into which Arthur Wellard or Harold Gimblett, occasionally Bill Andrews and later M.F. Tremlett deposited their straight-driven sixes; Hammond and C.J. Barnett too, on Whitsun Derby Days. Somerset cricket was gloriously haphazard then, ripe with character, swinging from humiliating obliteration to exhilarating giant-killing with forgotten names, Horace Hazel, Wally Luckes, Harold Stephenson, G.E.S. Woodhouse, M.M. Walford, H.T.F. Buse, John Lawrence, the unequalled idols of my adolescence.

In more tender years illness was always an event. Whooping cough meant dashes out on to the lawn through the french windows just in time. Chicken pox left its small scars, and mumps got me away from Barton St David C. of E. a few days before the end of my last term there. I was to go on to the grown-up grandeur of Sexey's Trade School, Bruton, (now simply Sexey's) to which my brother had again preceded me.

Home life was the farm. My father had no other interests. He got up at six o'clock to administer it and to start milking. In the late Thirties he bought a milking machine, the second for miles around. The drama was intense. At the first milking the cows could hardly be coaxed or cajoled into the stalls. Hours were spent on persuasion and the time for the next milking came round before the first was finished. My father fumed. The village sniggered. But the second performance halved the time ... the third was nearly a triumph.

There were always eggs to be collected, nestling behind stinging nettles or under haystacks and in corners of barns. Chickens to be fed. Ducks whose throats must be slit. Sheep to be moved. Cows to be driven seven or so miles to the moorland for summer pasture, and back before winter set in. Haymaking I hated; but it usually happened during term-time. Harvest I tolerated because of the orgy of rabbit-catching as the binder closed in on the few remaining yards of corn. Acres of wheat or barley or oats had to be stooked ('stitched' we called it) in groups of a dozen or so sheaves which had later to be pitchforked on to wagons expertly crafted by Lampert's of Catsgore, prettily painted in blues and pinks labelled with the names of the owner and the wagon-maker. They were pulled by Captain (white) or Jolly (chestnut) or Bonnie (speckled) or Blackbird (black), or Prince, a bay. The cows all had names too. We started with mixed Shorthorns and finished with Ayrshires – the only name I can remember is Primrose, a Shorthorn with a Jersey colouring, I think.

Old Henny, as Albion Henry Small was called, was cowman and sometimes kitchen gardener. He and his wife Florrie, and their son Roy, then a village Romeo and a natural aspirant for the glamorous role of tractor driver when the first Fordson arrived, had migrated from High Ham with us. Herbie Brown was the carter, right back to the days of polished brasses and ploughing matches where red, white and blue rosettes were the prizes. His son Arnold was second tractor driver. A wizened little man, Herbie was one of my favourites. He had exciting, sometimes lurid, stories of early life in Canada – camp fires and logging – and he pronounced cartridges kidderidges, and partridges pidderidges. He and Arnold encouraged me to swig the unpleasant-tasting sharp cider from their stone flasks.

At the end of every summer we collected the apples, despising the big yellow Morgan Sweets and going for the small red Kingston Blacks and the Russet Cider Apples that were preferred. Layer after layer of straw and fruit was piled on the press, flattened with creaking machinery and squashed into a monstrous straw 'n' apple cake which yielded up the sweet cider which my brother and I downed thirstily before it could be transferred to large barrels in the cellar where it matured.

Every day 'the men' filled their stone flasks and took them to the fields. At midday and in the evening they were refilled. During haymaking and harvest my mother produced huge open-air meals – more stone jars, now full of tea, doorsteps of fresh bread and butter and jam or cheese were driven out to the fields. Extra hands were co-opted for these seasonal bouts and whole afternoons had to be devoted to cutting and spreading and packing the piles of food.

The house was large, rambling and draughty. The floors of the corridors and practical rooms downstairs were flagged and freezing. The dining- and drawing-rooms were carpeted, the hall tiled. We lived in the dining-room except on Sundays when we invaded the drawing-room and tried in vain to make it equally warm and welcoming. Up a small flight of steps was 'the morning room', a title inherited from the previous tenants though we never used it morning, noon or night, except as a retreat for my brother and, increasingly, for me. It gave on to the 'toy room' – Hornby and Meccano. For some inexplicable reason the old wall telephone with its fixed speaker and detachable earpiece stayed in the morning room for inconvenient years.

The advent of war brought some changes. A party of evacuees arrived by bus and surveyed the village from the main road outside our farm. One said, 'No pub, no pictures, no fish and chips; get back in the bus. ...' and so they disappeared. Later a few were individually billeted.

Caleb Dickinson, who had served a short, enjoyable farming apprenticeship with my father, realized his ambition to join the Air Force and was reported missing presumed lost on his first active service flight. His picture with his delicate features looked out dreamily from among our few family photographs, stuck on the drawing-room table; inside the glass, a pair of his Air Force wings.

My father joined the War Agricultural Committee and occasionally brought colleagues back to tea. One very dignified old gentleman was my first drunk. He skewered his salad to my fascination, aimed it at his mouth and continued to miss.

More and more land was ploughed up. More harvesting. High in the sky above plane-spotting became more thrilling on hot summer days as swastikas appeared on some of the aeroplanes and we learned from our cigarette card identification kits to spot a Heinkel or a Messerschmit. Bristol was bombed and we stood outside the front door in the cold night air, looked north and watched the pink glow over the Mendips as it burned.

A great-uncle and -aunt evacuated themselves from Bristol – Uncle Ted, who had been the village grocer at Badminton, had, on one memorable occasion when my brother and I visited him, beckoned us to stand near the telephone and keep quiet. 'I am calling the Duke of Beaufort and if you listen carefully you will hear the voice of a real live Duke. ... Good evening, Your Grace. ...' They had hardly arrived in Kingweston before a hastening-home German dropped a stick of nine bombs across the village (casualties one sheep and a couple of rabbits). Together uncle and aunt dived for cover under the dining-room table before my family and I realized what had happened. Uncle Ted imported tins of Heinz chicken soup for supper, and as he slurped it down my brother and I watched open-eyed with envy between our mouthfuls of very good bread and cheese or cold meat.

Breakfast was large and traditional. Lunch was called dinner and was a substantial meat and sweet affair. Tea was solid and supper was cold. Ration books were a nuisance; but living on a farm meant poultry and eggs in easy supply and permits to kill two pigs a year, which my father then preserved in a large lead salter, providing an orgy of chitterlings and brawn and other goodies immediately after the slaughter. Hams and joints emerged over the next six months when he felt like it; and so did large pieces of meat from some deal which my father made with a friendly butcher, whose grandson now bats aggressively for Somerset. I am not sure if it was in contravention of legislation or not. I seem to remember journeys after dark, which probably means that it was.

Another wartime change in Kingweston was the advent of some sort of Searchlight Headquarters at 'the Big House' – the older Dickinsons moved to neighbouring Butleigh, where they stayed after the war when Millfield School took over Kingweston House and the rest of the family returned to the Dower House. Joy Dickinson had also gone to the war. Soldiers and officers and WRACS masterminded the fight against the Germans from the top of the drive.

As an even smaller boy I had been privileged to see one of the Dickinsons' theatrical performances as the highlight of a village fête held in the grounds. It was a one-act sketch called 'Brought Home by Broadcast', and for a long time my ideas of theatre were conditioned by it. Curtains were drawn back at the end of one of the larger rooms to reveal Captain Dickinson as a cantankerous old lady sitting in an armchair beside a large Bush wireless. From the opening soliloquy we gathered that his daughter had disappeared. He/she looked at a watch, moved to the wireless and switched it on. We heard a rustling backstage as the formidable figure of Mrs Dickinson tried to make her way as discreetly as possible past the scenery to a position immediately behind the wireless. In clear (and unmistakable) tones she read a BBC SOS: '... last heard of in ... please get in touch with ... etc.' With a look of satisfaction the old lady (or the squire, depending on whether you accepted the convention) switched off the wireless and returned to the armchair. Simultaneously Mrs Dickinson could be heard returning to her prompter's stool. After a very short second monologue a door, or rather a curtain, burst open and in bounced Miss Dickinson as the prodigal daughter. Her father/ mother feigned illness for a few moments, but then revealed that the SOS was simply a ruse to bring the erring girl home. In her turn she confessed that she had been lying low down the road all the time. This swift exchange of plot and counterplot brought the entertainment to a close. They took a couple of curtains and I rather think Mrs Dickinson's Wireless Announcer took one as well.

'Brought Home by Broadcast', my second toy theatre (the first was concocted out of cornflake boxes), a pantomime at the Playhouse, Street (*Cinderella*, with Dandini doing a paper-tearing act while they changed the scenery preparatory to the ball) – these were my early, live theatrical experiences. The year after *Cinderella*, we were travelling with some excitement to the Playhouse to book tickets for that year's panto-mime when my mother, who was driving AYA 422, was overturned by a friend of my father's in his larger car. My brother and I were uninjured, my mother had a few days in bed, and I emerged from the upturned car furious that we might miss the pantomime. We did. War broke out and there was no show.

During the war we made occasional visits to 'the pictures', at Glaston-bury or Street or, as our cycling grew more ambitious, to Yeovil. The first movie I remember was a skiing, skating vehicle for Sonja Henie at Wells. At about that time also my brother and I were taken to a film demonstration of tractors and balers at Yeovil: a screen was lowered, fields of hay were gathered before our very eyes and an insistent com-mentary accompanied the pictures. For one of my father's farmer friends it was a first. Eventually he could contain himself no longer – 'Tom, Tom!' he hissed to my father, 'where's thick feller talking from?' My brother and I felt very sophisticated in face of this adult naivety.

The wireless was a different matter. Alfred and I had played with a crystal set, but I only remember a few squeaks emerging from it. Eventu-ally my father returned home one day bearing a large Bush radio. (He always wore a sheepish look when he bought something new – tractor, combine harvester, radio, milking machine, eventually television; he was defensively prepared for ridicule and reluctant to betray pride in his purchase.) Most people of my generation and those which immediately followed have vivid, conditioning memories of radio. Mine are further focused by the programmes my father did not allow us to hear.

Band Waggon was 'not funny', and *ITMA* was 'a lot of rot'. Will Fyfe was always welcome and Gracie Fields was an event; however, some-times 'she made a fool of herself'. *Garrison Theatre* with Charles Shad-well and Jack Warner – 'blue pencil', 'mind my bike' – Joy Standing and 'programmes, chocolates, cigarettes' was acceptable; but Margaret Eaves's powerful soprano brought her into the despised class of 'screech-ers'. Crooners, on the other hand, 'bawled'. Count John McCormack was above reproach. The Western Brothers, Kenneth and George, were most agreeable, 'Murgatroyd and Winterbottom' – Tommy Handley and Ronald Frankau – 'daft'. Hymns were good listening and at the beginning of the war, when they played the National Anthems of all the Allied Nations before Sunday's nine o'clock news, the family stood rigidly to attention throughout the fifteen or twenty minutes. Very soon we reached a compromise by not getting to our feet until 'God Save the King', which was top of the bill.

A half-hour classic serial preceded the anthems. It was touch and go if it was Dickens – 'too many people. Can't make the story out'; Trollope was simpler and usually acceptable. *Barlasch of the Guard* is the first I can remember hearing in full, having spent months switching on earlier and earlier for the anthems in the hope of getting my father hooked on the serial. The names of the BBC repertory company come back as familiarly as the initials of Somerset cricketers. Gladys Young, Carleton Hobbs, Mary O'Farrell, Laidman Browne, James McKechnie, Frederick Lloyd, Belle Crystal were the stars, and the most vivid memory of all is the acute family embarrassment as Grizelda Hervey's Irene repeated her lament, 'Rape, rape', as she fled from her husband Soames Forsyte (Ronald Simpson) in *The Forsyte Saga*.

L. du Garde Peache's Sunday serials, which had some historical interest, were passed fit for listening, especially if Richard Goolden was appearing. *Toy Town* was 'silly'. My brother and I were keen on a short-lived show which had a signature tune, 'Rusty and Dusty Brown, they've got patches where they sit down'; but I shed a tear when it was taken off prematurely. J.B. Priestley's wartime speeches after the news were immediately switched off. My father did not like the accent.

It was an age of catchphrases. Even if you did not hear the series you soon cottoned on. 'TTFN', 'Can I do you now, sir?' ' "After you, Claude." "No, after you, Cecil" ', 'Don't forget the diver', 'This is Fumpf speaking' – all from *ITMA*; and others, 'Large lumps, they're lovely', 'Sarsparilla!', 'Hello, playmates', 'In our shed'; and then the new crop from the wartime series *Stand-Easy* and *Much Binding in the Marsh*.

The Searchlight Headquarters also brought live entertainment to the village. Occasionally officers were billeted on us at Lower Farm, and when ENSA parties came to entertain the troops we might be squeezed in to share the feast of entertainment. Eventually this got out of hand, and on the last occasion that I attended the audience consisted entirely of village children. The gallant entertainers had come from Wells, some ten miles away, to entertain the brave fighting boys, and made no secret of their displeasure. Some time later the village farmers were all invited to a cocktail party at the officers' mess. My father 'didn't hold with that nonsense', so he and my mother did not go, but Alfred and I turned up and, picking my way waist-high through various condescending officers' wives, I heard my first piece of theatrical gossip. 'I loved Owen Nares,' said one lady. 'So did I,' said another. 'I'm told that Ivor Novello has inherited his mantle,' said the first. I glowed at the idea of having such an important gobbet of information in my possession; but days went by and I could find no one in Kingweston to whom I could pass it on. It has been my secret until now.

During the week we read the *Daily Mail*. We did not see a Sunday paper for years. My father delighted to describe how his mother had hidden the weekday papers under cushions on Sundays. However, a semi-religious magazine called the *Quiver*, staggering in its dullness, was allowed. I retain one rare, enlightened sentence – a mother telling her tearful son, 'Don't cry, my dear. The little Jesus had an olive skin too.'

Sundays changed when Uncle Ted arrived and ordered the *Sunday Dispatch*, not to be touched by anyone else until he had peered at it through his owl-eyes. By the time he went back to Bristol my father had got the habit and the *Sunday Dispatch* stayed with us. Few of its contents linger, apart from, for some unfathomable reason, a column by Lord Vansittart; but I do remember a shuffle of papers when I came upon my father reading the serialization of *Forever Amber*.

Sundays also featured church. Kingweston shares a parson with the neighbouring Barton St David, so it was matins or evensong, but not both on the same Sunday. My father, though not changing his principles or his attitude to religion, certainly changed his mind about God's representatives here on earth as the years went by. As they grew younger and he grew older his respect for them diminished proportionately. We looked forward to the occasional exchange of parsons or a visiting preacher, perhaps for Harvest Festival. There was even a Rural Dean from Wells who made a joke and another who offered an enlightened interpretation of the story of Jonah. 'Modern science', he explained, 'has shown us that Jonah was not swallowed by a whale.' He paused while we assimilated this heresy. 'Jonah was not swallowed by a whale.... It was a shark.'

If my father had another religious prejudice apart from younger clergymen it was Methodist parsons – 'Chapel passons,' he preferred to call them. He identified his suspicions quite simply. A 'Chapel passon' was a man who would inquire with infinite concern about your wife or loved ones while simultaneously buying your cow for a few quid less. I often tested my father's theory in later years when dealing with David Frost, the well-known Methodist.

My mother's devotion was simple, complete and sincere. She carried her Christianity lovingly into her ordinary life and showed extraordinary patience with my father and her two sons. She had been brought up in gentler surroundings than the large, cold farmhouse where she spent most of her married life, but she worked as hard as only farmers' wives work without complaint for over thirty years. Thin, wasted and latterly racked by arthritis, she was the most unselfish person I have known. Just before I went off to boarding school she thrust a pamphlet into my hands, saying quickly, 'I'm sure you know more about this from biology at school: but I think you should read it.' Years later she asked me, 'What was Oscar Wilde's crime?' I sought for a suitable form of words and finally compared it to a notorious 1950s homosexual scandal. 'Ah yes,' she said, 'I thought so; but we were never allowed to discuss it when I was a girl.'

A decade later I heard Micheal MacLiammoir's father's answer to a similar question. MacLiammoir told me that as a child he had been fascinated by Wilde's fairy stories and wished to know more. All around him he met a forest of evasion. Finally he asked his father point-blank, using my mother's question, 'What was Oscar Wilde's crime?' His father wanted to know what he had already heard of Wilde. What had he read? MacLiammoir explained that he had enjoyed the fairy stories. 'Ah!' said his father triumphantly, seeing his cue, 'Well, you see, my boy, the trouble with Oscar Wilde was that he turned boys into girls.'

My brother had been established at Sexey's Trade School, Bruton, for three years when I joined him there as a weekly boarder. We came home at weekends, he willingly, I with some reluctance. I had too good a time at school and my hands stayed cleaner than on the farm. Sexey's was formed in the last years of the nineteenth century, named after Sir Hugh Sexey, a courtier of Queen Elizabeth I, who had endowed almshouses at Bruton. Down the road from us loomed the up-market shadow of King's, Bruton, the local public school, and in the other direction, Sunny Hill School for Girls, which my mother had attended. At Sexey's fee-payers and 'scholarship boys' were mixed, and spiced by some Londoners sent away from the Blitz, who seemed amazingly sophisticated.

As war filled up the boarding house, my brother and I were farmed out to the house of an old master, Mr Crowther, monstrously henpecked by his enormous, bedridden wife. She had one particular aversion – the BBC news phrase, 'mopping up', applied to human beings in wartime. Such sensitivity sat oddly on habitually violent lips, but every time the offending words were mentioned on the news, Mrs Crowther would shift her massive, silk-swathed bulk in her bed and splutter and growl, '"Mopping-up operations!" What words to use about human beings! "Mopping-up" indeed!'

The headmaster was Mr W.E. Page. He was only the second head the school had had, succeeding a local legend, W.A.K. (Whacker) Knight.

Mr Page was short and he bounced. The only time he beat me he took a little spring and bounced up and down, swished his stick and then bounced across his study and launched himself at me. Six sets of bounces and it was all over. The offence was pitch and toss played, for money, behind the bicycle sheds.

He bounced into prep one night and startled us all with the ungarnished announcement, 'It has come to my notice that some boys have been playing with other boys' penises . . . this has got to stop!' It was not as funny as Peter Bull's memory of his headmaster, 'You may have noticed between your legs. . . .'; but it was good enough for us to be going on with.

Food was often awful. My particular aversion was the rice pudding, my worst moment a midday meal when it was so inedible that nearly everyone left theirs. Expecting trouble from Miss Mudge, a mean marshmallow of a matron, I finished mine like a good little boy. Plates were passed up. Waste was perceived. The plates were sent back down the table and I got one of the full ones and was made to finish it. I nursed the sense of injustice. On one occasion we coveted the tomatoes which were filling the school greenhouse. Word of our moans got to Mr Page. He improvised infinite variations on his single theme, 'They are *my* tomatoes. They are not *your* tomatoes. You may think they are *your* tomatoes; but they are not *your* tomatoes. They are *my* tomatoes! . . .' Yes, we had no tomatoes! Another fit of phrase-making was inspired by his discovery of a group of boys slouching through Bruton, 'like a lot of mill girls, kicking salmon tins down the High Street'.

Old Mr Thomas coughed yellow damage from the First World War into a jam jar during arithmetic. Bill Barnes was a card, bald-headed and rumoured to be addicted to beer. D. J. Williams had a Welsh freedom with words and a great ability to provoke an affection for literature. He was later to be much shocked by *TW*3. Poor Miss Boome came to teach French during the war. She was, we learned, Miss K.A.M. Boome, daughter of General Boome, born in Trichinopoly. Baiting Miss Boome reached its peak one morning in Five (B). The desks were raised in tiers, Miss Boome stood in front of the class holding a large French dictionary. One of her persecutors, Klaus Blendsdorf, not only an evacuee but also a refugee, was in the front row. We watched fascinated as he crawled across the floor towards her in an attempt to peer up her skirt. Miss Boome appeared to be unaware until he reached his destination and was raising his sights – when she withdrew her hands from the heavy book and let it fall heavily on Blendsdorf's head. One up to Miss Boome.

From school we made occasional theatre outings to the Bristol Old Vic and Stratford. William Devlin's Lear at Bristol and, at the same theatre, Robert Eddison's Hamlet, which excited us a great deal. A full row of schoolboys watched, fascinated as a Wimbledon crowd, as great gobbets of saliva shot from side to side across the stage. To cap that, one of Catherine Lacey's breasts popped out of her Gertrude costume. Suddenly all eyes were fixed, riveted together in a single stare. Then, finally, Hamlet came to his '... motive and the cue for passion ...' speech. We had never heard the line in context before; but what we did know was that a much-thumbed novel called *Cue for Passion* had passed from grubby hand to grubby hand at school, and had provided us with extracurricular reading and unofficial sex education, luridly described on those pages at which the book fell open automatically. As Eddison spoke the line, an instinctive guffaw came from the solid row of schoolboys. I have often wondered if Robert spent painful subsequent performances trying to recapture that laugh.

The excitement of the occasion was confirmed when I was seduced by the head prefect in the back of the car in which two masters were driving us back to school. I did the same for a hitherto unavailable day-boy in the middle of Godfrey Tearle's 'Tomorrow and tomorrow' speech on my first Stratford visit, and then prayed that Edna Conquest from Sunny Hill Girls' School, up the road, would fall in love with me.

There was no dramatic tradition at Sexey's at that time, and the nearest we got to it was an annual end-of-term concert at the boarding house. I was particularly proud of a platinum-blonde wig made out of binder-twine from the farm, which I thought the last word in realism. Having finished school certificate, I moved up into the sixth form to specialize in Chemistry, Physics and Biology. It was a wasted term. I was well aware that I could do none of these subjects justice, except possibly the Botany part of Biology: I was still collecting pressed flowers and had developed a hobby of arranging them. Given a font or a pulpit at Easter or Harvest Festival and I was a regular little Constance Spry. An aunt once asked Caryl Brahms where she thought I had acquired this talent. 'From his mother?' Caryl offered. 'Certainly not,' said the aunt. 'What about his father?' The aunt pounced. 'Have you ever seen Uncle Tom arranging flowers?'

Manipulating my divorce from science was not easy. Mr Page, a physicist himself, was reluctant, but I had allies among the arts staff who had no one to teach above school certificate level. A quick conspiracy with Messrs Brockbank, Morgan and Williams (D. J.) led to a successful *coup* and I switched to English, History and Latin. I kept on pressing flowers as a subsidiary subject.

National Service amounted to a year at Catterick and Aldershot with the Royal Corps of Signals, followed by a year in Austria. For a country boy it was a crash course in the outside world. I had been to London with my mother and my brother, staying with an aunt and uncle in Upminster just after George VI's coronation – Southend, the Zoo, the underground, Piccadilly to Leicester Square, dropped and collected by Uncle Bert's chauffeur; and to *Tarzan and the Green Goddess* at the Odeon, Leicester Square. Once after the war we had gone to Bertram Mills's Circus with the local Young Conservatives. But the world outside Somerset was mainly perceived through the *Daily Mail*, the wireless and, for theatrical splash, *Picture Post*.

The Army helped a lot towards decountryfication. I am not aware of having changed my accent although there must, I suppose, have been some modification as I grew up. The only word with which I have been aware of tampering is 'garage'. In Somerset it was 'garidge'. I learned to say 'garage' as I emerged. Then when I went to America I had to change again to 'gar*awge*', if I hoped to get a laugh out of American audiences without making them stop off to consider the eccentric pronunciation.

My first Army lesson was simple. I learned it at my medical. Don't go to the loo before these occasions. I spent an embarrassed morning trying to contribute to a specimen bottle. I was drafted into the Signals and a great deal of family planning (not in the modern sense) was put into my safe arrival at Catterick. My parents had friends in Leeds so it was arranged that I could break my journey there. Donald Wolfit was appearing in *The Merchant*, and inwardly I cursed my hosts who dismissed the idea of going to see him.

Gallowgate Camp in Yorkshire, a training camp for potential Signals officers, was a lesson in combating the cold. The walls of the barrack room were abnormally thin. A contractor had laid bricks vertically rather than horizontally, producing a surplus which he flogged. It was little consolation to us to know that he was inside a warm, thick-walled prison.

Two more lessons followed on my arrival in barracks. School names were being swapped and for the first time I had to think twice about Sexey's – a *double entendre* that had never occurred to me. I also realized slowly that certain schoolboy practices were carried on outside school. Smartly, on lights-out, the recruit in the next bed whispered, in a very matter-of-fact manner, 'Race ya, Ginge!' Before I could puzzle out this terse challenge there was a frantic creaking of springs and then a contented mixture of gasps and sighs. 'Beat ya!' he said, before I had even solved the conundrum.

Next lesson. It seems incredible to realize that in all my Somerset life it had never occurred to me that Jews existed outside the Bible. Now, when I commented on the distinctive appearance of another soldier, the observation was dismissed loftily by one of the public schoolboys: 'Jewish, old boy.' Apart from my father's idiosyncratic conviction that Jews have a wickedly clever method of cooking old boiler hens so that they are as tender as young chicken, Jewishness had never touched my life. We had seen Blacks in Kingweston, the occasional tramp, and then the GIs, but nothing more exotic.

After a first spell at Catterick there were six weeks of infantry training at Aldershot, presided over by RSM Britten in the last few years of his reign of terror. I only tangled once and modestly with Britten. On some sort of royal parade I saw him breaking off from the main inspection party and taking a relentlessly straight line in my direction. As he drew nearer there could be no doubt that I was his target. He came to rest in front of me and loomed above. 'Get your left boot one half centimetre back, laddie!' was all he said before rejoining the officers.

At Catterick I had found that an unexpected reply usually threw a young inspecting officer off-guard. At least it worked on two occasions. 'Why isn't this button clean?' 'I didn't think you'd look under there, sir'; and, 'Your front buttons are filthy!' 'Not as bad as the ones at the back, sir.' Both produced convenient confusion. But I would never have dared to try that sort of approach on Britten or on CSM Bennett, who was more closely responsible for our discipline at Aldershot. Certainly not on the sadistic sergeant from the West Kents who ruled our platoon and went mad with the one that followed us. Bennett had particular aversions, especially public schoolboys, Roman Catholics, and people who bit their fingernails. When he found one officer-cadet who combined all these sins he had a field day.

The drinking lesson was the next. It was the age of gin and orange, about a decade before gin and tonic superseded it, and definitely pre-vodka. Back in Catterick for the rest of the officer training course, life was more comfortable, gin and orange more plentiful, and an involvement in amateur dramatics was revived.

Catterick ended with a passing-out parade to which my father and mother came by train. At least they came as far as Sheffield by train.

Here they were required to change. That meant crossing Sheffield to a second station. My father had had enough of a train by then. It was, I think, his first journey on the railway since his honeymoon in Torquay. Impatient, he did a deal with the taxi-driver to drive the rest of the way across Yorkshire to Richmond where they were to stay. Yorkshire is a large county. Guests once arrived at Chatsworth two hours late for dinner with the Devonshires. They had driven all the way from Scotland. 'Sorry,' they said, 'we forgot Yorkshire.'

I had the luckiest posting from Catterick to Austria, my first trip abroad: by train to Harwich, from Harwich to the Hook – first time at sea. On arrival at the Hook we were kept waiting a couple of days for a train connection. First exploration of foreign parts. Then the long train journey to Villach. First sleeping compartment – shared with a boozy captain. Waking in the morning to picture-postcard views of snow-clad hills which emphasized the exotic character the journey was taking on for me.

I was posted to Klagenfurt in Carinthia, the Promised Land where the Israelites of the Eighth Army had finished up at the end of the war. Few of the originals survived but there were a couple in the Signals Officers' mess in Beethoven Strasse, a fairly large house a short walk from the barracks.

My work was not onerous, just incomprehensible. I was Motor Transport Officer. Slowly I learned to drive and to fake vehicle inspections by crawling earnestly under the lorries and concentrating on dirt and dust. The great bonus was to have a car easily at my disposal during off-duty hours; the great hazard was to forget to send cars to pick up senior officers. I had two civilian drivers who were champion skiers, one for speed, the other for jumping. They knew the best slopes around Klagenfurt and we would go off on unofficial skiing trips at weekends. After one or two disastrous attempts on the lower slopes they would leave me happy with my tea-mit-rum by a blazing fire while they skied until darkness. Then they would put me between them like a sandwich and, keeping a tight hold, scream down the paths to the parked truck at a speed which took my breath away.

In retrospect I despair at how little I made of my time in Carinthia. It served as a buffer state between school and Oxford, and I know that I enjoyed Oxford more because I was two years older; but the sense of missed opportunity in those twelve months in Carinthia is heavy on my conscience. I did not take leave to see Venice. I visited Vienna only once. Not only did I not learn to ski, I did not learn to skate or swim either. I spent days lounging in the Werthersee, a large lake surrounded by holiday hotels. The more I tried to swim the less I succeeded. Old colonels would observe my efforts and swear that they had taught whole platoons of men to swim a couple of lengths in full-kit-and-marching-order in the course of an afternoon. However hard they tried to bring off the trick with me, it never worked and they would wander away disgruntled.

I did not learn to speak German, except in restaurants and tailors' shops where I ordered a lot of unsuitable clothes in lurid, shiny, foreign materials. My theatre-going was mostly confined to the Stadttheater at Klagenfurt. An unusually plump, blond male dancer appeared to feature in all the entertainments offered – Shakespeare, opera, operetta or ballet. The Klagenfurt *Merchant of Venice* was graced by a visiting star from Vienna and ended in a frenzy of curtain calls which went on longer and longer as he tried to achieve one on his own. The more he came back, the more he was foiled by one or other of the small part actors or the plump, blond dancer. Somehow the star never made it.

The routine of mess dinners and horseplay, films at the AKC and Saturday night dances at the Hotel Moser stole the time. The Moser was the centre of Army social life. Occasionally an Army Entertainment troupe would arrive – Joan Turner and Bob Harvey were a big hit. Outside the hotel stood a sad Austrian lady who had seen her husband go into the hotel just before the war and never emerge. She arrived each day at the same time, still expecting him to show.

The British troops in Austria Amateur Dramatic Society wasted a lot more time, but a second lieutenant's rank gave me much bigger roles than Ian Holm who was, after all, only a private, so rank had its advantages. An affair with a major's wife flared and fizzled, and one with a colonel's daughter foundered when, walking through the woods behind the mess, I tripped over her lying with one of my despatch riders who was making her extremely happy.

A gleeful memory is a ceremonial presentation of Colours to a regiment by the Princess Royal. It was performed on a parade ground surrounded by hills which produced a formidable echo. The echo and HRH's open vowel sounds reached a peak of eccentricity in a sentence which started, 'My fath.a.a.h in India.a.ah, in nineteen hundred and four-a.a.ah!' or noises to that effect, echoing round the mountains like an Imperial yodel.

The Army had become a tempting prospect, so easy and unchallenging were its disciplines. I would have been an appalling soldier, and I shudder at the thought that had not the Oxford place been assured I might have embraced that cosy career.

During my Army life I was lumbered with the name Ted, which I hated. When I went up to Oxford I adopted Ned, to my father's annoyance. He had always called me Ned and seemed to feel that he had some sort of copyright on it, but I was determined not to be Ted, and after a term Ned began to stick. At school my initials, E.G.S., had led to 'Eggy', to which I had no wish to return.

My father was never keen on the idea of Oxford, though he did nothing to hinder my progress. What puzzled him was how it was going to help. I intended to read History or English, and the only prospect into which his imagination could convert such a course of study was 'schoolmastering'. All farmers have a profound contempt for schoolmasters and he had no intention of letting me become one. However, my mother's father was a solicitor and my father held him in some awe. The loophole through which I slipped in order to avoid a family row was to choose Law as my subject.

So I went to Exeter College, Oxford, and had the very best of times. Emerging some way further from my country chrysalis, I plunged into all the freshman activities, playing football and cricket indifferently for the college – one day distant cheers just audible on the cricket pitch announced Roger Bannister's four-minute mile. I joined the OUDS and the Experimental Theatre Club as well as the Union, and wrote occasionally for *Isis*. Quite soon I was cast by John Wood for an OUDS production of *'Tis Pity She's a Whore* in the small but showy role of the Cardinal, who closes the play with the lines, 'Of one so young, so rich in nature's store, who would not say, 'tis pity she's a whore.'

After one rehearsal I was summarily dismissed and replaced by the Priest who spoke the opening lines of the play – one of the quicker promotions inside the Roman Church. Then I failed to get Sir Toby Belch in an OUDS production of *Twelfth Night* in which Maggie Smith played Viola. Discarded by the OUDS, I turned to revues and spent most of my theatrical time at Oxford producing them. Looking back on the old programmes, Nigel Lawson, as a chorus boy with extravagantly long eyelashes, seems the most eccentric casting.

There was one excursion into serious drama. Kenneth Tynan, recently down but already a legend, came back to judge a one-act play contest organized by the Experimental Theatre Club. I dramatized a short story by Somerset Maugham in which God featured strongly. It was a very moral tale and dramatized is an overstatement. I did little more than copy it out and make the lines shorter than the width of the page. I decided that this made it a verse drama and was duly impressed. I can't remember who won – it may have been Colin Shaw, who went on to become Director of Television for the IBA. He wrote a piece called *As Flies ...*, a tense little Central European frontier incident. Tynan remarked in his adjudication speech that he always distrusted plays with three dots in the title. My own piece he dismissed out of hand with one splendid swipe at God, who was played by Desmond O'Donovan, later a monk and even later a director at the Royal Court and the National Theatre. Desmond had a wonderful rolling 'R', a highly individual lisp. 'I couldn't understand', Tynan stuttered, giving his judgement, 'how, if the Almighty could create the consonant "R", he couldn't pronounce it.'

Oxford is a mellow memory. Exeter was a mellow college. A few mellow pages must wrap it up. Distilled are recollections of the ascetic Rector Barber's official welcome. '... Exeter is the second oldest college – fourth if you count lodging houses. ...' His first sherry party, when Mrs Barber, a charming Swiss, mixed up the sherry and whisky decanters and a dozen undergraduates, broke college ice quicker that usual. Later he took us round the college pictures. One eager freshman pushily claimed an early rector as a direct ancestor. 'Interesting,' said Rector Barber. 'Of course all rectors were celibate in those days.'

Dawkins, Baron Corvo's 'blubber-lipped professor of Greek', still haunted the quad. Atkinson, who loathed women and lectures, was still a walking legend. Nevill Coghill still had his rooms on No 1 staircase, gave leisurely lunches and produced an *As You Like It* in Worcester Gardens which opened with the University Society of Archers blasting a dozen arrows across the grass to within feet of the front row. I was too late for Ariel's famous walk across the water. An air of unfulfilment sat heavily on Nevill's melancholy shoulders for all the gleam of enthusiasm which occasionally lit up his eyes and his conversation. Most individual was Dacre Balsdon, long ago a Devonian, speaking now in some favourite but extreme version of an Oxford accent which tradition told us he had painstakingly assumed. He teased, challenged, cosseted and provoked his chosen undergraduates out of hobbledehoydom to some vantage point from which they could espy sophistication.

I forced myself upon him one day in the front quad. I was not his pupil, academic or moral, but I was ambitious to register with this college character. We fell into step and he asked where I had been to school. By now I was sufficiently self-conscious of the *double entendre* which Sexey's embodied to reveal the name as a joke and to wait for the expected laughter. He received the information with the straightest face and I felt properly gauche at having betrayed my old loyalties. I did not take a reaction for granted again. Just before he died, I did a BBC personal anthology broadcast from Sexey's, with Robin Phillips reading the more demanding bits. Dacre wrote from retirement outside Oxford to say how good he thought it was to choose to do it from 'a school for which you have such an affection'. I have lost the letter he wrote to break the news of a dear mutual friend's sudden death with simple care and concern. He was much disliked by some colleagues and some undergraduates, but to those whom he inspired he was the essence of their Oxford experience.

My grasp of the Law was not impressive and the late Derek Hall, my tutor, managed a reluctant tolerance which accepted that I was doing other things. I lived in Exeter for three years, two of them shared with a Welsh friend who had an instinct for setting fire to wastepaper baskets. He is now so distinguished and so respectable that he would rather forget that I once awoke to find him lobbing a burning basket at me which I just managed to punch away to safety out of the window, whence it dropped into the Turl past the window of two more undergraduates who thought they were witnessing a falling comet. The only time any real damage was done was when I inadvertently lit a wastepaper basket myself – and blackened a whole wall.

The Greek earthquake disaster shocked the country in the early Fifties. A wave of sympathy prompted fund-raising schemes all over the world and we staged a modest show at Oxford. I remember little about it apart from some sort of disturbance by Lord Weymouth and an excerpt from *The Importance of Being Ernest*. Daphne Levens, the wife of a don at Merton, gave her Lady Bracknell, and Maggie Smith, still emerging, contributed her Joan Greenwood impersonation as Gwendolen. We raised a substantial sum, and those of us who helped to organize it attended a committee meeting in London before the professionals' Midnight Gala at the Theatre Royal, Drury Lane, for which we had purchased comparatively inexpensive gallery seats. At the committee meeting, in a shipping magnate's house in Avenue Road, I found that I had lost my ticket. Observing my confusion, the guest of honour – Princess Katherine of Greece, Lady Katherine Brandram in this country – said kindly that this must be remedied. I had hopes of another ticket. Not at all. 'Stick with me,' she said, and I did, out of the door, into the car, out of the car into the theatre, up the staircases and finally and happily into the back of the royal box.

It was my first visit to the Theatre Royal. I thought the others were all remarkably blasé about the entertainment. After all, there was Olivier ripping off a specially written prologue, Alec Clunes giving forth, a Brazilian dance troupe, and Christopher Hewett performing a revue classic of which I had only heard, 'Hush, hush, if anyone calls/Sir Christopher Wren is designing St Paul's,' or words to wittier effect. I was enraptured. The midnight matinée sagged into morning. Deserters crept away from the royal box. Eventually my benefactress wafted out into the night. I would not be moved. At last the curtain fell. Calls were taken by those of the Graecophiles in the theatrical profession who remained, and the surviving audience in the stalls and circle began to look for the exits. Suddenly the band struck up a strange tune which, I saw as I peered over the lip of the box, stopped patrons in their tracks. They were standing to attention. The band was playing the Greek National Anthem and, loyally, I threw out my chest. Round came a spotlight, in which I basked – to the annoyance of my friends in the gallery who had not lost their tickets. I hung on for our National Anthem too.

I made occasional forays into semi-professional entertainment from Oxford. I auditioned for BBC Drama, West. I sold and read some short stories for the West Region of the BBC and made an inglorious trip to Birmingham to report on a football match at the Villa ground. They allowed expenses for a taxi to the studio but, thinking I knew better, I decided I could do it on public transport with time to spare. Emerging with the crowds, I got hopelessly lost and tried begging a lift from passing cars. 'I'm from the BBC,' I offered, and gained access to one car. They thought I was Wilfred Pickles or Richard Dimbleby. It took them about twenty yards to find out that I was not, and I was pitchforked on to the street again. Finally I jumped a bus which turned out to be the right one, and I made the studio just in time to give my account of the match. Several bits of colour I had added were inaccurate and I was not asked again.

One Sunday I was summoned to Bristol to do a radio play. As I remember it was about the invention of the steam engine and I gave 'an eighteenth-century voice' and 'the voice of inspiration'. It was a fascinating, low-key affair and the beginning and end of my career as a radio actor.

After Oxford I submitted a musical to Owen Reed, head of Drama at Bristol. It was based on a novel by Somerset's Thomas Hardy, Walter Raymond, and was called *Gentleman Upcott's Daughter*. The music was

by Leopold Antelme who had composed some revue music at Oxford.
The cast was led by Jane Wenham and Denis Quilley, supported by all
the west country actors whom I had heard for years braodcasting from
Bristol. The sound mixer was Paul Bonner, who later became second
in command on Channel Four. I was very proud of *Gentleman
Upcott's Daughter*, and especially of a riotously rural number called
'Grass':

> Yas! Yas!
> You must 'ave the weather for grass! Yas!

It was heady wine at that age to have a loving production, a perfect cast
and an enormous orchestra. Nothing could have come of it and nothing
did.

The much-travelled ground of Oxford hardly needs another road
map, and when I had covered it and it offered up a reasonable Second it
began to merge with London and legal cramming at Gibson and Weldon
in Chancery Lane, where I prepared hastily for Bar exams.

My parents were relieved and pleased as these various obstacles were
cleared. They had long since given up concerning themselves with
what my next move would be. As I moved into television, my father
had his favourite programmes and his *bêtes noires*. He proclaimed
the former loudly and kept quiet about the latter. *Ask Me Another*
and *Tonight* were all right. Everything else was suspect, especially
TW3.

On one occasion during the time I was directing *Tonight* I came home
for a weekend and found myself moving some sheep from one field to
another. During the quarter of an hour or so that we were on the main
road a car drew up behind me, and a man got out and walked along
with me. He had a clipboard and a list of questions. Did I, he wanted to
know, watch much television? 'All the toime,' I said in as broad an
accent as I could risk. 'What is your favourite programme?' 'Oi think
oi'd have to say *Tonight*.' He wrote it down feverishly. 'D'you like Cliff
Michelmore?' 'Yas.' 'Alan Whicker?' 'Yas.' 'Fyfe Robertson?' 'Yas.' So
it went on and he had a really good time filling in all these affirmatives.
Finally he said expansively, 'Well, what quality do you think makes
Tonight a good programme?' I pondered it for some time. 'Oi suppose
on the whole it's the outstandingly foine quality of the direction,' I said.
He was about to write it down when the pen hesitated. 'You aren't Tom
Sherrin's son, are you?' I confessed and he was very nice about the time
I had wasted.

On the London 'treasure' I am a long-time expert. My first brush – in the early Fifties – was a Mrs Dench. Mrs Dench was a stately lady who came with a flat I borrowed in Duke Street, St James's, for a few weeks. The owner was not poor and Mrs Dench was not a big saver on her employer's behalf. She was always eager to go to market to buy vegetables. Market was Fortnum and Mason's. 'Fortnum's is only two doors away,' she would say, and back she would come with everything elaborately packaged and hideously expensive. 'Dench', it turned out, was a 'freelance butler to Royalty'. He had been employed by the same class of person on a regular basis but had found that he was making much more money on a freelance basis on his nights off. Accordingly he had gone independent and made a mint. Every summer 'Dench' took Mrs Dench on a little European tour. That year they had gone down the Rhine, 'All them grapes', and returned 'via Paris'.

I asked, 'How did you like Paris, Mrs Dench?'

She was wonderfully dismissive. 'Very small to London!' she said.

When I moved into my first house, in Bywater Street, my baptism of fire was a Mrs O'Rourke. She started by explaining that she did not have to do the job. 'My husband is a builder in a very big way of business. . . . I don't need the money. I shall spend half of it on my personal appearance and the other half of it I shall give to the Catholic Church. If my husband knew I was coming here to work he'd be up the road in ten minutes and beating you around the face.'

Her Achilles heel was celebrity worship. 'If Mr David Frost should come to call I would be honoured to kiss the front door mat the moment he has stepped off it.'

The manner of Mrs O'Rourke's going was disconcerting. She failed to arrive one Monday morning so I telephoned to see if she was all right, risking Mr O'Rourke's wrath should he still be at home. She spoke only one sentence, 'You know very well why I didn't come this morning,' and slammed down the receiver. It was a bewildering puzzle, aggravated by a letter which arrived two days later. 'Mr Sherrin,' she wrote, 'you have a unique ability to make people around you unhappy.'

The words lingered reproachfully in my mind for three months, but when I finally got round to advertising for a successor to Mrs O'Rourke I picked up the telephone the next morning and heard her unmistakable voice. 'Hullo, Mr Sherrin?'

'Who is it?' I said, knowing full well and trying to think fast.

'It is a person of no importance,' she announced.

'Oh no it's not. It's Mrs O'Rourke.'

'Mr Sherrin, I want you to know that I've had two whiskies before making this call ... and I want to come back.'

Mercifully, that day the unique Miss Jean Godfrey came into my life and presided over it for its happiest years, so I was spared a second bout of Mrs O'Rourke and we were able to part friends.

My brother ran the farm with, and then for, my father whose strength began to fail. He moved up the road to a house he had had in his sights for some years. Set apart from the daily business over which he had presided autocratically for years, his energy diminished and he hugged his fireside. Cutting myself off from the farm left us little conversation that we could share unself-consciously.

In 1965 I drove down to spend a night in Somerset knowing that he would not live long. He had shrunk far into himself. He was very small and very frail. We spent a few unreal hours and I had to leave early on the Sunday evening. All his life he had been an undemonstrative man, with one exception. He assumed, expected, looked for a goodnight, or goodbye, kiss from his sons. My brother and I had gone through the usual stages of doing it happily when small, beginning to be self-conscious about it as we grew older, hating it, rebelling against it, and finally coming round to it. But as I got up to go that last weekend to say the goodbye that I knew was the last, a car drew up outside. By an odd coincidence the driver was the friend of my father's who had knocked us over years ago, before the war, on our way to book seats for the pantomime. The party came in, aware, gently consciously, genial. Suddenly the occasion became public and I did not like to go across to kiss him. I saw his sadness, but I left. I did it a week later when he was dead.

My mother lived a dozen years more, lovingly looked after by my brother and his housekeeper Nancy, and kindly and regularly visited by Joy, the Dickinsons' daughter, and other members of her Kingweston Mothers' Union, while I had a good time experiencing the earlier parts of this book. Towards the end she became very vague and would gaze intently at the television screen if I was on and say, 'I know that man!'

One Boxing Day we settled down in front of the set after lunch and watched the opening sequences of the American musical *The Unsinkable Molly Brown*. It starts with a long dance sequence choreographed by Peter Gennaro for Debbie Reynolds. Miss Reynolds, playing a tomboy, runs, jumps, dances and romps for some ten minutes with a group of equally energetic chorus boys. The scene is a farmyard and they cover haystacks, fences and barns, the routine building to an all-out climax designed to draw a round of applause in the cinema. As Miss Reynolds finished her stint with arms spread wide, and the scene faded, my mother leant forward with a look of faint disapproval on her face. 'Oh, dear,' she said, 'I do hope those aren't local children!'

Index

Adam, Kenneth, 61, 62, 66, 83, 92, 109
Addison, John, 167
Adler, Larry, 165-6, 185
Adrian, Max, 123, 202
Agutter, Jenny, 124
Albery, Donald, 8, 164
Albicocco, Jean-Gabriel, 153-5
Alexander, Marc, 197
Alexandra, Princess, 217
Allan, Elkan, 64
Allenby, Amy, 198-9
Allsop, Kenneth, 37, 42-3
Amis, Kingsley, 9, 58
Anatol, 52-3
Anderson, Daphne, 19
Anderson, Lindsay, 8, 9
Andrew, Prince, 10
Anouilh, Jean, 3, 205
Antelme, Leopold, 254
Antrobus, John, 77
Arden, John, 8
Arlon, Deke, 183, 227
Armstrong-Jones, Antony, 11
Arnold, Malcolm, 53
Around the World in Eighty Days, 44
Ashton, Ken, 34
Ashton, Pat, 179-80
Ask Me Another, 51-2
Aspel, Michael, 200
ATV, 18-19, 20-1, 22, 32

Baddeley, Angela, 170
Baker, Lenny, 216
Balsdon, Dacre, 251-2
Banda, Dr Hastings, 4
Barclay, Humphrey, 63, 84
Bardot, Brigitte, 44
Barker, Ronnie, 41, 111
Baron, Lynda, 116
Bart, Lionel, 46
Bassett, John, 58-9, 80
Bates, Alan, 158
Bates, Michael, 170
Batty, Peter, 91
Baverstock, Donald, 34, 36, 37, 40, 47, 55, 57-8, 66, 68, 83, 90, 93, 94, 96, 108
Baxter, Stanley, 15
BBC, 2, 6-7, 12-13, 22, 33-4, 37, 41, 47, 48, 49-50, 86, 127
BBC-3, 80, 111-16
Beatty, Warren, 103
Beaumont, Roger, 157
Beckinsale, Richard, 149
Bee Gees, 179
Beecham, Sir Thomas, 202-3
Beerbohm, Sir Max, 163
Behan, Brendan, 8
Benbow Was His Name, 172
Benjamin, Arthur, 165, 175
Benjamin, Louis, 229, 231
Benn, Anthony Wedgwood, 73
Bennett, Alan, 8, 59, 111, 159, 178

Bennett, Hywel, 130-1, 134
Bentine, Michael, 149
Berlin, Irving, 227
Berman, Shelley, 140-1
Bern, Tonia, 40
Betjeman, John, 6
Beyond the Fringe, 8, 59, 86
Billington, Kevin, 34
Bird, John, 60, 61-2, 63, 64, 86, 98,
    102, 104, 111
Birdsall, Timothy, 67, 85-6
Black, Peter, 58, 108
Blackton, Jack, 200
Blake, Josephine, 102
Blake, Robert, 226
Bloom, John, 4
Blue Angel, 62
Bodyguard Man, The, 153, 155-8
Boisset, Yves, 153
Bolam, James, 41
Bond, Christopher, 191
Bond, Derek, 37
Bonner, Paul, 254
Bonynge, Richard, 46
Booker, Christopher, 59, 60, 77-8,
    93
Booth, James, 149
Borwick, George, 190
Bonsanquet, Reginald, 32
Boulting, John and Roy, 139
Boussac, Marcel, 3
Bowen, Muriel, 2
Bowers, Lally, 170
Bowie, David, 130
Bowles, Anthony, 175
Box & Cox, 45-6
Braham, Beatrice, 62
Brahms, Caryl
    meets Sherrin, 164
    collaboration with Sherrin, 21-2,
        52-3, 74, 119, 123-4, 150, 159,
        164-84, 202-4
    TW3, 62, 76, 80, 93
    anecdotes concerning, 99, 100
    TV programmes, 116
    Wolfit obituary programme, 121
    No Bed for Bacon, 163, 164-71

Side by Side, 186
    mentioned, 33, 40, 45
Braine, John, 9, 58, 77
Breslin, Jimmy, 221
Bresslaw, Bernard, 143
Brickman, Marshall, 221
Brien, Alan, 7, 8
Briers, Richard, 149
Bron, Eleanor, 8, 60, 64, 86, 98, 102,
    107, 116, 151
Brooke, Henry, 79
Brown, George (later Lord George-
    Brown), 28, 88
Brown, Georgia, 123
Browne, Coral, 74
Browne, George, 173
Bruce, Lenny, 60
Bryant, Anita, 196
Bryant, Chris, 153
Buchanan, Pat, 221
Buckley, William, 221
Buddy Bradley dancers, 23
Bullmore, Jeremy 12, 13
Bunn, Douglas, 218
Burgess, Anthony, 41
Burke, David, 171
Burton, Richard, 122, 123
Bury St Edmonds theatre, 189
Bush, Harry, 30-1
Butlin, Roger, 179
Byrne, Michael, 120

Cage of Water, 153-5
Caine, Marti, 230
Caletta's Restaurant, 17
Cambridge University, 8, 58-9, 63,
    163
Cameron, John, 181
Campbell, Patrick, 98-9, 102, 103,
    107-8
Camus, Albert, 9
Cantor, Arthur, 203
Capp, Al, 107, 108-9
Carden, George, 19
Cargill, Patrick, 124, 143
Carr, Carole, 40
Carson, Johnny, 220

Cassandra, 4
Casson, Sir Lewis, 74, 75
Cavett, Dick, 220, 225
Channing, Carol, 230
Chapman, Graham, 148, 150
Chatto, Tom, 19
Chichester Festival Theatre, 207, 208, 210–11
Chin, Tsai, 105, 149
Churchill, Randolph, 5
Cilento, Diane, 164
Cindy-Ella, 172–3
Clark, Jim, 139, 149
Clarke, Oz, 210
Cleese, John, 63, 111, 148, 150
Clifton, Bernie, 230
Clore, Charles, 3
Codron, Michael, 61, 173, 189
Coghill, Nevill, 251
Cohen, Nat, 10, 144
Colin, Sid, 143, 144
Collins, Norman, 20
Columbia Pictures, 126, 181
Come Blow Your Horn, 100
Come Spy With Me, 127
Connery, Sean, 3
Connolly, Cyril, 73
Cook, Peter, 8, 59, 60, 61, 64, 86
Cook, Ray, 185, 186
Cook, Roderick, 15
Cook, Barbara, 227
Cooper, Dame Gladys, 124
Cope, Kenneth, 67, 149
Corbett, Ronnie, 111
Corbucci, Sergio, 156–7
Cornwell, Judy, 140
Cotton, Bill, Jr, 92
Courtenay, Percy, 176
Courtenay, Tom, 121, 171–2
Coward, Noël, 7, 77, 182–3, 189, 200, 213, 227
Cox, Patricia, 32
Crawford, Michael, 100–102
Crawford, Susan, 204
Craxton, Anthony, 12
Crewe, Quentin, 71
Crosby, John, 70

'Cross-Bencher', 69
Cutler, Ivor, 45–6

Daily Express, 84–5
Daily Mirror, 4
Dale, Jim, 151
Dallas, Ian, 109
Daniel, Ben, 215
Daniels, Maxine, 40
Dankworth, John, 74, 80, 185–6
Davenport, Nigel, 148
Davidson, Ian, 63
Davidson, Jim, 230
Davies, Ray, 136
Davis, John, 149
Davis, Carl, 80
de la Tour, Frances, 140
Dean, Basil, 172
Delaney, Shelagh, 8
Delfont, Bernard, 229
Demongeot, Mylene, 44
Dench, Mrs, 255
Dennis, Nigel, 73
Desmonde, Jerry, 19
Devlin, Lord, 72
Dexter, John, 128, 129, 132
Diaghilev, Sergei, 89
Dickinson, Caleb, 233, 238
Dickinson, Joy, 233, 239, 256
Dickinson, Captain W.E., 233, 239
Dickson-Wright, Arthur, 15
Dilhorne, Lord, 72
Dimbleby, Richard, 40, 67–8
Dobereiner, Peter, 71, 101–2, 114
Dodd, Ken, 182
Dods, Marcus, 54
Donaldson, William, 59
Dors, Diana, 8–9
Dorté, Philip, 23, 24, 25, 28
Dotrice, Roy, 202, 203
Douglas-Home, Sir Alec, 67, 78–9, 107
Dowson, Graham, 149
Drabble, Phil, 30
Duncan, John, 59
Dunlop, Frank, 170
Dunn, Michael, 56

Dunn, Nell, 16
Durrell, Lawrence, 9
Dylan, Bob, 109

Eades, Wilfred, 58
Eastwood, Clint, 123
Edmonds, Noel, 230
Ege, Julie, 140, 149
Eisenhower, Dwight D., 2
Elizabeth II, 10
Elliott, Michael, 121
Emney, Fred, 145
Engelmann, Franklin, 51
Ephron, Nora, 221
Essex, Tony, 34, 36
Establishment Club, 60
Evans, Barbara, 102-3
Evans, Dame Edith, 73-4
Evans, Philip, 153
Every Home Should Have One, 138-41
Evita, 152

Farson, Dan, 178
Feldman, Marty, 127, 139-41
Felix, Julie, 111
Fielding, Harold, 182
Fields, Dorothy, 227
Fields, Gracie, 19
Fields, Happy Fanny, 177-8
Fisher, Doug, 98, 111
Fleming, Ian, 2
Foot, Michael, 215
Foot, Paul, 59
Foreman, Carl, 128, 138
Fortescue, Kenneth, 15
Fortune, John, 60, 64, 98, 111, 116, 149
Foulkes, Frank, 6
Fowlds, Derek, 171
Fox, Paul, 67
Francis, Arlene, 199
Francis, Clive, 150
Fraser, Bill, 143, 145
Fraser, Ronald, 122, 149
Frayn, Michael, 41
Freeman, John, 6

Freud, Clement, 70
Friday Night, Saturday Morning, 226
Frischauer, Willi, 63, 70, 78, 96, 110
Frost, David
  at Cambridge, 8
  cabaret and stage appearances, 60, 62-3, 85, 92
  early TV career, 64
  meets Sherrin, 63
  TW3, 63-9 *passim*, 77-9, 83, 84, 91-2, 93
  Not So Much a Programme, 96-7, 99, 103-5, 107-8
  American version of *TW3*, 103-5
  later collaboration with Sherrin, 105
  anecdotes concerning, 105-6
  leaves BBC, returning to Redifusion, 110-11
  mentioned, 27, 109, 148
Frost, Rev. Paradine, 83
Fury, Billy, 45

Gabor, Zsa Zsa, 145-8
Gaitskell, Hugh, 6, 69
Gallico, Paul, 152
Galway, James, 230
Garland, Judy, 228-9
Garland, Patrick, 152, 203, 207, 208
Garnett, Tony, 8, 102
Geidt, Jeremy, 60
Geis, Tony, 195, 220, 222, 226
Gentleman, Abe, 159
Gentleman Upcott's Daughter, 253-4
Getty, John Paul, 3
Gibb, Maurice, 179
Gielgud, Sir John, 122, 202
Gilbert and Sullivan, 204
Gilliat, Leslie, 128, 129, 132, 138
Gilroy, John, 220
Gingold, Hermione, 195, 199
Gypsy, 2
Girl Stroke Boy, 141, 150
Gish, Lillian, 44
Glasgow Citizen's Theatre, 181
Gleeson, Colette, 210

Glinwood, Terry, 141-2, 148, 150, 151
Glock, William, 6
Godfrey, Derek, 170
Godfrey, Jean, 141, 256
Gold, Jack, 34, 150-1
Goldie, Grace Wyndham, 33, 34, 35-6, 41, 47, 55, 56-7, 66, 72, 89-90, 92
Goldilocks, 126
Goodwin, Dennis, 23
Gordon, Noele, 19, 22, 23-4, 28
Gordon, Ruth, 17
Gorrie, John, 97
Grade, Lew (later Lord Grade), 18, 20, 27
Graham, Colin, 100, 174-5
Grainer, Ron, 62, 80, 116, 123, 178, 183
Grant, Cy, 39, 172, 173
Gray's Inn, 14
Green, Harry, 22
Greene, Hugh Carleton, 6, 47, 56, 61, 68, 72, 107, 109, 114
Greenfield, Jeff, 221, 226
Greenwell, Peter, 40, 116, 136, 206
Greenwich Theatre, 178-80
Greenwood, Joan, 117-18, 118, 124, 150
Griffiths, Derek, 145, 181
Grimaldi, Alberto, 155
Grimaldi, Marion, 40, 170
Guinness, Sir Alec, 122
Gulbenkian, Nubar, 44
Guthrie, Sir Tyrone, 17, 122
Gwynn, Michael, 68

Hall, Henry, 50-1
Hall, Peter, 7, 37
Hall, Robin, 39, 119
Hall, Willis, 68, 71, 74-5, 82
Hamilton, Irene, 54
Hammerstein, Oscar, 227
Harburg, 'Yip', 227-8
Harnick, Sheldon, 227
Harris, Wee Willie, 45
Harrison, Noel, 39
Hart, Derek, 34, 37, 44-5, 46

Hart, Lorenz, 227
Harty, Russell, 199
Hastings, Macdonald, 34
Hattersley, Roy, 73
Havergal, Giles, 181
Hazell, Hy, 54
Hearne, Richard, 23
Heath, Duncan, 80
Heath, Edward, 79-80, 88
Hello Dolly, 17
Helpmann, Robert, 99
Hemingway, Ernest, 112
Hemmings, David, 100, 169
Henry, Buck, 104
Hepburn, Katharine, 159-60
Herlie, Eileen, 17
Hewitt, Slim, 42
Heyman, John, 142, 221
Heyward, Leland, 103-4
Hicks, Colin, 45
Highet, Gilbert, 87
Hill, Arthur, 17
Hinge and Brackett, 230
Hinton, Pip, 54
Hoare, Tony, 41
Hobson, Harold, 8
Hobson, Sir John, 214-15
Hodge, Patricia, 210, 212
Hoggart, Richard, 8
Holland, Julian, 71
Holloway, Stanley, 124
Holm, Ian, 74
Holmes, Nancy, 104
Holt, Seth, 65
Hood, Stuart, 62
Hooper, Ewan, 178
Hope, Bob, 39
Hopkins, Anthony, 124
Hopkins, John, 129
Hordern, Michael, 118, 119, 143, 150
Horne, Lena, 227
Howar, Barbara, 226
Howard, Michael, 60-61
Howerd, Frankie, 60, 68-9, 142-5
Hudd, Roy, 98, 99, 145
Humphries, Barry, 60, 175
Hunt, Sir David, 5

Hush and Hide, 203-4
Hutt, William, 53, 54

Ingrams, Richard, 59, 61
Irwin, John, 98
Iselin, Jay, 221

Jackson, Gordon, 124
Jackson, Pamela, 208
Jacob, Sir Ian, 47
Jagger, Mick, 28, 130
James, Dick, 21
Jay, Anthony, 34, 58, 63, 96
Jebb, Julian, 205
Jeffrey, Peter, 170
Jesus Christ Superstar, 152
Johnson, Celia, 121
Johnson, Lyndon B., 114
Johnson, Paul, 36
Johnston, Brian, 12
Jones, Leslie Julian, 19, 165, 166, 167
Joseph and His Technicolor Dreamcoat, 152
Judah, Cynthia, 34, 39

Kast, Pierre, 154
Katherine, Princess, of Greece, 252
Kauffman, George S., 88
Kaufman, Gerald, 69, 71-2, 97
Kavanagh, P. J., 97
Keel, Howard, 227
Keith, Penelope, 140, 149
Kellett, Bob, 150
Kendall, Marie, 177
Kennedy, John F., 2, 76, 90-95
Kernan, David, 40, 66, 68, 185-6, 187-8, 192, 229
King, Alan, 228
King, Dave, 145
King's Road, 16-17, 38
Kinnear, Roy, 61, 66, 68, 70, 82
Kissinger, Henry, 217
Kitt, Eartha, 145
Kluge, Die, 174-5
Knight, Peter, 172
Kotcheff, Ted, 58
Kotlewitz, Bob, 221

Kretzmer, Herbert, 71, 80-82, 126
Krupp, Alfred, 3

La Fresnais, Ian, 129
La Rue, Danny, 126
Labour Party, 5-6
Laine, Cleo, 102-3, 116, 173, 185
Lamour, Dorothy, 44, 199
Lang, Harold, 65
Lang, Robert, 93, 170
Langford, Bonnie, 182-3
Laugh Line, 52
Lee, Dave, 71, 80, 84-5, 170
Lefeaux, Charles, 169, 172
Lehrer, Tom, 104
Lerner, Alan Jay, 205, 227
Lester, Dick, 133
Lett, Anna, 20
Levene, Sam, 17
Levin, Bernard, 26-7, 41, 59, 64, 65, 66, 72, 84, 90, 93, 107-8, 110, 218
Levy, Ben, 215
Levy, Stuart, 10
Lewsen, Charles, 83
Lewis, C. Day, 10
Lewis, Peter, 71, 101-2, 114
Lieber and Stoller, 204
Little Beggars, The, 100, 169, 171
Littler, Prince, 20, 23
Littlewood, Joan, 178
Lloyd, Harold, 44
Lloyd, Marie, 175-81, 229
Lloyd-Weber, Andrew, 151, 152
Longford, Lord, 3
London, Dorothy, 52
Lowe, Arthur, 124, 202-3
Lynley, Carol, 106
Lynne, Gillian, 181
Lyon, Barbara, 23

McCarthy, Mary, 112-13
McCowen, Alec, 17, 169
McGivern, Cecil, 33
McGrath, John, 128-9
MacGregor, Jimmy, 39, 119
MacInnes, Colin, 3

McKenzie, Julia, 185, 186, 187, 190, 192, 229
Mackintosh, Cameron, 188, 190
Macleod, Iain, 107
MacLiammoir, Michael, 202, 243
Macmillan, Harold, 4, 4–5, 11, 88
Macmillan, John, 64
Mankiewicz, Christopher, 155, 158
Mankowitz, Wolf, 125, 175
Mansfield, Jayne, 44
Marceau, Marcel, 44
Marcus, Frank, 77, 148
Margaret, Princess, 11, 217
Marks, Simon, 3
Martin, Millicent
  early career, 7
  Tonight, 40, 61
  TW3, 61, 65, 67, 80, 82, 83, 93
  stage and cabaret appearances, 85, 179, 185, 186, 194, 229–30
  Not So Much a Programme, 116
  Side by Side, 186, 188, 192, 193–4
  marriage, 197
  anecdotes concerning, 217, 219
Martin, Vivienne, 170
Mary, Princess, 108
Maschwitz, Eric, 48–9, 52–3
Matchmaker, The 17
Maudling, Reginald, 88
May, Elaine, 52
Mayne, Clarice, 177
Mayne, Mildred, 164
Mboya, Tom, 4
Melly, George, 65
Mercer, Johnny, 227
Merman, Ethel, 2
MGM, 153
Michael, Patricia, 210
Michelmore, Cliff, 34, 37, 42
Miles, Sir Bernard, 167–9, 190, 191
Miller, Jonathan, 8, 35, 37, 59
Milligan, Spike, 59, 149
Mills, Richard, 146
Milne, Alasdair, 34, 36, 37, 47, 55, 66, 83, 93, 96, 108, 220
Milton, Ernest, 73
Minster, Jack, 172

Minnelli, Liza, 152
Mitchell, Warren, 150
Mitford Girls, The, 185, 204–13
Molinaro, Edouard, 153
Monday Night at Eight, 51–2
Monkhouse, Bob, 23
Montagu, Helen, 190, 202
Monty Python team, 148–9
Moore, Dudley, 8, 59
Moore, Stephen, 170
Moorfoot, Rex, 92
Morgan, Barry, 80
Morley, Sheridan, 200
Morse, Robert, 104
Mortimer, John, 7, 76–7, 107
Mosley, Sir Oswald, 25, 208–9
Moult, Ted, 52
Moxey, John, 58
Mr Tooley Tried, 175–6
Muggeridge, Malcolm, 94, 110
Murray, Barbara, 143

Nabarro, Gerald, 28
Nathan, David, 71
National Health, The, 141, 150–1
Nessen, Ron, 226
New Cross Empire, 21, 98
Newman, Sydney, 58
Nichols, Mike, 52, 98
Nichols, Dandy, 124, 150
Nichols, Peter, 15, 141, 150
Nicholson, Nora, 124
Nickleby and Me, 181–4
Night Music, 205
No Bed for Bacon, 163, 164–71
Nobbs, David, 71
Norden, Denis, 97, 103
Norman, Barry, 89
Normanbrook, Lord, 109–10
Not So Much a Programme, 80, 90, 96–110
Nye, Carrie, 223

O'Brien, Jack, 224
O'Connor, John, 223
Oddie, Bill, 110
O'Donovan, Desmond, 12, 251

O'Flaherty, Terence, 224
Olivier, Sir Laurence, 122
Onassis, Aristotle, 3
Onassis, Jackie, 217
Only in America, 204
Oom Pah Pah!, 173-4
Orkin, Harvey, 37, 97, 103, 105
O'Rourke, Mrs, 255-6
Osborne, John, 8, 58, 77, 213
O'Toole, Peter, 73, 74
Owen, Alun, 58
Oxford University, 5, 8, 12-14, 59, 63, 163-4, 248, 250-4

Paddick, Hugh, 145
Page, George, 221
Page, Nicholas, 76, 145-6
Panorama, 67
Paper Talk, 24-5, 107
Parasol, 54
Parkinson, Michael, 199
Parkinson, Norman, 3
Parnell, Val, 25
Parnes, Larry, 45
Parr, Jack, 55-6
Peacock, Michael, 108
Peck, Gregory, 217
Pedlar, Stuart, 186
Pennell, Nicholas, 171
People are Funny, 21
Percival, Lance, 61, 65, 66, 75, 85, 143, 145
Peter Pan, 151-3
Pettifer, Julian, 15, 43
Phillips, Robin, 97, 148, 170-1, 179-80
Philpott, Trevor, 42
Pickering, Donald, 170
Pickles, Vivian, 124
Pinter, Harold, 7, 122
Poole, Frank, 149
Porter, Cole, 227
Porter, Eric, 122
Porter, Ngaire Dawn, 7
Potter, Dennis, 6, 71
Power, Tyrone, 23
Prince, Hal, 193, 205

Prisoner, The, 174
Private Eye, 59, 60
Profumo affair, 85

Quant, Mary, 38
Quayle, Anna, 145
Queen, 2-3
Quilley, Denis, 35, 179, 185, 254
Quiz of the Week, 215, 220

Radio Times, 7
Raincoat, 155-6, 158-62
Rank Organization, 149
Rantzen, Esther, 38-9, 99
Raper, Michel, 15
Rappel 1910, 176
Rattigan, Terence, 77
Ray, Robin, 199
Raymond, Walter, 253
Read, Al, 85
Reading, Bertice, 172-3, 204
Redford, Robert, 217
Redgrave, Lynn, 151
Redgrave, Sir Michael, 74, 75
Redgrave, Vanessa, 195
Redhead, Brian, 65
Redmond, Moira, 54
Reed, Owen, 253
Reeve, Ada, 176-7
Reeves, Richard, 221
Reid, Beryl, 107
Reid, Elliot, 104
Reisz, Karel, 9
Reith, Lord, 6
Rentadick, 141
Resnais, Alain, 10
Reynolds, Burt, 218
Reynolds, Debbie, 256-7
Rhodes, Zandra, 145, 147
Rice, Tim, 151, 152-3
Richard, Cliff, 3
Richard, Cyril, 199, 200
Richardson, Sir Ralph, 121-2
Richardson, Tony, 9
Rix, Brian, 122
Robbins, Denise, 215
Robertson, Fyfe, 34

Robertson, Johnston Forbes, 176
Robertson, Liz, 210
Robertson, Toby, 203
Robinson, Robert, 110, 112
Robson, Dame Flora, 118
Rodgers, Richard, 181-2
Rogers, Keith, 18
Roper, R. St John, 28
Rossiter, Leonard, 98, 99-100
Rothwell, Talbot, 143
Routledge, Patricia, 106-7
Royal Command Performances, 229-31
Royal Court Theatre, 7, 8, 58
Royal Family, 10-11, 84, 108
Royde, Frank, 15
Rushton, William, 59, 60, 61, 75, 97, 106, 170, 226
Rutherford, Dame Margaret, 124

Sadoff, Fred, 74
Sallis, Peter, 54
Salter, James, 155
Sandford, Jeremy, 15, 16
Sardi's restaurant, 196-7
satire, 58-60, 86-8
Saville, Philip, 58
Scales, Prunella, 41
Schlesinger, John, 15, 139
Schonn, Bonnie, 200
Schwartz, Arthur, 182-3
Scofield, Paul, 74
Scott, Alan, 153
Scott, Janette, 106
Scott, John, 80, 170
Secombe, Harry, 182
Sellers, Peter, 37-8, 50, 159
Setton, Max, 126
Setty, Max, 62
Shaffer, Peter, 77, 197
Shaffer, Tony, 197
Shales, Tom, 224
Shapiro, Helen, 105
Shaw, Colin, 251
Shepherd, Sandra, 111
Sherrin, Alfred (brother), 233, 235, 236, 240, 243, 256

Sherrin, Dorothy (mother), 233, 240, 242-3, 256-7
Sherrin, Thomas Adam (father), 52, 232-3, 234, 236, 238, 240-2, 247, 247-8, 250, 254, 256
Shevelove, Burt, 97, 103, 189
Shulman, Milton, 126
Shut Up and Sing, 171-2
Shutta, Ethel, 187
Side by Side by Sondheim, 35, 103, 185-201, 216, 218, 218-19
Sigal, Clancy, 9
Sillitoe, Alan, 9
Simon, Neil, 100
Simon, S. J., 163, 164, 165
Simpson, N.F., 8, 116
Sinden, Donald, 149, 151
Sing a Rude Song, 179-81
Sitwell, Dame Edith, 42
Skelhorn, Norman, 14
Sklar, Robert, 224
Sleep, Wayne, 130
Slevin, Tom, 221
Sloan, Tom, 48, 110-11
Smith, Geoffrey Johnson, 34, 37, 47
Smith, Maggie, 12, 14, 250, 252
Smith, Tony, 214, 215
Sokolova, Lydia, 123
Sondheim, Stephen, 191, 192, 197, 205; see also *Side by Side by Sondheim*
Soper, Gay, 210
Spicer, Joanna, 66
Staughton, Bill, 15
Steele, Tommy, 3
Stephens, Olive, 52
Stevas, Norman St John, 27, 107, 215
Stevens, Marti, 228
Stigwood, Robert, 144, 150, 151, 179
Stockwood, Mervyn, 146, 215
Stoll, David, 19
Stoppard, Tom, 159
Storey, David, 9
Storr, Anthony, 215
Straker, Peter, 150
Sunday Telegraph, 69-70
Sunday Times, 3, 8, 9, 125

Susskind, David, 64
Sutherland, Joan, 46
Sutton, Julia, 210
Swarbrick, Carol, 200
Swift, Clive, 151

Tabori, George, 37
Take a Sapphire, 127
Tanen, Ned, 152
Tatler, The, 2
Taylor, Elizabeth, 44, 123
Taylor, Ted, 39
television, 6-7, 18, 33-4, 41, 48
  breakfast, 18-19, 22
  see also ATV
That Was The Week That Was
  (*TW3*), 2, 24-5, 27, 55-95, 125, 254
  American version, 95, 96, 103-4
Theatre Royal, Stratford, 178, 183
Thomas, Leslie, 128
Thomson, Lord, 43-4
Thorndike, Dame Sybil, 74, 75-6, 93,
  122, 124, 216
Tillstrom, Burr, 199
Tilly, Vesta, 177
Times, The 2, 4, 7, 9
Tinniswood, Peter, 71
Todd, Diane, 40
Todd, Mike, 44-5
Tonight, 33-47, 55-7, 89-90, 91, 254
Took, Barry, 127, 139
Towers, Harry Alan, 20
Toye, Wendy, 35
Toynbee, Polly, 212
Trevelyan, John, 127
Trinder, Tommy, 19-20, 98
Truffaut, François, 10
Tuchner, Michael, 34
Tutin, Dorothy, 19
TW3, see *That Was The Week That
  Was*
Tynan, Kenneth, 59, 65, 77, 98, 112-
  13, 250-1

Universal Pictures, 152
Unsinkable Molly, Brown, The, 256-
  7

Up The Chastity Belt, 144-5
Up The Front, 145-7
Up Pompeii, 143

Van Dyke, Dick, 52
Van Essen, John, 126, 150
Vance, Dennis, 58
Vertue, Beryl, 144, 151
Vicar's Wife, The, 159
Vidal, Gore, 92, 105-6, 112, 226
Vietnam, 114
Viking Studios, 19, 34-5
Vinaver, Stephen, 61, 80, 82
Virgin Films, 141, 150
Virgin Soldiers, The, 105, 128-37,
  138
Vosbrugh, Dick, 100, 181

Wade, Stephen, 18
Waldman, Ronald, 13
Wale, Terry, 203
Walsh, David, 60
Walton, Tony, 173
Wanderer, The, 153-4
Ward, Bill, 23, 32
Ward, Dorothy, 28
Warner Brothers, 155
Warth, Douglas, 24-7, 107
Washbourne, Mona, 124
Watergate theatre, 14
Waterhouse, Keith, 9, 68, 71, 74-5,
  82
Watkins, Alan, 111
Watkins, Gordon, 34
Watson, Bishop, 27
Watson, Reg, 23, 24, 28
Watt, Hannah, 19
Waugh, Evelyn, 9
Wavendon, 185-9
We Interrupt This Week, 220-7
Webb, Rita, 94
Webster, Professor, 29-30
Webster, Donald, 106
Webster, Reginald, 52
Welch, Elisabeth, 123, 172, 173, 185,
  230
Welensky, Sir Roy, 4

Welles, Orson, 19, 73
Wells, Dee, 107
Wells, John, 59, 61, 98, 159, 226
Wenham, Jane, 254
Wesker, Arnold, 8
West, Timothy, 203
Weston, David, 97
Wheldon, Huw, 73, 108, 109-10, 112
Whicker, Alan, 34, 43
Whitehead, E.A., 151
Wilding, Michael, 124
Williams, Kenneth, 15, 61
Williams, Pat, 69
Williamson, Malcolm, 169-70
Wilson, Colin, 58
Wilson, Sir Harold, 78-9, 114
Wilson, Sandy, 80
Wiman, Anna Deere, 59
Windsor, Barbara, 61, 178, 179-80
Windsor, Duke of, 108

Winn, Godfrey, 145
Wolfit, Sir Donald, 19, 117-23, 215
Wood, John, 119, 123, 170
Wood, Peter, 178
Woodthorpe, Peter, 164
Woodvine, John, 170
Worsthorne, Pegrine, 36, 112
Worth, Irene, 148
Wyngarde, Peter, 68
Wynn, John P., 51-2
Wynyard, John, 118-19

Yakir, David, 204, 224, 227
Yarwood, Terry, 26
Yew, Lee Kuan, 135
Young, Andrew, 195
Young, B.A., 108
Your Witness, 214-15

Zuleika Dobson, 163-4